Patrick O'Conor
19th March 1983

By the same author
RESTORING THE IMAGE

AS TREES WALKING

Roger F. Hurding

Roger, Joy and family, April 1982

As Trees Walking

by

Roger F Hurding

EXETER:
THE PATERNOSTER PRESS

AUSTRALIA:
Bookhouse Australia
P.O. Box 115, Flemington Markets, NSW 2129

SOUTH AFRICA:
Oxford University Press, P.O. Box 1141, Cape Town

British Library Cataloguing in Publication Data

Hurding, Roger
As Trees Walking.
1. Hurding, Roger 2. Christian biography—Great Britain
I. Title
280'.092'4 BR1725.H/

ISBN 0-85364-354-7

Set in 12pt Bembo by Busby's Typesetting & Design, Exeter, Devon and printed by Pitman Press Ltd., Bath, Avon, for THE PATERNOSTER PRESS LTD, Paternoster House, 3 Mount Radford Crescent, Exeter, Devon

To

Fred 'n' Mary

'And he took the blind man by the hand, and led him out of the town; and when he had spit on his eyes, and put his hands upon him, he asked him if he saw aught. And he looked up and said: I see men as trees, walking. After that he put his hands again upon his eyes, and made him look up; and he was restored, and saw every man clearly.'

Mark 8:23-25 (KJV)

CONTENTS

ILLUSTRATIONS

PREFACE

"As Trees Walking" is a book that demanded to be written. During the years 1978 to 1980 I experienced long periods of blindness, a complication of the diabetes I have had since 1951. These years gave a great deal of unanticipated time for reflection on the themes of light and darkness—in both the physical and spiritual senses of these words. Many, many hours were spent alone, listening, thinking, praying and meditating.

Important relationships were somehow simplified, refined and enriched. With regard to family and friends, the loss of visual communication increased the importance and significance of physical contact and the spoken word. I shall always be grateful to Joy and our three children for their imaginative and reassuring understanding throughout our time of family plight, as well as to my dear parents (to whom this book is dedicated) and to my sister, Anne, and her family.

My gratitude extends outwards to a circle of very special friends who visited me regularly, often overwhelming my emotions by their practical love, their depth of identification, their warmth of feeling and their sense of humour. I am thankful too, to other friends who were supportive and prayerful in the background, enquiring about our situation over the phone, putting short stories and Scriptures on to tape, chauffeuring me to keep various engagements and helping us, both individually and as a family, in scores of different ways. More generally, though no less specifically, Joy and I owe a great debt of love to the church leaders and other fellow-Christians of Christ Church, Clifton, where we have worshipped regularly since 1974. The love and prayers of God's people in Bristol, and other areas with which we have had extended contact through the years, have undoubtedly sustained us throughout.

Behind the months of blindness stretches back over thirty years of diabetes, years of coping—for the most part—with a condition harnessed enough to be only minimally disruptive. The advent of this disease at the age of seventeen was instrumental in my call to Medicine. Over the years since, its presence has curtailed and channelled my abilities and energies. Again, I am grateful to many for their understanding through the more difficult periods of diabetic control, especially to my colleagues at the Student Health Service at the University of Bristol during the years 1974 to 1978, when they had to close the ranks a great deal while my eyesight deteriorated towards blindness. We are, of course, greatly indebted too to the medical and nursing care that I have received through the decades. Amongst those physicians who have advised and helped with the general problems of diabetes I would like to thank Drs Kenneth Black, formerly of St Bartholomew's Hospital, London, Hugh James Galbraith of Chelmsford and Martin Hartog of Bristol. In recent years the patience and skill of the ophthalmic surgeons Mr Vincent Marmion of Bristol and Mr John Scott of Cambridge have been inestimable.

My thankfulness to God is expressed throughout the pages of this book, especially for His continual proving of His words to the apostle Paul, 'My grace is sufficient for you'! As a family we unite to give praise to Him for His all-sufficiency through the days of both light and darkness.

As I emerged from blindness in the spring of 1980, I felt a pressing need to write about the experience of the preceding months. In some ways, there had been a book growing out of the thirty years of diabetes for a long time. There seemed to be a story to tell—not a dazzling one of sensational miracles but one of God's power to keep through the long years of coping with illness. I felt that the theology of healing had been given a justifiable airing in the previous decade or so in Christian circles and it could be helpful to redress the balance and explore the theology of suffering too.

I approached The Paternoster Press with the possibility of writing *As Trees Walking* and they responded with the comment, 'We are interested—if you make it dangerously personal!'. And so the book has a strongly autobiographical flavour. Many friends, acquaintances and colleagues are mentioned in its pages, as well as, of course, members of our more immediate families. At times, I have obscured the identity of certain individuals, particularly those with whom I am now out of touch, in an effort to respect past (and, perhaps, present) sensitivities. I apologise to them now if any offence has been given unwittingly. However, the book is essentially factual although so much of it is seen through the subjectivism of a 'dangerously personal' view!

I am indebted to certain very good friends who have laboured with me and on my behalf in the production of *As Trees Walking*: to Esmé Nourse and Pam Lapraik for typing some of the earlier and later chapters respectively; to Penny Touhy for her industry and secretarial thoroughness in producing the final draft; and to Janet Croysdale for helpful advice on some of the knottier problems of the text.

My greatest thanks goes to my dear wife who has been a very patient co-partner through the last twenty years, surviving the exasperating ways of her individualistic husband with, for the most part, equanimity. At our wedding we sang the hymn whose first verse begins: 'Father, hear the prayer we offer: Not for ease that prayer shall be.' We have sometimes wondered whether we had made a wise choice of hymn since God seems to have answered that prayer abundantly! However, both the positive and negative aspects of the hymn's prayer have been experienced, so that 'living fountains' have been released 'from the rocks along our way'. Moreover, Joy has been a steadfast and companionable rock-smiter while we have tackled together the sometimes stony ground of long-standing diabetes and recurring blindness.

Portishead, 1982 ROGER F HURDING

MEN AS TREES WALKING

Trees walking?
I remember the warning:
DANGER! HEAVY PLANT CROSSING—
A vision of lumbering timber, stalking.

Do trees walk?
Willows weep and pining pines sigh;
Who knows, when we avert our gaze,
Perhaps even a heavy plant might try?

Men as trees walking?
Many treat others as if they were
As cursèd as a blasted oak
Or an embarrassment, like a shuffling fir.

'There's a tree strolling up the lane.
Let's choose another route;
It might be a tree we know
Or, worse still, some stranger shoot.'

I see men as trees walking;
Not through fear that I am needed
(though that is in me too),
But through eye-sight's loss impeded.

'That shadow there; is it man or tree?'
With searching eyes the mystery
Is probed on steadying stick.

The tree moves and, with branches splayed,
Engulfing, loving, unafraid,
Rushes to embrace me.

Rooted to the spot, I yield,
While far out in the vision's field
The trees dance for joy.

CHAPTER ONE

SWEETNESS AND LIGHT

'Here is my servant . . . A bruised reed he will not break, and a smouldering wick he will not snuff out.'

Isaiah 42:1,3 (NIV)

'The urine of the sick is so wonderfully sweet, or hath a honeyed taste. . . . As to what belongs to the cure, it seems a most hard thing in this disease to draw propositions to curing, for that its cause lies so deeply hid and hath its origin so deep and remote.'

Thomas Willis, 1679

AT ABOUT HALF-PAST-TWO IN THE AFTERNOON OF FRIDAY, 2 November 1951, a farm-hand at Court Farm, one of those remote holdings which sit a mile from the sea-wall and the great North Sea beyond, might have noticed a noisy band of six teenage cyclists trundling out on the rough track which runs eastwards to the vast expanse of mud, sea and sky which is the coastline of Essex. He had seen at least some of this strange crew before, usually arriving on Saturdays in winter, bedecked with gum-boots, rucksacks, binoculars and telescopes, and vanishing for hours on end somewhere beyond the sea-wall; later, they would return, tired and silent, their boots caked with mud, and then cycle wearily away towards the setting sun. If he had been observant on this particular Friday, he would have noticed that one of the six was already trailing the others.

The bird-watching côterie, April 1951. *L. to r:*
Derek, Stan, Dave, Rob, Roger and Mick

Rob, Dave, Derek, Mike, Mick and I had just cycled thirty-five miles from our homes in Hornchurch and were all set for three days' bird-watching. Our immediate destination was 'R.S.', a disused, ex-army hut mounted on concrete piles to the seaward side of the dyke and the only break in the eastward horizon for miles. This hut, linked by five miles of sea-wall to the Saxon chapel of St. Peter-on-the-wall to the north and by over two miles of the same sea-wall to Holiwell Point to the south, was to be our home for the next two nights. Standing by this erection, the view to the west was an expansive one of low-lying land, interspersed with farms and small copses and intersected by meandering brooks and regimented drainage-channels. To the east, the eye was drawn over the intervening saltings and tidal mud-flats of Ray Sands to the inhospitable North Sea and, so, on to the painfully distant horizon where water met sky. In all directions, the sky dominated.

The skyscape on the late afternoon of the day in question arrested attention. The vault of heaven shaded from a smudge of misty grey low in the sky through a soft rose-pink around the sun, and so via the palest of pale greens to the wintry blue of the sky overhead. The sun itself was veiled by a dark patch of cloud so that the wisps of cirrus above were suffused with pinks and oranges, while a long bank of lower cloud was flushed a warm pale yellow, its sunward flank glowing the colour of an almost ripe orange. The appreciation of all this beauty was dulled by a simple fact that would not go away: I was feeling unwell and had felt increasingly ill during the last six months.

Life at 16 and 17 can be difficult. Although very much a ringleader in my early teens, a delayed puberty, a tendency to introspection and an over-sensitive nature led to strong feelings of inferiority over the next few years. My commitment to Jesus Christ at the age of 15 complicated the issues, because of the battle between my old and new natures which raged within. My mind and imagination were set to accept the advent of physical symptoms as further evidence of an intrinsic deficiency. And so the insidious onset of increasing tiredness and weakness was acquiesced to as part of the order of things. I recall the extreme effort of mounting the double flight of stairs at school, especially as the day wore on, and the comments about 'Hurding's round shoulders' as muscle tone decreased and a sense of inadequacy increased. Even three months' abnormal thirst and some loss of weight were not enough to bring the much needed reality into the situation. I must have held an all time record for hand-raising, accompanied by the request, "Please sir, may I be excused?", as the thirst eventually could not be slaked for more than fifteen minutes and was accompanied by an increased frequency of passing urine. My parents were worried by my repeated dashes to the kitchen tap, but I played down the severity of my symptoms, desiring to keep out of the limelight. Somehow, following weeks of illness, I had willed my push-bike all the way to the Essex coast along with five very good friends for a few days 'away from it all'.

That Friday night we slept well, muffled against the cold on the concrete floor of the hut, shrouded by the silence. Rising soon after 6 o'clock to the call of a curlew, I trudged the few hundred yards to the mains tap to collect water for cooking our breakfast porridge. The sun was rising on a frost-bound landscape and we were keen with anticipation for a good day's bird-watching. Our expectations were met as we later made our way south to the mouth of the River Crouch and back, enjoying the company of 800 to 1,000 wigeon feeding along the tide-line, the sighting of flocks of curlew, golden plover, oyster-catcher and turnstone, and the thrill of watching a female merlin hunting. Although I had coped reasonably well with the physical exertions of this modest expedition, the next day, Sunday, was to prove one of crisis.

Waking to a rather cold, blustery morning with strong gusts of wind blowing in from the south-east, we set about our various chores to prepare a cooked breakfast. While Rob tended the fire in the confines beneath the concrete floor of the hut, I went foraging for dry wood amidst the carcase of a wrecked car on the seaward side of the dyke. My nausea at the smell of frying bacon and eggs did not promise well for the day ahead.

Leaving Rob to wash up the breakfast things, the rest of us set out to cross the saltings towards the distant mud-flats. Mike and I lingered behind the others, discussing that subject which is so all-absorbing to ornithologists: birds of prey. After a while, I was relieved to see Mick turn back from the group of three way out in front of us, as this might give me the chance to slip away and make progress at my own curtailed speed. Once Mick had joined us, I took my leave and waded along a creek back towards the sea-wall. I felt extremely weak and unnaturally tired, and longed to sit, or, better still, lie down somewhere. I remember feeling that life could not go on much longer like this and that the most desirable thing was to fall asleep and simply cease to exist. Suddenly, a flock of ten golden plover careered low overhead, the swish of their wings breaking my reverie!

Somehow, I walked laboriously back to the hut, and so on to the welcoming tap to quench my raging thirst. Struggling within as to whether to battle on with life or not, I stripped to the waist, dowsing my body with the cold water, while the wind drove in great gusts across the fields. Perhaps this was a symbolic act of defiance against this strange wasting disease that had gripped me.

Back at the hut, we demolished the remains of our food in preparation for the long ride home. I vividly remember being offered the last few spoonfuls of a tin of Golden Syrup and, although my body chemistry sounded some ill understood warning, I was too tired to refuse any solace, real or imaginary.

There now followed the one mile trek of wheeling our laden bicycles to the waiting car of Dave's parents, on to which we would load our more cumbersome equipment. Dave had been delayed by a faulty tyre and, on reaching the small Standard saloon, proceeded to strap his bike to the back of the car. He then offered to ride my steed home, and I was bundled into the car for a most welcome lift. In those days it was a great novelty for me to be in a car, and so it was doubly a treat to be whisked through familiar, autumnal lanes at three times our cycling speed.

Apart from my strange behaviour, another reason for the lift home was to help me reach St. Peter's church, Harold Wood, by 6.00 p.m., as I was on duty to chime the set of eight bells for Evensong. Somehow, by God's grace, I managed to ring my way through the requisite half-hour, although there were a few slips and the rate of chiming was exceptionally slow!

That evening, while I drank innumerable cups of tea, my father, always one to wring some humour out of the most unpromising situation, insinuated that I had drunk a loofah! Sleep was very good that night, and so was the breakfast in bed the next morning. At 10.30 a.m. my mother and I were sitting in the crowded and airless waiting room of the general practitioner, Dr. Siddhanta, our kindly Indian doctor. Suspecting 'sugar' diabetes, he referred me to the local hospital to be seen the next day.

'Sugar' diabetes is a common disease of bodily function. It is also known as *diabetes mellitus*; the word 'mellitus' is from the Latin word for honey and indicates the sweet taste of the urine, in contrast to that passed in *diabetes insipidus*, quite a different and much rarer condition! The word 'diabetes' is from the Greek, and means literally, 'a passer through, or siphon', indicating the frequency of passing urine in both these disorders.

Diabetes (throughout the rest of the book *diabetes mellitus* is referred to as 'diabetes') is essentially a condition in which there is an abnormally high level of glucose in the blood-stream. This state of affairs is, in turn, due to the relative lack or complete absence of a substance called insulin in the diabetic's body. Normally, insulin is produced by the pancreas and is used to burn up glucose to give the individual energy. In the untreated diabetic the unusable glucose in the blood spills over into the urine, taking a great deal of water with it, thus producing dehydration and extreme thirst.

The diabetic's body has its own energy crisis! Alternative sources of energy are sought out, so that protein from the body's muscle is changed into more glucose, leading to muscle wasting; and, more seriously, the deposits of fat are burnt up, producing toxic substances in the system and loss of weight. The latter development is known as ketosis and is sometimes recognised by the sweet smell of acetone in the breath. If this state is unchecked, there can be a laboured form of breathing known as 'air hunger' and progressive drowsiness, which can lead to coma and, on rare occasions, death.

There seem to be two distinct forms of diabetes: 'juvenile-onset', usually starting below the age of 40 and, if untreated, leading to the ketosis just described; and 'maturity-onset', which is much commoner, and usually found in the over-40's, quite often associated with obesity. It is less serious and can quite often be treated by diet alone. The causes of diabetes are still unknown, although certain individuals seem to be predisposed to develop the condition. The actual onset of the diabetes is then perhaps triggered by some factor in the environment, including the possibility of infection.

Dr. Siddhanta's suspicion of 'juvenile-onset' diabetes was soon confirmed at the hospital by urine-testing and a general medical examination. 'Diabetes mellitus, with a severe degree of ketosis' was the firm diagnosis made by the dumpy, bespectacled physician and his team of younger doctors. Armed with this statement of fact, a friendly nurse led my mother and me the length of the central corridor to Ward 11, one of those single-storey, pre-fabricated units which mushroomed in so many hospital grounds during the Second World War. Mum, who had cried a little while I was with the doctors, agreed to bring me certain books during the evening visiting time, and left me sitting on a chair at the threshold of the ward.

I was soon swept up by Len. Most male medical wards have a 'Len'. He has usually been on the ward a fair while, but is now mending well and rejoices in his new-found mobility. Extroverted, even cocky, he likes to be liked. Up first in the morning and to bed last at night, he is indispensable to both nurses and patients. He is a bringer of tea-trolleys and is the one to cry, "Nurse!" when a fellow patient is in unexpected distress. This particular Len soon whisked me around the ward and left me sitting beside Charlie, a short, dark-complexioned man with a very friendly manner, who sat up in bed and belched continually.

Ward 11 was to be my home for the next six weeks and proved to be an excellent training-ground in the art of listening to people while they expressed their problems, both real and imaginary.

In the small hours of the next morning, a good-humoured Irish nurse descended on me with an injection of insulin, the first of a few tens of thousands of similar jabs over the coming years. Although the effects of the insulin made me rather restless for the rest of the night, the breezy awakening at 5.00 a.m. to wash, and drink a cup of tea, heralded the beginning of a very special day.

For most people, Wednesday, 7 November 1951 was much as any other day. However, for me it had all the significance of a suddenly discovered bonus birthday. The insulin was beginning its restorative work and, for the first time for many months, I began to feel well again. It was as if I could sense the strengthening process coursing out through my limbs. My mind began to sharpen and concentrate, and I could sense the return of many half-forgotten motivations. Life was worth living after all, and the future seemed to present a kaleidoscope of new opportunities. To the rest of the ward I must have offered a slightly inane picture—this youth with a mop of tousled hair, who sat up in bed and grinned ecstatically as he consumed a boiled egg with evident relish!

The following weeks on Ward 11 were busy, as anyone who has been a patient in hospital will appreciate. The day started briskly at 5.00 a.m. with the resounding clanking of enamel washing-bowls and the more welcome clatter of a trolleyful of clustered china mugs and the slurping of hot, strong tea. There then followed a bewilderment of purposive manoeuvres. Ward orderlies would appear and the air was filled with the smell of polish and the sound of moving lockers. Announced by the cry, ''Here come the bed-wreckers', a bevy of nurses would descend, interrupting the swopping of symptoms, the earnest application to crosswords and the fitful sleep of the more ill, to remake the beds yet again. The arrival of the 'blood-suckers' from the Path. Lab. was a more insidious affair—a sudden awareness of a white-coated figure busy with test-tubes and hypodermics at one's bedside. Best not to resist but to give in quietly, roll up a sleeve and bare a vein.

As well as these daily routines, there were the scarcer ward-rounds when one of the two consultant physicians and his team of junior doctors would still the patients into reverential silence. Then there were the more welcome interruptions: the attention of your favourite nurse, the arrival of meal-times, and the advent of family and friends during visiting hours.

On the fourth day of my stay, I was allowed out to explore the hospital grounds. My ornithological interest magnetised my steps towards the ploughed fields to the west of the hospital where, during the following weeks, I spent up to an hour most days observing the movements of gulls, watching flocks of lapwings and studying a host of smaller birds in a leisurely and thoroughgoing way. Most mornings would find me traipsing the muddy footpaths along the hospital's perimeter, notebook and binoculars in hand, gazing intently at God's world as if seen for the first time.

However, I did not *have* to flee the ward to find times of respite. There were lulls in the frenetic activity of the unit's routine, times for reading, thinking and praying. Certain biographies were particularly influential in moulding my thoughts and Christian commitment at that time. My particular hero was Edward Wilson of the Antarctic and the quiet strength of this artistic, intelligent Christian doctor, who perished with the rest of Scott's team on the fateful journey back from the South Pole, sank deep into my mind. The other life which moved me greatly during those ward-based weeks was that of Hudson Taylor. A good friend lent me the two volumes: *Hudson Taylor in Early Years* and *Hudson Taylor and the China Inland Mission* by Dr. and Mrs. Howard Taylor. The single-minded trust that took God at His word and the individuality of this great pioneer missionary were an abiding challenge and stimulus.

Another privilege of those hospital days was the time available to try my first hand at oil-painting. Doing Art in the Sixth Form at the local grammar school had encouraged my skills with water-colour, and now, through the generosity of two older friends, I was given a whole range of oil paints, brushes, a palette and a set of Daler boards. As a result, my bed, half way down the ward, was marked out by the pile of biographies and school text-books on the locker, and by the distinctive aromas of linseed oil and turps.

It has been interesting to look back on the way God spoke to me during those crucial six weeks. He reminded me of what a truly great Creator God He is as I watched a lapwing in flight, flickering black and white against the dun-brown of a ploughed field, or observed the copper-yellow crowns of the hedgerow oak trees, motionless in the cold November air. He challenged me through Hudson Taylor's profound appreciation of Christ's words: "It is finished!", shouted victoriously from the cross. He inspired me through 'Bill' Wilson's giftedness and unselfish commitment to God and others. And, furthermore, He spoke to me through my fellow-patients, both Christian and non-Christian.

Mr. Clark, the quiet, gentle father of two sons and two daughters, all good friends of mine and involved at the local church, was admitted the day following Armistice Day, with pain from a heart attack. We had many chats, albeit brief ones, as he had to lie flat and be disturbed as little as possible. One day, he told me how much his faith had meant to him during the previous few years and how he found particular comfort in the words of Isaiah 30:15, 'in quietness and in confidence shall be your strength' (KJV). The evident peace of this man, humble enough to ask a 17-year-old to pray for him and facing death with a quiet confidence in his God, has lodged happily in my memory.

Another person of very special influence, quite unbeknown to both of us at the time, was the young man Harry, who occupied a bed next to mine. Having had a leg amputated as a result of the complications of war wounds, he had, nonetheless, a cheerful and warm personality expressed through a most colourful vocabulary. One day, following the consultant's ward round, he brightly announced to all and sundry that, while the doctors were quizzing him on his care over diet, he felt that his 'belly was touching his backbone'. He had observed my growing interest in the possibility of studying Medicine and, knowing my Christian commitment, he once said, "If you ever want to be a doctor, then go to Bart's—it's full of Christians!" Five years later, I took his advice.

When my diabetes was diagnosed, I had recently entered the Upper Sixth and was reading Geography, Geology, Pure Maths and Art for 'A' levels (then called the Higher Certificate of Education). These subjects, on the one hand, reflected a dilemma between studying the Arts and the Sciences, and, on the other hand, dovetailed quite appropriately for my prospective future as a land surveyor. My ambitions as a youngster had moved steadily from a desire to be a big game hunter (at the age of ten, I used to gather quite an audience at school behind the air-raid shelters to hear my blood-curdling rendition of a lion's full-throated roar) to becoming a surveyor of little-known tracts in deepest Africa, a pioneer situation where I could evangelise for Christ in territories closed to official missionaries—or so I fondly imagined! The only other serious claims on my future had been: ordination, which my mother and an ancient clergyman friend aspired to for me; and a career as an artist, which was generally discouraged as being too much of an unknown quantity.

However, a number of factors were operating within me as I listened to the men on Ward 11. I was vaguely dissatisfied with the idea of working with maps for the rest of my life, although the prospect of the intended degree in Geography at King's College, London was attractive. Somehow, the physical, emotional and spiritual needs of people seemed to be pressing in on me and I desired increasingly to be involved in the world of trying to meet those needs. The thought of switching from my beloved Earth Sciences to Chemistry and Physics did not appeal, although my love of Natural History made the prospect of Biology seem more inviting. The shining example of Edward Wilson was never far from my thinking. After all, he had combined Artist, Natural Historian, Doctor and Explorer, all undergirded by Christian conviction! More realistically, I could see that a life of diabetes would almost certainly prevent me from pushing the frontiers of pioneer mapping in Africa.

And so the decision was made to, at least, nudge the doors that led in the direction of a career in Medicine. A bargain was struck up with God on the basis of one of those adolescent convictions that can be so unshakeable: "If, (a) I achieve a State Scholarship in Geography and Geology; and then, if, (b) I can use that grant to finance studies in Medicine; then, God, I'll know that I should become a doctor". The Lord honoured that pledge; and, through the advent of serious illness, brought me into richer fellowship with Him and into a completely unanticipated career.

The questions of, 'Why does God allow suffering?' and, 'Why not claim God's healing?' were barely raised in the Christian circles we frequented. Evangelical Anglicans seemed to talk little about these important issues, perhaps partly in reaction to Catholic and Pentecostal emphases. The writings of people like Dorothy Kerin had hardly penetrated through to the reading of the Christians I best knew. We did, however, have a visit from the Revd. Jim Wilson who talked about healing at a church fellowship meeting some months after my discharge from hospital. As he was the younger brother of my hero-explorer, I went to hear him gladly. In the event, my mind was filled more with images of men hauling sledges across Antarctic wastes as I tried to listen, rather than the possibilities of healing from diabetes.

Basically, I was so delighted with my new-found health, maintained by self-administered, daily injections of insulin and dietary care, and the different direction that life was taking, that I did not carp at God for allowing me to become ill. There were so many compensations in what God had shown me through the experience that I saw this affliction as a very gentle one indeed, which I could live with in His strength and to His glory.

The only adverse comment from a fellow Christian that I recall was a remark, heard second-hand, that so-and-so thought that the diabetes was the result of sin or sins that I had committed. My own new-found freedom in Christ did not permit me to linger over this line of thinking as, in all good conscience, I could not see its relevance in what had happened.

It was still a decade or more before the 'charismatic movement' began to bring the whole debate about healing to the fore, and so it is best to keep the theological and practical issues concerning suffering and healing to the later sections of this book.

Meanwhile, how was it that this seventeen-year-old, with his faltering faith and faltering body, came to be part of a gang of exuberant, mud-bespattered young bird-watchers who explored the creeks of the Essex coast-line during a windy weekend in November 1951—tiny figures in a vast, level landscape? To answer this question I would like, over the next three chapters, to look back in time to trace God's hand on our emerging family unit.

CHAPTER TWO

ROOTS & SHOOTS

'Here is the Register, musty and dusty, but nevertheless a thing of great meaning. In these brief sentences, curiously written in the old flourishing hand, is contained the sum of the human life of two centuries and a half.'

Richard Jefferies:
The Future of Country Society, 1877

'Who has performed and done this, calling the generations from the beginning? I, the LORD, the first, and with the last; I am He.'

Isaiah 41:4

MY MOTHER HAD 'FLU ON HER WEDDING DAY. THIS MUST BE A risk for any mid-winter marriage and Boxing Day 1929 saw the 19-year-old Mary Chapman, slim and beautiful in white, shivering on her step-father's arm while her eyes streamed and her body ached. Disappointed and exposed by the vagaries of fashion (the 1920's hem-line had taken a sudden lift), her knee-length gown and short veiled head-dress, crowned with waxen 'lilies of the valley', trembled as she clutched a huge bouquet of white and gold chrysanthemums. Behind, stood Emmie, Alice and Marie, three of her five sisters, eager in light blue cotton dresses, their nervous hands clasping smaller posies tightly. Flakes of snow, freshly fallen on the bridal party, lingered in the chilly atmosphere of the church.

My father, dapper in double-breasted jacket and pin-striped

My parents on their wedding-day, Boxing Day, 1929

trousers, cleanshaven with his black hair brylcreemed and brushed back, waited in a line of four bridegrooms at the chancel steps, for this was to be a 'four for the price of one' wedding. Four couples were to be married at the same time that snowy afternoon, sharing a common ceremony beneath the echoing arches of the half-empty church. There was to be no organ, no singing and no official photograph, although my father's best man had arranged for a surprise camera to appear from the shadows. In fifteen minutes, four groups of newly-weds would emerge into the chilly murk of Arbour Square, Stepney, East London, to face uncertain futures.

This was a home-made wedding in many ways. The days leading up to Christmas had been hectic with dress-making and the planning of the food. The scullery at No. 57 Jamaica Street, my father's home, had been vibrant with the chat and clatter of preparation as my mother and her sister Bess cut bread, filled sandwiches, baked cakes and sausage rolls, and set jellies for the wedding breakfast.

Brought back the half mile or so from St. Thomas's in the luxury of a hired car, my parents joined the general festivities from mid-afternoon onwards while the food vanished and the beer began to flow. Amidst the hubbub of voices raised in shouting exchanges and increasingly inebriated singing, my mother and her sisters tackled the washing-up.

The 'flu was taking its toll and so at about 9.30 p.m. Fred and Mary Hurding prepared to slip away by bus to a rented top flat in King's Avenue, Clapham, six miles away across the river, to begin their married life. Privacy was not to be part of their lot, because one of Dad's married brothers and his wife insisted on coming too!

In terms of God's hand upon our lives, weaving the complex tapestry of our inter-relationships, it is interesting to look back further in time to see how it was that these two young people, whose fathers had come from remote rural areas 250 miles apart, 'chanced' upon each other in a hospital corridor in South London.

'. . . another Englishman Herding'. So runs the translation of a simple statement in the Domesday Book (1086) under the entry for Berkshire. This Herding (a common variant of the surname Hurding) was probably one of the officers under Queen Edith, King Harold's second wife. The name seems to belong to Wessex and was quite dominant in Dorset from the Middle Ages onwards. There were several Hurdings who were Collectors of Taxes in that county during the 15th century.

Certain of these were men of some influence, an ancient coat of arms was displayed and, as with so many 'middle men' of the Tudor period, a section of the family moved in at the Dissolution of the Monasteries, taking over land in the Bride valley, west of Dorchester—land which had belonged to the monks of Cerne Abbas, with lush meadows for dairy cattle and chalk uplands for grazing sheep. In this beautiful setting, these more prosperous Hurdings were lords of the manor till the beginning of the 18th century when, in spite of two influential marriage alliances, the male line failed. The surviving sisters sold the family seat to a merchant recently back from Spain.

My father's ancestry may be traceable to a Peter Hurding who died during the reign of Charles I and was a second cousin of the landed gentry. Whether this is so or not, the family generally moved into very hard times from the early 18th century onwards.

At that time, another Peter Hurding died leaving his wife Catherine and their young children to the beneficence of her brother. She was from a Roman Catholic family which held land as part of the manor of Chideock in West Dorset. With the help of her brother, the bereaved family moved to Stourton in Wiltshire, another area strongly influenced by catholicism.

Stourton is well known today as the tiny village huddled along the edge of the great estate of Stourhead, near the point where the counties of Dorset, Somerset and Wiltshire meet. This is a well-timbered upland region forming the southern fringes of the ancient Selwood forest, which once crowded the crown of the sandstone scarp running northwards from Pen Selwood to the market town of Frome. The upper reaches of the Stour have been contained to form a string of small lakes which bejewel the valley below the imposing house of Stourhead.

Seven years after the elegant Palladian house was completed and just over ten years before the gardens were landscaped in the revolutionary new English style of gently curving lines, the small band of impecunious Hurdings arrived from Dorset-shire.

The Catholic Lords Stourton dominated the vicinity so much that by the end of the 18th century about 10% of the villagers were catholic. As the country's laws against papists eased, Bonham chapel was built on land owned by Lord Stourton, and many infant Hurdings were baptised there from the 1770's until the early 19th century. Amongst these was my father's great-great-grandfather, Luke, born in 1797, the son of Stephen and Mary Hurding and the youngest of seven children. His mother died when he was only two years old and his father died five months' later.

These were exceedingly hard times, especially in agricultural areas and amongst the poor. One only has to read the Overseers' Accounts for the neighbouring parish of Pen Selwood to find frequent mention of Luke's uncle and cousins, victims of the Settlement Act. Under this law, some of them were forcibly and repeatedly removed from the parish to another, ten miles away in Dorset, where they had settled previously. In this way, the local parishes sought to control the amount of poor relief they each had to provide 'for their own paupers'. This matter-of-fact entry barely conceals the heart-ache that there must have been in such situations:

April 21st, 1813 ... Conveying Frances, Helen, Charlotte and Rachel Hurding by an Order to Charlton Horethorne and delivering them to the Overseer Henry Baker and Expenses with a Cart and Horse ... £1 - 0 - 6

These four 'Hurding maidens' were quite an expense for the parish; they seem to have been carted away from Pen Selwood on a number of occasions and been involved at the Quarter Sessions several times, until they were gradually married off! All, that is, except Fanny (Frances), who never married. She was last removed to Charlton Horethorne in September 1827 at the cost of eighteen shillings. However, the Settlement Act had been repealed three years before and so, from 1828 until her death in 1837 at the age of 58, she depended on charity through the local workhouse for her existence.

Luke somehow survived. His signature, on the certificate marking his marriage to Anne Mounty in the chalkland village of Maiden Bradley, shows a bold and legible hand. His possible proneness to absent-mindedness is etched for all time in the Overseers' Account for Pen Selwood for March 29th, 1823, two years after his wedding:

Gave William Hurding pair of shoes 10/-
Lost by Luke Hurding 3/4

Marrying at the age of 23, he and his wife settled in a rented cottage back at Pen Selwood for the next ten years or so.

It has been said that the repeal of the Settlement Act in 1824 was very much in the interests of the burgeoning industrial parts of the country since they needed a greater mobility of cheap potential labour. Luke, Anne and their growing family of five children were thus released to move away from Pen Selwood in search of a livelihood. In the early 1830's they settled in Wanstrow, Somerset, and continued to 'bring forth their kind'—another four little ones.

This was a desperately difficult period for the one million families working in agriculture in England. The enclosure of open fields and common land proceeded apace and the standard of life deteriorated, especially in the south away from the wage-competition of the factories and mines.

However, Luke managed to find some work. The clay soil at Wanstrow is suitable for both brick-farming and pottery and he was soon making bricks to support his family. At other times his labouring probably took him away from home, 'navvying' on the roads and building embankments and tunnels for the new railways.

He eventually died in a nearby village at the age of 82, described as a Farm Labourer. This was in August (1870), a bad time of year for an old man to experience the dehydrating effect of 'Diarrhoea 4 days'; for so the laconic entry of his death certificate records his last few days.

His eldest son, another Luke, carried on similar outdoor employment during the 1840's and 1850's, while his wife Charlotte brought forth three sons and a daughter. The eldest of these, Alfred, was my father's grandfather.

Not far away from Wanstrow is the largely unspoilt village of Nunney, nestling around a crossing point over the Nunney Brook and dominated by its four-towered, medieval castle ruin and the 15th century parish church. It was here that Alfred, in his teen years, found work as a 'general servant' at the home of a General Practitioner with the stylish name of Augustus Marsh. As far as I can tell, this is the nearest we have been to a medical tradition in the family!

Perhaps Alfred had an eye for history as well as the medical profession for in 1864, eleven days after his nineteenth birthday, he married Sarah Dallimore, three years his senior. We have traced Sarah's ancestry in Nunney back to the end of the 16th century and it is possible that she was a descendant of the Delameres who built Nunney castle in the 14th century. (To this day there is a family tradition to this effect and Delamere recurs as a forename amongst present day Hurdings). If she was, the connection may have been the 'wrong side of the blanket', because the official line of these particular Delameres passed into oblivion long before.

If Alfred's interest in Sarah had historical overtones, it was expressed at some stage in unbridled human passion and a 'shotgun wedding'. Their eldest child, Harry was born four months later.

This family unit was fortunate, at least for a while; for the Mells and Nunney area was the centre of the internationally reputed Iron Works belonging to the Fussell family. A series of streams set in steep-sided valleys run north-east to join the river Frome. These declivities were ideal sites for damming the rivers and thus for the production of water-power. The proximity of coal-pits close to Mells allowed the eventual use of steam in the manufacture of iron tools. With work thus available, Alfred found a job as an 'edge tool' grinder, 'keeping his nose to the grindstone' as he helped in the production of spades, shovels, hoes, scythes, hay-knives, reaping hooks, bill hooks and axe heads. In about 1876, Alfred and Sarah moved to nearby Chantry with their six children, living for a while in the ominous sounding district of Dead Woman. They attended the local church, built in the 1840's in the grounds of the classically designed house, The Chantry, to accommodate the rising population employed by the iron works. There are sculpted reminders of the presence of this industry on the outside of the church, for, between the gargoyles, angels have been carved, some carrying edge tools.

However, there was trouble on the horizon. The sudden collapse of English agriculture in the 1870's must have affected the edge tool industry badly; business declined steadily in the early '80s and in 1894 the Nunney works were declared bankrupt. This great agricultural depression led to a massive abandonment of English villages in the early '80's onwards. 70,000 British farm-workers and their families left for the colonies aided by Union funds. These economic pressures led to the break up of Alfred and Sarah's family in the last twenty years of Queen Victoria's reign. Of their ten children, three crossed the seas to the United States: Hugh, Alfred Delamere and James Edward; one boy died; and six remained.

Sometime in the mid to late 1880's, Harry, the eldest of the offspring and my father's father, left the winding lanes and wooded valleys of Somerset to try to secure a future in London. At some stage, his father Alfred found his way to the metropolis; for he died in 1905, at the age of 57, in Fulham. One wonders whether he took a few prized edge tools engraved with the name Fussell with him, as he was designated 'domestic gardener' on his death certificate. Sarah, reputed to descend from the aristocratic Delameres, died in obscurity at the work-house at Frome, Somerset, at the great age of 92, in 1934, the year of my birth. It is extremely unlikely that the news of the advent of this great-grandson leaked from the streets of S.W. London to the Somerset-shire market town, with its vestiges of the Poor Law and its dying old lady who had lived through the reigns of three monarchs and thirty different parliaments.

Harry, carrying his West Country burr into the alley-ways of cockney London, signed on as a police constable and found, courted and married Jane Emily Fitzsimmons, the daughter of a local coffee-house-keeper and erstwhile gun-maker. Harry and Jane moved into No. 57 Jamaica Street, one of a long line of terraced tenements, in Stepney, to raise their brood of seven children, the sixth of whom was my father, Frederick Reginald, born in 1905.

While Luke Hurding the elder was making bricks at the upper end of the common in Wanstrow, Somerset, my mother's great-grandparents, William and Ann Chapman, were farming on the breezy uplands of North Norfolk. Their son, Richard Henry and his wife Sarah had a family of three sons and a daughter. Thomas Watts Chapman, my mother's father and the middle of the three sons was born in 1868 in the tiny village of Edgefield, like his father before him.

Edgefield lies at a high point alongside the 'B' road that links Norwich and Holt and the wild reaches of Cley marshes and Blakeney Point beyond. Bounded to the north by Edgefield Heath, with its linnets, gorse and ancient Bowl Barrow, and fringed by the shallow valley of the river Glaven, it is a displaced village. The western edge of the local heathland was colonised late, leaving the original church almost isolated. All that now remains of this former centre of worship is the octagonal 14th century west tower. In 1883, to serve the shifted concentration of population, the present church of St. Peter and St. Paul was erected a quarter of a mile to the south-east, using material from the older church and building in a similar style.

The great fields of East Anglia were hit badly by the slump in agriculture in the late 1870's. A series of poor harvests, the development of the American prairies producing cheaper cereals and the invention of the binder and other machinery, all contributed to the decline; and thousands lost their jobs. Thomas Watts Chapman, his hair powdered white, found some security working as a footman, probably at Melton Hall, four miles away to the west and described as one of the most perfect of the 'Sir Christopher Wren' style houses built in the 1660's. However, this situation did not last and so, in his early 20's, he joined the great exodus and followed his older brother, Robert Henry, south to London.

It is interesting to reflect that Harry Hurding made his way from Somerset to the capital just a few years before Thomas Chapman's journey from Norfolk, both part of the widespread wanderlust for work, both carried to the great hub of attraction and opportunity by the converging spokes of the new railways, and both finding employment in the Metropolitan police force. Tom spent about ten years in London before his marriage. As a 'bobby' on the beat, he was based at Old Street police station. Not far away, in City Road, Islington, there was a strategically placed Newsagent's where he could leave his police cape when the weather was settled.

Minnie Louisa Davis, living with her parents in the flat above, was an added attraction at the shop. She was the daughter of the newsagent's clerk, 'Charley' Davis, well known in racing circles for his successes in training whippets and greyhounds. Minnie had left school at the age of 11 to serve an apprenticeship as a dressmaker. Sewing jet beads on bonnets and capes, she worked a 62 hour week to bring home 3s. 6d. (now 17½p). Three shillings were handed over to her parents, four pennies were paid into the local Penny Bank and tuppence was kept as the weekly pocket money. She became Tom's wife in 1901 and my mother's mother nine years later.

Believing firmly in God's election, choosing his people from eternity,[1] it is fascinating and humbling to look back over the centuries to the apparent vagaries of human choice and circumstance. God only knew where the vicissitudes of a tough life in rural corners of the West Country and Norfolk would eventually lead. The quest for work in order to keep a wife and children alive, the ignominy of Poor Law charity and the work-house, and the basic human needs which drove individuals together to form new families, were all strong influences checking and releasing the movements of Hurdings and Chapmans across the rural landscape. Some may have found forgiveness and new life in Christ, experiencing, even through the hunger pangs of poverty, that 'in all things God works for the good of those who love him, who have been called according to his purpose'.[2] Probably most were unregenerate, simply following their human passions, groping after some security, some foothold on the earth's crust that they could call their own, some happier existence.

Somehow, through the whims, decisions and circumstances of the generations, the Lord God brought these two families together at a fourfold wedding in a draughty Victorian church in East London on Boxing Day, 1929, when Fred married Mary; and my mother had the 'flu.

1 Ephesians 1:4,5 (NIV): 'For he chose us in him before the creation of the world to be holy and blameless in his sight. In love he predestined us to be adopted as his sons through Jesus Christ, in accordance with his pleasure and will'. (see also: Romans 8:28-30; 1 Thessalonians 1:4,5).

2 Romans 8:28 (NIV).

CHAPTER THREE

SURVIVAL OF THE FITTEST

'The value of marriage is not that adults produce children but that children produce adults.'
Peter de Vries: *Tunnel of Love*, Ch. 8

'Thou dost see; yea, thou dost note trouble and vexation,
that thou mayst take it into thy hands;
the hapless commits himself to thee;
thou hast been the helper of the fatherless.'
Psalm 10:14

THOMAS WATTS CHAPMAN WAS A GOOD MAN. POLICING THE streets of Islington in the 1890's must have been demanding work. There was a substantial crime rate in the area and parts of the borough were notorious for a thriving trade in prostitution. He was commended for bravery on several occasions, was said to have saved a young woman from drowning in the Regent's Canal,[1] and when, after nine and a half years' service, he resigned from the Metropolitan police, Finsbury division, a month after his marriage, he carried away a small certificate bearing the comment, 'his conduct was good'.

Tragedy struck the Chapmans early on; the first child, Frederick Charles, died at the age of ten months, within the first two years of their marriage. Minnie Rebecca was born later that year and lived to be the family's big sister. Moving from Islington with his two

1 On checking some of the few, surviving family letters, it seems likely that T.W.C. was *not* the hero of this event.

My mother's parents (*left*) with Bessie (*on lap*), Tommy and Minnie Rebecca. *Above*: My mother (*sitting*) and her sister Bessie, 1912

Minnies, Tom rented a series of rooms at different addresses in the vicinity of Lavender Hill, Battersea, where, over the next fourteen years, Minnie Louisa bore six more children.

The girls seemed to be stronger than the boys; for the third child, Sidney Edward, died in 1906, at the tender age of one year and two months.

All seemed to be set fair after this and by 1915 Tom and Minnie had a 'quiverful', comprising another boy, Thomas Watts the younger, and four more girls: Bessie, my mother Mary, Emmie and Alice.

Called 'Doll' by the family from birth because of her symmetrical good looks, my mother's early childhood in the streets of Battersea was a happy one. She has fond memories of the hurly-burly of childhood games out in the alleys, of racing after hoops and balls, of skipping to breathless chants, and of clustering around street vendors with her mates. Particular favourites were the man who carried apple fritters in a wheelbarrow and the character who sold hot doughnuts, fried over a brazier at the street corner.

Another highlight, this one an annual one, was on Derby Day, when Mary and her friends would join countless other children to line the routes linking Epsom Downs with the City. A square-foot of pavement was secured by each eager child at a pre-judged interval before the last horse-race finished, and the crowds of spectators returned homewards. The frenzied welcome was ear-splitting when the 'toffs' appeared in horse-brakes, traps and donkey-carts. As the cavalcade drew level, Mary would yell out with the waves of excited voices, "Throw out your mouldies!" There would be a mad scramble, sometimes dangerously near the flying hooves of the horses, as the 'street urchins' scuffled for coins. There was a special glow of victory for the child who snatched up a threepenny bit or a much prized piece of silver.

My mother's earlier childhood was given focus and significance by the love her father Tom had for his family. Although he often seemed to be sickly, Tom's home and children filled his limited horizons. Saturday was specially memorable as the day of preparation for the first day of the week. Father played a key part in the routine. This was the one day of the week when he had a shave. The visit to the local barber's for the removal of his week's old stubble enhanced his magnificent Kitchener's moustache, trimmed and isolated by the gleaming smoothness of his shorn jowl. During the afternoon, this transformed father mended, cleaned and polished the shoes and boots of the entire family in readiness for the Lord's Day. There was never *any* excuse permitted for missing Sunday School and the church services, although Father, as he became increasingly ill, seems to have been exempt from the latter. Mother and the eldest, Minnie Rebecca, would attend the Evening Service. With this arrangement, Min held the family record for frequent attendance, visiting the parish church three times every Sunday. In time, the first day of the week must have become a haven of peace for their tired, unwell father, while his choirboy son and five daughters stepped out for hallowed ground in their gleaming boots.

Tom's illness foreshadowed the serious lung condition (possibly tuberculous) which plagued him during the coming years, and his departure from the Metropolitan Police was on medical grounds.

For a while, he found less strenuous work as a Station Policeman at Victoria Railway Station, wearing the red and white striped armband of this humbler occupation. His father-in-law, 'Charlie' Davis, now a porter at the same station, relied almost entirely on tips from Boat Train passengers for his income.

Even this limited form of policing was too demanding for Tom's failing health. Lady Frances De'Lisle and Dudley proved to be a caring benefactress and managed to secure him the job of gatekeeper at the fashionable Army and Navy Stores in Artillery Row, Westminster. Lady Frances was a much loved member of the aristocracy and deeply involved in charitable work amongst the girls and women in Hoxton, a few streets away from the Chapmans' earlier Islington home. Her Memorial Service at St. Pauls', Knightsbridge on 8 November 1926, nearly two decades later, was attended by a Mrs. Chapman, representing the Girls' Guild of Good Life. This mourner may, just conceivably, have been a relative of the Norfolk Chapmans.

After more periods of paternal illness and absenteeism, the growing family had to rely on the vagaries of Tom's work as a timekeeper at one of the gates of the massive London Docks. This work was paid on a daily basis and was extremely precarious as a source of income. He had to appear at the appropriate dock gate each day to wait for employment. If this was not forthcoming, he battled back to his family in Battersea without a penny. Some days he was obliged to walk to and from work, and the six or so miles home must have been wearisome in the extreme without the jingle of the daily wage of two shillings in his pocket.

Cruelly, it seemed, the security of this home-based haven, already threatened by Tom's increasing illness, was to be torn apart. The day after Mary's sixth birthday, this lovingly-remembered father died of an overwhelming lung infection at the age of 48.

As if this was not enough, little Tommy, with a place at Christ's Hospital secured for the autumn, became ill with meningitis and pneumonia within six months of his father's death. These were very serious diagnoses in an era before effective antibiotics and the six-year-old Mary caught something of the foreboding in the household. She remembers her loving and much loved brother lying on a bed in the front room, asking her in a weak voice to close the door as he felt so cold. She recalls putting the pitifully meagre supply of coal on the fire in an effort to comfort him. He died on 14th April 1917 at the age of eleven, the last of their 'menfolk'.

My mother's family soon after the death of her father.
L. to r: Mary, Minnie Rebecca (standing), Bessie, Minnie Louisa, Alice, Emmie and Tommy

Minnie Louisa must have been in desperate straits with the death of her husband and the loss of her only surviving son, both in the space of six months. Minnie Rebecca, aged thirteen, took the Labour Examination to see whether her level of education was adequate for her to go out to work. She passed; and so, with her hair pinned up at the back, she began clearing and scrubbing marble-topped tables and washing mustard-pots at the busy ABC restaurant at London Bridge, a haunt beloved of scores of medical students from the nearby Guy's Hospital, a teasing throng which terrified the teen-age girl fresh from primary school.

The eight-year-old Bessie and the four-year-old Emmie were sent to foster homes in Basingstoke. The sixty miles from South London must have seemed an unbelievable distance. Alice was still in her first year and so stayed at home with mother.

On a fateful morning a week or so after the funeral of the younger Thomas Watts Chapman, Mary was woken up with, "You're goin' into a Home today". She can recall no word of explanation—simply the grim reality of a most sudden uprooting—here today and gone tomorrow. Her destination was an orphanage for 300 girls, mostly daughters of soldiers killed or severely wounded during the First World War, which was raging at that time. This establishment, formerly a hospital and run by a Miss Sharman, was in Australl Street, Lambeth, and, although only three miles from home, might as well have been the other side of the world to the frightened child.

My mother's memories are crowded with vivid pictures of her two years in the orphanage. One of her first experiences there was the removal of her crowning glory. She was proud of her dark, curly hair which swept down to her shoulders. Suddenly it was no more, shorn in the interests of hygiene. She recalls her urgent, anxious question to the other inmates, "Will my hair ever grow again?"

The impact of this wrench from home was profound, leading to an embarrassing stutter by day and to the horror of bed-wetting by night. Nagged at by the 'helpers' for her newly acquired impediment of speech, there was worse to come for the shame of a wet bed. Tucked beneath a single blanket, the urgent prayer: "Please God, don't let me wet the bed. Please God, don't let me wet the bed. Please God ..." served instead of counting sheep. If she woke in the morning damp and sticky, there was no escaping the outcome: a long, long wait, shaking with fear, outside Matron's office for the final insult—a slipper vigorously applied to the offending rear-end.

Hunger was also memorable. The day started with a breakfast of a piece of black bread, the size of a small hand, and a mug of tea. Mid-day 'dinner' meant something more filling—some boiled potatoes, boiled rice or a wedge of sweet bread pudding. This was washed down by a mug of water. For the younger ones, four o'clock was the time of the last official meal of the day—another piece of black bread with margarine and, as an occasional treat, a small portion of jam.

There are redeeming features in the bleakest of situations and Miss Sharman's orphanage was no exception. Bed-time was six o'clock, and sometimes one of the older girls could be persuaded to tuck the younger ones up in a special way. The cry from the bed was "*Please* make me a 'boat' tonight!" This was, in the circumstances, a luxury—a 'back to the womb' experience of mother comfort. The fortunate child was tucked in very tightly by the solitary blanket so that the thin mattress could be rocked in consolation—'like a boat'.

My mother's bed was near the door of the dormitory and this

enabled a friendly, older girl to be a Good Samaritan. Soon after 7.00 p.m., she would bring Mary a precious, extra morsel of bread, presumably taken from her own meagre ration.

Another unexpected 'friend' was the Air Raid, when the German Zeppelins loomed huge over London. The children would be roused out of sleep and hurried down into the basement. Here was 'manna from heaven', for at some stage during the excited waiting, an outsize tin of mixed Huntley and Palmer's biscuits would appear and (dear Germans!) each child would have one—but only one. Some nights, the prayer for an air-raid was almost as pressing as the prayer for a dry bed!

Beyond the simple creature comforts of being tucked up in bed by a caring older girl, and the bonus of an extra 'air-raid' biscuit, there was another occasion which has imprinted itself deeply on my mother's mind as one of providential kindness. This took place during the rare treat of a railway trip to the coast at Herne Bay. Mary was squeezed into the crowded carriage at the end of a line of girls from the orphanage, on the outward journey. The bench seat opposite was packed equally tight, saving for the far end, which was occupied by the more ample figures of two well dressed ladies. Mary, in the diagonally opposite corner, was the object of careful scrutiny by these figures from another world. Like another Mary before her, caught up in the profoundest of encounters, this seven year old was 'highly favoured'. Beckoned over for an audience, she was cross-examined with: 'What is your name? How old are you? Do you have a father? Is your mother still alive? Which orphanage are you from? ..." The two completed their kindly inquisition with: "Watch out for a parcel through the post". A few weeks later, two great stone jars of mixed acid drops and bulls' eyes arrived at the orphanage for Mary Chapman. They were held at Matron's office under the edict that Mary could report there each morning for two sweets from each jar. Furthermore, she could bring any of the other girls with her for the same luxurious quota. My mother's popularity rose steeply with the advent of the bulky parcel; and then declined relentlessly as the jars emptied!

There is no knowing the battle for existence that my mother's mother experienced while three of her five daughters were away at foster-homes and the orphanage. Every Monday morning she had to walk to the Waifs and Strays' Office at Kennington Cross to pay something towards the cost of keeping Bessie and Emmie at Basingstoke. However, as part of the 'war effort', she managed to find work cleaning the windows of the Underground trains at a nearby station.

Within ear-shot of the orphanage, ran the busy Southern Railway lines to and from both Waterloo and, across the river, Blackfriars. Mary knew that her Mum worked 'on the railways' and so, during the early weeks of her stay at the orphanage, whenever she heard a steam train, she would run out to the Matron crying, "There's a train going through! Please take me to my mother!"

Mary's mum's visits to the orphanage were based on the statutory 'one visit every month'. However, her duties on the Underground would sometimes prevent her from coming. On these occasions, Mary would sit in the Waiting Room, while the names of girls who had visitors were called out, until she was the last one, left with the knowledge that it would be another four weeks before her mother might come.

One visiting day, towards the end of Mary's captivity, she was summoned by name from the Waiting Room to descend the stairs to the Receiving Room, with its lining of wooden locker-seats upon which sat both visitor and visited, to find her mother accompanied by a strange man, Arthur William Mellows. Soon after, she was told, "Tomorrow you will go home".

The excitement experienced by this eight-year-old, eager for the love and security of home, was quenched by a series of 'cultural shocks'. As she and her mother approached their destination, she was puzzled by the unfamiliarity of the neighbourhood, for, while Mary had been in the orphanage, the family had moved from beloved Battersea to Kennington, only a mile or two away but strangely different to the eyes of a child searching for friendly landmarks. "This is a *different* house!" was her hurt accusation as they arrived.

More bewilderment followed when the 'strange man', Arthur William Mellows, whom my mother's mother had met during her work on the railways and had married, appeared, apparently very much part of the family. Mary was standing in the corner of the stark kitchen when her step-father entered, empty cup in hand, his steel-rimmed glasses resting on the tip of his nose and his braces dangling down below his collarless shirt. His acknowledgement of her was a grunting nod.

Quite soon, Mary was looking back wistfully at the predictable order of the institution, highlighted by the love of the older orphaned girls. There was a security there that seemed lacking in this unfamiliar place in Kennington, where the effects of poverty and unhappy relationships played havoc with the growing family of Chapmans and Mellows.

Arthur Mellows, or the 'Old Man' as he became called, could only find casual work as a painter and decorator during those difficult post-war years. Every Friday night, his anxious wife would watch for his approaching figure. Her heart sank if he was carrying his bag of brushes and overalls, for this meant he would be out of work for at least another week. And being out of work meant many unwelcome things.

It would lead to the shame of the visits by the Relieving Officer. He would bring the pink tickets which, in turn, would mean the regular lunch-time journey for Mary to the local fire station. There the tickets were exchanged once a week for a sackful of meat, bread, margarine and tins of condensed milk.

It would also mean an exacerbation of the appalling rows between Mary's mother and the 'Old Man'. The less work, the more aggravation between the warring parties. My mother has vivid memories of hearing the anger and pain downstairs late into the night, and of rushing down to her mum's defence. At this time, she sensed the 'Old Man's' hatred of her spirited interventions and can recall his harsh words wrung out of their extremity: "You've no right in this house; here I am asked to keep another man's children! . . ."

Although these nocturnal shouting-matches were feared, day-time brought the delights of school. Mary attended St. Gabriel's, a local church school on the western side of the Elephant and Castle. There had been little Christian instruction at the orphanage, although Mary had learned the glorious statement of John 3:16[2] by heart, and in Spanish! This legacy of doubtful usefulness had been taught to her by a visiting missionary. Now, however, there was the regular teaching of scripture at the Morning Assembly and Mary, thirsty for truth, soaked up the Bible stories as a dry sponge absorbs water.

At school, she escaped from the squalor of home-life into the past world of history and the present creativity of writing essays. At the age of twelve, one of her compositions won a competition on the subject of Safety First. The teacher, Miss Lennard, treated her to tea

2 John 3:16 (KJV): 'For God so loved the world, that he gave his only begotten Son, that whosoever believeth in him should not perish, but have everlasting life'.

at Lyon's Corner House in the Strand, a scarcely believable luxury. This delight was followed by the awe-striking experience of the presentation of a certificate to her by the Lord Mayor of London at the Kingsway Hall. Her predilection for literature was shown by her choice of Rudyard Kipling's poem *Recessional* as the prize-winning subject of another essay.

In her last year at school, Mary became the headmistress's monitor, the responsibility of which included the task of running from one school to another with letters, during the lunch-break. This brought the comment: "Yer'll be runnin' the shoe-levver off yer feet!" from her distracted mother. Min's and Bessie's earnings, and the unreliable income from the 'Old Man' were not enough to supply the family's simplest needs, as, by now, there were two sons, a daughter and another boy on the way by the second marriage, as well as the five daughters (all now based at home) by the first. There seemed to be little alternative; Mary would have to go out to work as soon as possible. As a result, her mother appeared before the School Board to argue the case for removing this thirteen-and-a-half-year-old girl from school, before the statutory minimal age for leaving of fourteen years. Perhaps the school authorities did not want to lose every connection with this promising pupil and so a job as a maid 'of all work' was found in Brixton at a boarding house for teachers, one of whom was the headmistress of St. Gabriel's Infants' School.

Starting at 6.30 a.m., and with only one half-day off a week, Mary worked a long day for her £1.00 a month. Lighting fires, cleaning bedrooms and washing up all day were heavy duties for a thirteen-year-old girl. After nine months or so, finding the work a great strain physically, she slipped on the stone stairs, jettisoning a heavily laden tray of china. Behind the scenes, wisdom prevailed, and she was soon able to relinquish this job with its onerous duties.

Within this year at the boarding house, another step in my mother's spiritual pilgrimage was taken. The scripture lessons at St. Gabriel's School had whetted her appetite for more, and so, when the owner of the house suggested that she should be confirmed, she agreed eagerly. Paradoxically, the employers would not release her from her work to attend the preparatory classes. However, special instruction was arranged for Mary with the vicar each Sunday afternoon at the vicarage. These tête-à-têtes with the Cloth of the Church were terrifying to the confirmee. Fear was mixed with perplexity, as my mother found her clerical mentor quite unintelligible. Whatever the inadequacies of the preparation, her confirmation by the Bishop of Kingston meant a great deal to Mary and the hymn sung on that occasion, '*O Jesus, I have promised . . .*', has had special significance for her ever since.

After a few months at home, Mary was sent to see a Miss Priestley in Kennington to be 'fitted into service'. Miss Priestley ran an agency to link potential young servants with their well-to-do employers. During Mary's day with her, she was asked to answer the door to an elegantly dressed lady, who was bedecked in furs and wearing a fashionable, wide-brimmed hat, and who had just arrived in a chauffeur-driven Rolls Royce. My mother ushered this grand dame into the drawing room and then retired discreetly. Ten minutes later, the visitor emerged with a flourish, pointing at the overawed maid-to-be with, "I want that gel!"

So began my mother's service to Miss Maude Aline Hay-Drummond, then in her early fifties. The youngest daughter of the fourth son of the tenth Earl of Kinnoull, she ran the London Hospital for Unmarried Mothers from her residence, the President's Lodge, Sunningdale, in Berkshire; and she had been looking for a personal and general maid.

One week after this first encounter, Mary was instructed to meet Miss Hay-Drummond at Victoria station, before being driven to Harrods to be measured for her uniform. It was to be pink and white linen with thick leather shoes for morning wear, and mauve alpaca with muslin and black patent shoes for duties in the afternoon and evening. After this dizzying experience, she was regaled with a box of fondants and sent home by taxi.

The winter season was under way, and so Mary started work at Miss Hay-Drummond's London flat at 172 Ashley Gardens in Westminster. Although sniggered at by the rest of the staff for her home-made underwear, she soon settled to the routine of the privileged!

Miss Hay-Drummond was a devout Anglo-Catholic with a genuine concern for her staff. In due course, she urged my mother towards church attendance, and private confession at Easter, Whitsun, Advent and Christmas. As that first Easter in her employ approached, Mary became increasingly fearful of the pending confession. What sins could the unsophisticated fifteen-year-old girl offer to the attentive priest? One day, when Miss Hay-Drummond was out, she searched the impressive books in her lady's bedroom for ideas for the confessional. There, in Thomas à Kempis and in more recent books of an Anglo-Catholic tradition, she tracked down a formidable list of sins. These were jotted down on a scrap of paper and duly recited into the burning ears of the invisible priest!

Spring came, Harrods descended for the annual inventory, Miss Hay-Drummond's household staff packed up in readiness for her departure to Berkshire, and the flat was let out to visiting Americans for the summer.

During her first Summer season at Sunningdale, my mother found working for this kindly benefactress an enriching experience. Her duties were wide-ranging, since she and the cook made up the modest complement of staff at the Lodge. Apart from the general household work, her special commitments included polishing the silver in the pantry and brushing her mistress's hair at night.

Miss Hay-Drummond took a continuing and concerned interest in Mary. She advised her on deportment while out walking and on how to wear her hair. Regular attendance at the Thursday morning Eucharist, held in the Lodge's private chapel, was insisted on; my mother soon became accustomed to the genuflections, the signing of the Cross during the Creed and the aroma of incense. The young chaplain, sporting a large, mobile Adam's apple, became a source of amusement to Mary and her older sister, Bess, who was employed as cook during the second Summer. His clerical mauve and Mary's uniform became the subjects of giggling comparisons between the two sisters while they sat in the maids' pew, Mary resplendent in mauve alpaca, mauve stockings and black patent shoes.

Amidst the frivolity, there was a genuine desire for spiritual reality on my mother's part. Although she had no Bible of her own, Mary prayed daily to the Lord God for strength to cope with life's demands.

Sadly, during Mary's second summer at the President's Lodge, sister Bess was dismissed for talking with the local newsagent's boys. Out of family loyalty, Mary said that she would leave too, and so, after working one month's notice, she returned to South London.

Now sixteen, she found more menial work, this time as a nurses' maid at the General Hospital, Lambeth, with responsibility for making beds and cleaning in forty bedrooms. This proved to be the happiest period of her life up to that date, as both confidence and friends increased.

One day, while approaching the dining room with two of her workmates, her attention was taken by two men working on the lighting in the corridor. Full of bravado and egged on by the response, "Dare you!", she said to her friends, "I'm going to take that young man up the ladder an apple!" She did, and by giving away her lunch found herself a husband.

The large parish of Stebenhithe, now called Stepney, was situated just east of the London Wall and, in the 16th Century, was an area of woodland, broad pastures, fields of cereal, orchards and scattered farmsteads. In 1504, Thomas More wrote to the Reformer, John Colet, then vicar of Stepney, describing Stepney in these words: 'Wherever you look, the earth yieldeth you a pleasant prospect. ... Here you find nothing but bounteous gifts of nature and the saint-like tokens of innocence'.

Stepney has been the point of arrival for countless immigrants down through the centuries. The Huguenots, persecuted by Catholic France, arrived in their thousands in 1685, many settling in Spitalfields where they developed a flourishing silk industry. Throughout the 19th Century there was a great influx of Irish, desperate for some form of work; and the burgeoning industries and busy docklands provided the magnet. Although Jews settled in East London from Spain and Portugal as early as the 17th Century, the great invasion began in the 1880's, as Jews were displaced by cruel victimisation in both Poland and Russia. By the end of the century they were arriving at the rate of 4,000 a year.

The massive inflow of people into the area led to conditions of extreme overcrowding and insanitation. In the cholera epidemic of 1866, nine out of twelve deaths in London occurred in the parish of St. George-in-the-East, Stepney. At the end of the century, the average density of population throughout London was 54 people an acre. In Stepney the figure was 290 per acre.

In the 1880's, into this cosmopolitan and congested conurbation came Harry Hurding from Somerset. Joining the local police force, he must have walked straight into the scandal of the unsolved and macabre murders of Jack the Ripper, all taking place within a mile of where he and Jane were living. Stepney was a dangerous and difficult place to police in the 1890's, although by then the Christian influence of men like F. N. Charrington, General Booth and Dr. Barnardo was relieving the miserable lives of many.

Frederick Nicholas Charrington, who at the age of twenty had renounced his share, worth £1¼ million, in the family brewery, opened the Great Assembly Hall in the Mile End Road in 1886. This building, the largest prayer hall in Europe at the time, was packed to capacity most Sundays. Prayer was of paramount importance to F. N. Charrington, so much so that his friends nicknamed him 'Doyk'. This tag referred to his habit, when faced with a special need, of crying out, "Down on your knees!" This man of prayer was also a man of action and he was instrumental in the closure of over 200 back street brothels in the area.

Similarly, Dr. Barnardo and General Booth, labouring for their Lord, brought love and relief to countless down-and-outs throughout the East End. The uniforms of the Salvation Army became an especially cheering sight to the deprived, as they caught the humanising message that, if a man was poor, he was deserving too. It seems that these two Christian reformers greatly respected each other. Booth once said to Barnardo, "You look after the children and I'll look after the adults, then together we'll convert the world."

My father, Frederick Reginald, was born in 1905, the year that Dr. Barnardo, the champion of the homeless child, died. With three older brothers and two older sisters, he needed to be a born fighter. He was! However, his earliest memory of the war of retaliation was a skirmish aimed at his younger brother, Frank. The scene was the family parlour, occupied by two small shivering boys still dressed in smocks, since they had not reached the age of 'breeching'. Fred, aged three years, and Frank, about eighteen months, were jostling for the warmth of the open fire. Frank taunted, "It's *my* fire! It's *my* fire! It's *my* fire..." Fred, his toleration at a modest level, exclaimed, "Right! If it's your fire, yer can 'ave it!" and with that, he pushed his younger brother into the flames. Frank's smock flared up, burning his face badly, his shrieks bringing all and sundry to the scene. The pain in Frank's face was almost matched by the pain in Fred's backside as his father's wrath brought down his heavy police belt again and again.

Nicknamed 'Golliwog' by his father because of his shock of black hair, Fred seemed to move from one drama to another. A further incident involving fire took place in the 'Off Room', a small room off the landing where the two younger brothers shared the same small bed. It was fun playing beneath the sheets, but, as there were no gas-lights in the room, Fred had to provide his own source of illumination. In those days long before the electric torch, the obvious aid was a lighted candle. One particular night, Fred and

Frank were enjoying shadow monsters cast by the flickering candle-light beneath the tenting of the upper sheet. Suddenly the bed linen ignited and chaos was let loose. The boys cried for help, their mother shrieked with alarm and father dowsed the flames with buckets of water. The smouldering mattress was hurled from the window on to the scullery roof; and the brothers received the anticipated belting.

Injury, both accidental and deliberately inflicted, seemed to be the order of the day. Fred flew off a swing in Victoria Park, landing on his face and knocking himself out. His sister, Grace, fell down the stairs at home, breaking a hip. The fracture set badly, leading to leg-shortening and two or three years in the nearby Treloar's Home for Cripples. Punctuating these events, the older sister, Rose, had a penchant for sticking a hat pin into any available part of her brothers' anatomies. This unprovoked needling built up a store of resentment inside one particular, brotherly pin-cushion. At the age of sixteen, Fred learnt how to box, beat up his sister and chased her over a series of neighbouring backyard walls and fences.

During my father's earlier years, he remembers his father Harry as a jolly and large-hearted man. His ebullience had a musical outlet through the local Police Brass Band, in which he played that most extrovert of instruments, the tuba. Fred's acquaintance with this awesome piece was less creative, as it was his job to clean and polish its valves, cup-shaped mouth-piece, convoluted tubing and huge conical bell.

Harry's duties as a policeman were, of course, mostly of a non-musical nature. In January 1911, he was posted, along with his son Charlie, who was serving with the Territorial Army, as part of the siege of nearby Sidney Street. Two self-styled anarchists, possibly connected with the recent murder of a policeman in Houndsditch, opened fire on the besiegers, wounding another police constable. Compared with the protracted kidnappings and sieges of more recent times, this famous incident seems a modest affair. The situation was resolved in the space of one day, not, however, before the arrival of Winston Churchill himself, the Home Secretary of the day. Fred, then aged five, and the other younger children lay shivering in their beds with excitement and fear at the staccato sounds of gunfire only two streets away.

The First World War brought full employment to the East End as its menfolk flocked to the colours. Fred's eldest brother, Alf, joined the Middlesex Regiment and, by the end of the war, was a second lieutenant. Charlie, already in the Territorials, enlisted in the Royal Engineers and eventually became a corporal.

Fred, only nine at the outbreak of war, in due course joined the 23rd Stepney Scout Troop, attached to the ancient parish church of St. Dunstan's. He put all his pent up energy into this new venture, and his uniform was soon festooned with eagerly acquired badges, twenty-three in all. The first of these, the Electrician's badge, foretold the nature of his future work. Singlemindedly, he achieved a Bushman's Thong on the way to becoming one of the youngest King's Scouts in London by the age of fourteen.

As scouting led to many good friendships, so did attendance at St. Thomas's Colet Elementary School in Arbour Square. Fred prospered there, enjoying algebra, composition and drawing in particular. Just as Mary Chapman did in Kennington five years later, Fred became Head Monitor. This was sometimes a doubtful privilege as many school hours were given up, running errands and shopping for the headmaster's wife!

While Mary was longing for nocturnal Zeppelin raids over the orphanage, to bring that welcome bonus, a Huntley and Palmer's biscuit, to quieten an empty stomach, the Hurding family in Stepney were also experiencing the gnawing pangs of hunger. A doctor examining children at St. Thomas's School wrote on Fred's medical report that he was 'undernourished'; his weight scarcely rose above six stones throughout his teen years.

There was no rationing of food and so its acquisition became precarious. Fred remembers his father pushing proudly into the scullery on one hungry occasion to throw a bulky parcel on to the table with, "Look what Oi've got! A bit o' bacon!" One of Fred's regular chores was to queue up at the London Hospital for a basin of beef dripping for the family, costing two pennies. The standing joke passed along the line of waiting children, basins in hands, was that the dripping was 'boiled down Germans'.

The week-ends were set apart as something different. On Saturdays, Fred would light fires for the Sabbath-keeping Russian Jews, earning a farthing or a ha'penny at each crowded tenement. On Sundays, Fred and his younger brother Frank were packed off to the parish church for Morning Prayer, Sunday School in the afternoon, and then Evensong. The older brothers were away fighting for King and Country, Grace lingered in the Home for Cripples and Rose was busy courting.

The presence of the three great breweries of the Black Eagle, the

The presence of the three great breweries of the Black Eagle, the Albion and the Anchor, darkening the skyline to the north of Stepney, was a continual reminder of the great rivers of beer that flowed through the local taverns and so down the gullets of vast numbers of East Enders, seeking solace from the ugliness of poverty, hunger and deteriorating relationships. Drink played havoc with the lives of Harry and Jane Hurding. With a public house just across the road from Number 57, Friday nights were a special problem. The weekly wage packet was washed away with mild and bitter, an overture to the cacophony of intoxicated squabbling which lasted into the small hours.

As the Great War drew to an end, so did the life of this once robust Somerset man, Harry Hurding. Engulfed by 'double pneumonia', he died after only one week's illness. He was laid out, waxen white and cold in the front parlour, and the bereaved family crowded round to pay their respects. Fred, now an imaginative fourteen-year-old, found the experience nerve-racking. A few nights later, he woke up in the 'Off Room' in a clammy sweat, his startled eyes glimpsing a white, wraith-like shadow which seemed to float through the bedroom.

The sudden death at the age of fifty-four of the main breadwinner of the family jeopardised Fred's education. Like his older brother Harry, he had won a scholarship to attend the newly erected Raine's Foundation School in Arbour Square. Henry Raine, one of a long line of beneficent brewers, founded the school in the early 18th century. The motto 'Come in and do your duty to God and man' over the main entrance was an invitation that Fred was unable to take up.

He found a job at a general ironmonger's in Fenchurch Street, and was soon assisting a carpenter, a plumber and an electrician in turn on their assignments in local offices and warehouses. Within a year, he had graduated from being an 'odd job man' to working as a shop assistant for the firm. However, after a few months, along with countless others, he lost his job as part of the Post-War Slump. He was fortunate and soon moved into an interesting apprenticeship with H. J. Cash and Co., an electrical firm with work all over the country. The next two years were spent assisting an electrician with fitting generators and batteries in private and public buildings as far apart as Liverpool and Brighton, contributing to the advance from gas to electricity.

While working up a ladder in a corridor at the Lambeth Hospital, South London, an apparently trivial encounter became distractingly significant to this 21-year-old East Ender. A small bevy of giggling nurses' maids had caught his eye as they approached the dining room. One in particular, clearly the ringleader, dark-eyed and with hair swept up at the back, was looking in his direction. Fred glanced down at his work-mate, confiding, "Smashin' bit o' stuff comin' along 'ere!" As she approached, they exchanged, "'Ello darlin' " and, "Hello!" In spite of her excited friend's, "Don't trust them, Mary; you know what electricians are!" she soon returned and offered Fred the succulent love-gift of her modest lunch.

My father, Frederick Hurding, at twenty-two, and my mother, Mary Chapman, at seventeen

CHAPTER FOUR

A FAMILY COMES TO FAITH

'Thou knowest me right well; my frame was not hidden from thee when I was being made in secret, intricately wrought in the depths of the earth. Thy eyes beheld my unformed substance; in thy book were written, every one of them, the days that were formed for me, when as yet there was none of them.' *Psalm 139:14-16*

'High in the air soared the fighter pilots, or waited serene at a moment's notice around their excellent machines. This was a time when it was equally good to live or die.'
Winston Churchill: *Their Finest Hour*

WHO CAN TELL WHAT INFLUENCES LEAD A FAMILY TO FAITH IN Christ? How was it that twenty years after Fred and Mary's wedding, their family unit: father, mother, son and daughter should, one by one, become Christians? At one level, we can answer 'through the work of the Holy Spirit, surely!' This reply tempts me to query further 'Yes, but why *this* particular family at *that* particular time?' And this question is, in human terms, unanswerable. We are back into the inscrutable terrain of a sovereign God who chooses.

Nonetheless, the concept of God's election is counterbalanced in the Scriptures by Man's free will. Men and woman are not automata—they also choose and make decisions. God through his Spirit calls, coerces and challenges; Man either responds or rebels.

It may be instructive, then, to look at some of those influences that may have contributed to the Hurdings' commitment to Christ.

As we have already seen, attendance at church for Sunday worship was a routine part of both my parents' childhoods. These habits were reinforced, for my father, by his involvement with the scout troop attached to St. Dunstan's church, Stepney, and, for my mother, by her confirmation during her teen years. Although the significance of this latter milestone was barely understood by Mary at the time, there seems to have been a genuine longing for a spiritual perspective in life, at least during the next few years.

Following the wedding, Fred and Mary spent the first eighteen months of their life together based in the top flat of 28 King's Avenue, Clapham. Church attendance had *not* been part of their courtship and, apart from the marriage service in the draughty nave of St. Thomas's, Arbour Square, there seemed to be no reason for re-establishing one of the routines of childhood. However, the lack of this particular involvement was compensated to some extent by some good friendships forged during their years in South London.

The door across the landing from their flat was ornamented by a silver horse-shoe. Behind this charmed threshold lived Mr. and Mrs. Gibson. Through Mrs. Gibson, my mother had fresh reminders of her own cherished links with a more privileged way of life. Glimpses of this other world were afforded by an exquisite bone china tea-set, black cherries against a soft cream background, and by portraits of the babies of various aristocratic families that peeped out from mantelpiece and sideboard top. Mrs. Gibson had penetrated the households of the upper class through her training as a Truby King nurse.[1]

The Slump of the early '30's continued and Fred lost his interesting job with the electricians, H. J. Cash & Co., after only a few months of marriage. Mary managed to boost the income a little by some part-time work. One of these jobs was found through her sister Bess, who was then cook at a fashionable house in Cheyne Walk, Chelsea, the residence of the Dramatic Critic to *The Times*, Sir Charles Morgan, and his wife, the novelist Hilda Vaughan. My mother's work of laying tables and waiting at table for dinner parties gave her another taste of a more exalted life-style. One personal link with the Morgans has survived in my first Christian name. Their two-year-old son Roger quite frequently found his

1 Sir Frederic Truby King (1858-1938) was a doctor from New Zealand who pioneered mothercraft, reducing infant mortality greatly in the English-speaking world.

way to the kitchen, enticed by the prospect of titbits of food and the company of two friendly young women. Bess and Mary became so fond of their young visitor that one day my mother suggested: 'Look, whoever has a son first, let that one call him Roger!' A few years later, when Bess gave birth to a boy well before my mother's first pregnancy, she said to Mary: 'You thought of the idea first; you call yours Roger—I'll call mine Alec.'

On the first floor of 28 King's Avenue lived another couple who became good friends to my parents—a second 'Fred and Doll'—the Bakers. Dolly Baker was a dress-maker and made clothes for the actress Polly Ward, a daughter of the Poluskies, Music-hall artistes who had been well known in South London. One day Dolly told Miss Ward that there was a young couple upstairs at Number 28 who had 'fallen on hard times' and, further, she asked her whether she knew of any possible work for them.

For a while, Mary crossed King's Avenue regularly to earn a little by keeping Polly Ward's flat clean for her. Polly's husband, Robert Freeman, had contracted tuberculosis, had been sent to a Swiss sanatorium, where he became a Christian Scientist, and had then in turn been convalescing in Canada. On his return to England, the couple moved to Mitcham, only four miles south of Clapham but in a more genteel area where the air was at least a little cleaner. Their needs and my parents' dovetailed. Mary was asked to be their uniformed general maid, while Fred was offered work as chauffeur, gardener and odd-job man. However, my father had just found re-employment as an 'unestablished skilled worker' at the GPO, and this seemed to promise more security for the future than the Freemans' offer. Nonetheless, my parents moved into a small but comfortable flat at the Freemans' new house, while mother worked as a 'maid of all work' and father commuted to and from the City.

There were two exuberant wire-haired fox terriers, called Turko and Smith, at the house in Mitcham. One week, my parents were left in charge of the dogs while their master and mistress were on holiday. All went well until one evening Turko and Smith were locked in the kitchen, their comfort assured by a generous supply of soft cushions, while Fred and Mary enjoyed the snug exclusiveness of the sitting room. Before retiring, they cautiously opened the kitchen door to make sure that the dogs were all right for the night. The dogs were fine, but the kitchen was in a state of some devastation! The rumbustious terriers had attacked both carpet and cushions, tearing the former and disembowelling the latter of their ubiquitous feathers.

In the summer of 1933 my mother became pregnant and so my parents left Mitcham to return to Clapham—this time to a flat in Sandmere Road. Towards the end of January, 1934, Mary was admitted in labour to Knight's Hill nursing home, West Norwood, where, on the stroke of midnight of 29th January, I was born. From the moment of birth, I was a complicator of other peoples' lives. My mother was adamant that my date of birth was the 29th, while the midwife was equally insistent that I had arrived on the 30th. For the first fifteen years I celebrated my birthdays on the earlier date until, checking my birth certificate, I discovered that the 30th was the day it all officially began. I suddenly became one day younger to conform with the paper work. Bureaucracy and the midwife had the last word!

Polly Ward kept in touch with my parents and visited mother one day at the nursing home. A flamboyant personality, she arrived at the door of the ward dressed in a bright red ensemble, her arms laden with flowers and books. Having gained her audience, she flung her arms out wide scattering their contents with largess. This affect achieved, she rushed across her 'stage' to its other focal point —my mother, islanded in bed and accompanied by her product, snug in an adjacent cot. There then followed one of those ritual dialogues, nursed in the memory by many fond mothers. Looking down at me in the cot, Miss Ward asked my mother, 'What are you going to call him?' 'Roger Frederick Hurding!' replied mother proudly. Arrested by the tone of the maternal voice, the actress turned and said, 'Mary, it sounds as if he is going to be Prime Minister, the way you say that!'

In spite of this loving fantasy, I was far from a 'model' baby. From the very first days, I would return my mother's milk with interest, at times producing a jet of projectile vomiting. My mother's excessive supply was regarded as a bane and a blessing by the midwives. On the one hand, they chided her for my unsavoury behaviour with, 'What do you expet with the huge amount of milk you've got?' On the other hand, they came to her bedside, when I had finished a feed, with the needs of others in their minds, saying, 'Can we draw more milk now from you, for the twins?'

Once back home, mother pushed me out, rather shamefacedly, in a small, shabby and rickety pram. One day, as we were passing a junk shop, she noticed a massive Dunkley pram for sale for ten shillings. Perambulators of this make sheltered aristocratic charges and were proudly pushed out by Truby King nurses. The temptation was too much. Mary Hurding returned to the flat, counted out the pennies and rushed back to the dealer to buy the magnificent vehicle.

Although this great pram was a nuisance, blocking the passage at the entrance to the flats where my parents lived, mother was justifiably proud of this possession. Owning 'the only Dunkley in Clapham', she polished the black body-work till it gleamed and reflected, and lovingly sewed over the frayed edges of the canopy. The motto: 'As supplied to the Royal Family' was held in special esteem and received the maximum amount of polish and elbow grease.

When I was seven months old, we moved back to 28 King's Avenue but this time to the ground floor. This change of level came about from an apparently casual contact between mother and the district nurse in the street. Something about this young mother made the nurse query a history of rheumatic fever and, although the answer was negative, the ground floor was recommended as being less strain 'on the ticker'.

For the first nine or ten months of life, while being breast-fed, I was the sort of child that would have raised a great deal of sympathy towards the parents in a case of baby-battering. My crying was relentless at all hours. Seemingly, colic was a great problem as was the vomiting, presumably caused by a 'lax oesophagus'. The Bakers, in the flat just above the nocturnal howling, said to my mother, 'Mary, if you do anything to that child, we'll come and defend you in court!' My father, who had a reputation for loss of temper under modest provocation, felt *extremely* provoked. His reaction on one occasion was quite uncomplicated: 'I'll throw him out of the window!' At another time, when Nestlé's milk with malt was thought to be the perfect balm for such antisocial behaviour, he cried, 'This is what you're gonna have!', and dropped the tin on my head. I suspect that these shock tactics led to at least three seconds of stunned silence!

Fred was a very keen and able darts player and, in the cramped conditions of the previous flat in Sandmere Road, he had felt obliged to place the dartboard just above my cot!. I have since wondered whether he was trying 'to kill two birds with one stone' by this strategem. Mary's confidence that Fred's darts always found their way soundly into the board had been shaken on several occasions when metal hit metal and the lethal weapons ricocheted into the cot beneath. My mother's logic was simple: 'Fred must have his darts; I must have my son!' And so the cot had been moved into the main bedroom.

Life became a little easier for my parents over the next year or so. Mother made little vows to herself on how to bring me up. Although, as already indicated, she found herself protecting me against the understandable reactions of others, she was keen to establish certain principles. One of these related to a beautiful biscuit barrel which she loved to display on the sideboard. Friends advised hiding the barrel and its contents away from me as the temptation was surely too much. She rightly argued, 'He has to learn that he can have a biscuit at certain times only'.

I became a happier child once I could use my hands in a controlling way. I was absorbed in drawing 'tick tocks' and 'puffa trains' before I could walk. However, sleep was a continuing problem. I have a vivid memory of one night when I was probably only eighteen months old. I was standing up in my cot, which was placed in the large living room of the ground floor flat. I recall a large window in front of me with darkness beyond. To the right was a wardrobe with a long mirror. As I stood, I clutched the side of the cot in a state of fear. It may have been a windy, yet moonlit, night as there was an impression of a howling wind, the flapping of curtains and a kaleidoscope of light and darkness dancing through the room and reflecting off the mirror.

A few months after a miscarriage, my mother became pregnant again. One day in July, 1937 she went away 'to have a baby'. I was looked after by the kindly Mrs. Gibson, the experienced Truby King nurse. The Gibsons and Dad took me on one or two trips during that week or so, the most memorable being a voyage by steamer from Westminster Bridge to Southend-on-Sea and back. I think that flying darts and dropping tins had made me an apprehensive child as I remember the feelings of great trepidation as the ship's hooter was about to announce our departure.

After a week or so, Mum returned with a little bundle called Anne. I remember her climbing the stairs to show this precious addition to the admiring Bakers. While she did this, I asked Dad, man to man, where Mum had found the baby. 'In a shop window' was the rather puzzling reply.

Sleepless nights were a recent memory and there was a determination to achieve a quieter life with this second baby. If Anne's crying did not respond to a feed and a changed nappy, she was speedily removed to another room out of earshot. However, she was as placid as I had been fractious and, enhanced by her beauty, she soon developed a warm-hearted 'fan club' amongst Fred and Mary's neighbours.

Memories of that last year in Clapham seem tranquil enough at this distance. For me, remembrance includes distant visions of a huge weeping willow tree at the foot of the shared garden, a beautiful Old English Sheepdog owned by the other 'ground floor' family, and regimented rows of Darwin tulips, which I decapitated systematically as I could not abide the straightness of their planting.

The specialness of Sundays in the summer was not in church worship but in the cricket matches played at places like Wadden and Morden. Fred was a medium fast bowler, playing both for the Clapham Corinthians and for the Engineering Department of the GPO.

My father not only played hard, he worked hard too to improve his status at the GPO. Working as an electrician and a full member of the Trade Union, his work lost its initial temporary nature as he moved to the grade of 'skilled worker (Class II)' and so on to become an Assistant Executive Engineer.

In the late '30's, two of my father's brothers moved out of London with their families to the cleaner air of the Home Counties. The older of these brothers, Harry, had settled in Romford, Essex, where his wife Nell's father lived. Through them, Fred and Mary heard of the Nash houses, recently built at Collier Row nearby. There one could actually buy a house by depositing £5 and then paying 10 shillings a week. Alternatively, one could rent one of the properties for £1 a week. My parents, unable to afford the deposit, chose the latter course. And so, following one week's notice, the flat at King's Avenue, with its one guinea rent and expensive heating requirements, was vacated on my birthday, 1938.

51 Carter Drive, Collier Row, was to be the centre of our childhood for the next six years. A semi-detached brick house, with a garden of its own lovingly cultivated by Dad, it was on the perimeter of the estate. Clambering over the high, thoroughly creosoted fence at the foot of the garden, I was in a new world. Here ran—wonder of wonders—a stream, the River Rom, brimful with mysterious creatures eager to nibble the naked feet of a curious boy from the Big City. Beyond the brook with its attendant

brambles and alders lay inviting, hedge-bound arable land, and orchards 'set fair for scrumping'. Upstream, but barely half a mile away, was a small wood flanked by an area of rough pasture, tall with seeding grasses in high summer and a perfect hiding place for marauding Red Indians.

Starting school in the autumn of 1938 and so making one or two good friends, life at Collier Row seemed a happy one for a five year old boy with this world of river, field and wood at his feet. Living midway between North Weald and Hornchurch aerodromes, plane spotting became an obsession. During the coming war my commitment to these 'machines of the air', both British and German, was unwavering.

Meanwhile, Mum and Dad, along with countless other parents, heard and read the news of Hitler's opportunism, with apprehension. Rumours of war in September 1938 led to sand-bagging and the digging of shelters in gardens. Dad installed our Anderson shelter, a half cylinder of corrugated iron and roofing concrete over a dug-out, which contained bunk beds to sleep four to six people.[2]

When war was declared on 3rd September 1939, the mothers of Collier Row were requested to attend the local school for briefing. My mother remembers being told that, as it lay on the outermost ring of London's protective screen of barrage balloons and gun-belt, and was flanked by strategic aerodromes, Romford was a 'target area'. With foreboding in her heart, she knelt at the foot of the bed that night, praying that no harm would come to her family unit. One wonders how many other parents knelt similarly and prayed for the first time for years on that fateful day.

On hearing that war had begun between Britain and Germany, I recall the thrill of a five-year-old anticipating a ring-side seat at the most exciting dog-fights between Spitfire and Messerschmitt. My disappointment was profound as the protracted silence of the 'Phoney War' continued.

However, preparations for trouble were speedily made. Apart from the Anderson shelter, obscured by earth and plants in the garden, Mum and Dad prepared the front sitting room against the grim possibility of gas warfare. All the house's windows had been 'blacked out', but this front window was further sealed and criss-

2 The Anderson shelter was designed by Dr. David Anderson and coincidentally advocated by Sir John Anderson, the Chairman of the Air Raids Precaution (ARP), who later became Lord Waverley.

crossed with one inch brown tape to trap splintering glass. As much food as possible was stored in the room and every available utensil was filled with water. This voluntary seige was maintained for seven whole days and nights. There were no air-raids and so the precautions were gradually eased.

Eventually, my long awaited dog-fight was at hand. The sky was all commotion overhead, and the hall was all commotion at Number 51 as my mother drove my sister and me, and our visitor, an elegant and elderly spinster, into the cupboard under the stairs. I still remember my indignation at being so prevented from watching the skirmishes above. A Messerschmitt fighter plane (surely a BF 109E!) was brought down in the fields near a small lake a mile away, its pilot descending more serenely beneath his parachute.

The Battle of Britain continued during August and the first part of September 1940 in the skies above us. A mile to the west of us were key Anti-Aircraft gun placements, while beyond these we could see the light grey flotillas of the Barrage Balloons. Four miles to the south lay the Spitfire squadrons of Hornchurch, and six miles to the north was North Weald with its equally strategic Hurricanes.

As the Battle of Britain merged into the Blitzkreig on London and as the day-raids increasingly gave way to night bombing, the scurry down the garden path to the hidden shelter became a nightly routine. As we ran, with glimpses of a night sky criss-crossed by searchlight beams and with the dull drone of aircraft flying at great heights, I would shiver, my feelings a mixture of slightly puzzled fear and boyish delight.

We endured the ritual of my father banging his head on entry into the shelter, the trickles of rain penetrating our hide-away, wet beds from nervous excitement, and the persistent company of spiders. After some weeks, it was generally felt that the horrors of the Anderson were too oppressive and so, as the chances of a direct hit on Number 51 seemed slight, we began to risk sleeping indoors on the ground floor. Sometime later, Fred and Mary had become even more venturesome and slept in their bedroom upstairs. One night of heavy bombing, two large pieces of shrapnel penetrated the house. One fragment perforated the hot water tank causing immediate flooding, while the other came through the bedroom window and impaled the wall just above the headboard of my parents' bed.

On another night of bombing, Mum had great difficulty in

Mother with my sister Anne and me. *Right*: Mr. and Mrs. Pugh, our saintly neighbours

rousing Dad, who had been exhausted by his fire-watching duties in the City on the night of the so called 'Second Great Fire of London'. This conflagration had been started by incendiaries dropped by German 'pathfinder' aircraft to illuminate the targets for the discharge of High Explosive bombs from Heinkel and Junkers bombers. This same device was now being used over Collier Row! A string of incendiaries had been dropped in almost every garden in Carter Drive. Mercifully, mother's prayer for safety was still being answered, and the only damage we sustained from the ensuing HE bombardment was the severing of the power cable that supplied the light in our garden shelter.

The uncertainty and physical danger of war must have caused many to cry out in desperation, 'O God, save us! . . . save our nation, my family, me! . . .'. Perhaps mother was particularly determined in this respect, for on National Days of Prayer she would visit the parish church to find the building invariably empty.

Undrowned by the strident noise of war, there was 'a still, small voice' speaking to my parents through the quiet serenity of our immediate neighbours, Mr. and Mrs. Pugh. When the war started, Number 49 Carter Drive was soon occupied by lighthouse people from Felixstowe, billeted under the care of Trinity House. As the threat of invasion by sea diminished, they were returned to the coast. The house next door stayed empty until, one day during the early part of the war, mother saw a dignified, grey-haired couple approach Number 49 purposefully. Mary, eager to welcome, took round a tray of tea to meet the Pughs for the first time. Moving in a few weeks later, my parents soon realised that they had exceptional neighbours who showed a fine, gentle courtesy backed by a convinced Christian commitment.

Although in their mid- to late- sixties, the couple had only recently married; Mr. Pugh had waited a long time for his 'dear Sue', now released by the death of her mother. They were a carefully groomed and distinguished pair: Mrs. Pugh, a saintly little woman, short and rotund, her white hair swept back into a bun, emphasising her rosy, smiling face and rimless glasses; Mr. Pugh, taller than average, white-haired and white-moustached, his upright bearing evocative of distant trumpet-calls and gun-fire, and crowned by a black Trilby hat which seemed to be worn indoors as well as out. My parents watched them with keen interest as they lovingly tilled their garden and as they walked away to the local Mission Hall each Sunday, arm-in-arm, to worship their God.

My mother was deeply impressed by the cumulative effect of the contacts with these loving neighbours. One day, Mrs. Pugh asked my mother whether my father would buy some brandy for them, 'for medicinal purposes only . . . I ask as I know that your husband goes into the public house'. On another occasion, Mary was asked by this gentle lady whether she would buy a birthday card for her, 'but not with the word "Luck" in it. We don't believe in luck, only in God's overruling.' Mary Hurding has not bought an anniversary card with this condemned word in it since!

Along with these pointers to another and deeper dimension to life, my mother was further influenced by the complete absence of censoriousness in the Pugh's attitudes. Although their own attendance for Sunday worship was impeccable, they never remonstrated with my parents with: 'You ought to go to church—and take those children too!'.

During the harsh winter of 1941 and 1942, Mr. Pugh became seriously ill and, while his wife went shopping, mother was asked to sit with him. She recalls him staring at a rather nondescript painting on the wall of the bedroom near the window. To break the silence, my mother asked: 'Is that a very special picture that you keep looking at?'. His reply was simple and moving: 'No!. I see my dear wife reflected in its glass, as she goes to the shops and comes back again.'

The greatest impact from this saintly couple came soon after, when Mrs. Pugh called to my mother that her beloved husband had just died. The statement: 'He's with the Lord,' said with simple conviction by this serene neighbour, was quite unanticipated. Mary offered her meals and the share of a bed for a while. Mrs. Pugh replied, 'I've no fear of being in the house with his body, but I *will* come and stay with you.'

The awe that this Christian lady produced amongst her neighbours at Number 51 continued. She knelt to say her prayers before climbing into the double bed with my mother, and—miracle of miracles—we found ourselves saying Grace before meals. The greatest mystery of all overwhelmed my mother on the day of the funeral, when she witnessed Mrs. Pugh standing and singing at the top of her thin voice as she rejoiced in her dear Bert's presence with the Lord.

Following Mr. Pugh's death, Anne and I were plied with Christian books and bookmarks, displaying biblical texts, from his kindly widow. In time, this very special person moved back to relatives in Tottenham, but her loving contacts were maintained through regular letters to my parents, invariably closing with: 'God be with you and the children.' Once a month, the current copies of Boys' Friend and Girls' Friend were sent through the post for Anne and me. This faithful ministry continued until well after the war.

The love and prayers of Mrs. Pugh over nearly a decade were probably the most determining factors in the gradual turning of our family to Christ during the following years.

Thinking back to the war years, I remember, as a boy of seven or eight, being convinced of the reality of God. That conviction was of a loving and yet judging God who could see everything—the furtive cigarette in a hedge beyond the river, the helter-skelter across the fields after 'scrumping' apples and the dark thoughts I had towards a particularly priggish boy of a similar age. I recall seeing my mother as a god-fearing person, mainly through her anger when I let drop a swear word in the kitchen one day—I had no idea of the word's blasphemous content until her brown eyes flashed down at me.

I suspect there was a well established self-righteous streak in me, as was shown one day following a Sunday School service which Anne and I attended. During a rather protracted recital of the Lord's Prayer, I peered through my fingers across the wooden floorboards of the church hall to where my young sister was sitting.

To my horror, she was gazing across the hall rather than sitting with 'hands together and eyes closed', the pose prescribed for attentive prayer! Righteous indignation knew no bounds when I recounted this appalling discovery to our parents and one or two others a few days later. Anne's quiet rejoinder, that to have seen her during the prayer my eyes must have been open too, only *just* found its mark. It took me some time to see the justice of her comment!

In the course of those earlier war years, illness, which was to play such a dominant part later, was an intermittent distraction for mother. Following a severe bout of whooping cough while we lived in South London, I was prone to recurring pneumonia during the early '40's. One memory that my mother recalls was a particular visit of the local general practitioner, a smiling and gentle Indian, Dr. Siddhanta. Coming into the "Vick"-vapour-laden atmosphere of the childrens' bedroom, where my sister slept, aglow with the fever of measles, and I lay coughing with pneumonia, he apologised to mother for his 'black face' and the effect it might have if Anne woke suddenly. The caring and care-felt encounters with this kindly doctor did a great deal to encourage us to warmth and openness towards people of other races and backgrounds.

At about my tenth birthday we moved to a 3-bedroom semi-detached house on the busy Southend Arterial Road at Harold Wood, to be nearer to my father's brother, Harry and his family. A slightly bigger house with the same rent of £1 a week was an attractive prospect.

The allied invasion of Europe on 6th June of that year, 1944, was soon followed by the first of the Nazi 'Revenge' weapons, the V1. Also described as the Pilotless Bomber and the Buzz Bomb, the name Doodle Bug, first coined by New Zealand fighter pilots recalling a noisy insect from back home, seemed to catch on. The rattling of the pulse jet of these 'planes' is a sound I can still remember and imitate with little difficulty nearly four decades later. The initial impressions of a bewildered population reacting to these new weapons included: 'Like a Model-T Ford going up a hill', 'Like a motor-bike with a two-stroke engine', 'Something black, trailing a strong flame' and, perhaps the most colourful of all: 'Little aeroplanes with a light up their backside'!

Like so many puzzled listeners at the beginning of this 'Second Battle of Britain', Mum and Dad lay awake one night that summer hypnotised by the laboured chugging of these unfamiliar engines. From time to time they endured the ominously prolonged silence as an engine cut out. They soon learnt the sinister pattern: pulsatile engine noise; silence; and explosion as the war-head hit its chance target.

During the following months, we saw quite a number of these sinister-looking monoplanes belching fire from the rear. I remember the boyish mixture of fear and pleasure on seeing one just above the roof-tops while I ran parallel with it on my way to a friend's house. On another occasion, the element of pleasure, and even triumph, was strong when two of us boys watched a Spitfire shoot at a V1.

The flying bombardment increased in intensity to a climax in August and, as it did so, the publicity for evacuating children built up once more. The sheer thrill of chugging away, pulled by a steam train, was too much for my curtailed spirit. Although my parents were keen to keep the family together, they gave way to my persistence and I was soon part of an excited group of boys from the local school, grimy noses pressed to grimy windows as we gazed at the unfamiliar landscape and as the GWR train steamed to some unbelievable utopia.

The 'unbelievable utopia' was the rather grim town of Wrexham in north-east Wales, near enough to the English border to be partially accessible to our southern and suburban minds, and yet Welsh enough to be proud of its challenging language, its singing and its adjacent coal-mines. The Gresford disaster of 1934, with its 265 deaths, was still spoken of with hushed voices by the respectable family that I and another boy were billeted with.

My two to three months of evacuation was a bitter-sweet experience. On the one hand, we were not allowed to forget our Englishness and the mother and teenage daughter of the family I stayed with seemed particularly critical of this tongue-tied boy from Greater London. On the other hand, I enjoyed the attempt to learn some Welsh and rejoiced greatly in saying 'Rhosllannerchrugog', the name of a nearby mining town, with enviable accuracy.

Perhaps the greatest compensation was the proximity of a 'real mountain', which could be seen from the upstairs window as a smudge on the western horizon. This 'mountain' was the upland area of Millstone Grit moorland called Eclusham Mountain, rising to barely 1500 feet but, nonetheless, something mystical and enticing to my imaginative mind. Disappointed that an older Welsh girl did not keep her word to take me 'to the Mountain', I made my way by various buses to the village of Minera and later sprawled amongst the bilberry-covered slopes with a new-found exhilaration.

One influence I am grateful to my 'fostering' family for was the matter of Sunday worship. Mr. Evans, let us call him, was a tall, dark-haired man with an upright build and an upright life. He used to take me to the chapel he attended in the nearby mining village, where the pews fairly reverberated with the lusty singing of the dark-suited men. My sensitive English ears and attitudes were offended by Mr. Evans' rich, vibrato bass voice, which he used with great gusto as he tackled the hymns. I remember catching his slightly disapproving eye one Sunday as I looked up in sheer wonder at the volume of sound that poured from his frame. Later that day, I risked his wrath by announcing that I did not wish to go to the chapel any more. To my amazement he assented, although he was clearly puzzled by my criticism of the exuberant singing.

After this, I took the plunge and attended the gaunt, Victorian Anglican church, Sunday by Sunday. Encountering the sombre remoteness of the place, I sometimes wondered whether I would have been better off gazing up at Mr. Evans, while the chapel shook to the strains of Cwm Rhondda and Blaenwern. I even ventured to go to a mid-week meeting at the Church of England, such was my determination to find a spiritual home. My composure received one of its stiffest challenges when the highlight of the evening proved to be a rendition of the 'Lost Chord' played and sung by a very intense Welshman. The transportation of the singer, as he searched for his lost chord, the attentive admiration of the middle-aged around me and the overwhelming burst of applause as he finished did not seem to be meeting my emerging sensibilities, and my church-going was thus concluded for a few years.

Homesickness prevailed; and I was eventually rescued by Dad for a long, long journey home with numerous diversions and delays, a sleep-walking trek through a strangely silent London at about 1.00 a.m. from Paddington to Liverpool Street, and a wanderer's welcome from Mum and Anne on entering the hall at home.

On 7th September 1944, people living in the Epping Forest area were startled by what sounded like a double explosion 'coming out of the blue' and leaving a crater 8 feet across and 8 feet deep. The Government kept a conspiracy of silence about this new, German offensive weapon, and rumours about the 'flying gasometer' abounded. These V2's, the progeny of Dr. Von Braun's 'Rocket', the 'Dove of World Peace' built fifteen years earlier, were fired from launching-sites on the occupied coast of North-west Europe. Their trajectories, reaching a height of fifty miles, were sometimes pin-pointed by sinister vapour trails, the only indication of the imminent hail of destruction. More usually, the first awareness of a V2 was the double boom, the first of a sonic bang (as the rocket descended at a speed faster than sound) and the second the explosion of the one-ton war-head on impact.

That winter, a few days before the Christmas holidays, Anne and I had the rare treat of a day off school in order to travel up to London with mother to see a pantomime on ice at the Stoll, Kingsway; we were to meet father in the City, where he had been on fire-watching duty over the previous few nights.

It was a cold December day when a thick layer of snow obscured the familiar houses and gardens seen from my bedroom window. Mother had been up early and a welcoming fire crackled in the hearth of the rear room, where we were to have breakfast. Eager for the day ahead, we sat round the table, waiting for the small knob of rationed butter to melt a little in front of the fire. Suddenly, we felt the ground beneath the house tremble, saw the French windows belly inwards and splinter, and witnessed a cascade of soot, loosened from the chimney, fall on the precious butter. Almost simultaneously, the explanatory bang of an exploding V2 shattered our startled silence. Maternal instincts up and down the road sparked into action as mothers rushed into the snow with cries of, 'The school's been hit!'. Our own mother, protectively but understandably, muttered, 'Thank God you're safe at home!'.

Ardleigh Green School, both Infants' and Juniors', lay only a quarter of a mile away beyond several rows of houses. It comprised single-storey buildings, that morning full of non-pantomime-going children, and it had mercifully escaped the main impact of the rocket, which had instead devastated an adjacent button factory, hurtling myriads of tiny button missiles into the neighbourhood.

Life must go on, especially where an annual treat is concerned; and so the three of us boarded the train for London. With noses glued to the carriage windows, we silently observed the cityscape of East London, pock-marked with fresh craters from this most recent visitation; a whole fleet of V2's had been unleashed that morning to fall, with the snow, from leaden skies.

Returning home in the dark from the glowing fantasy-world of the pantomime, we found we were locked out in the snow. The rocket's explosion had caused enough shift in the house's structure to jam the locks and no key would budge them. My father's brother, Harry, had, unintentionally, sealed off another point of entry by boarding up the shattered glazing of the French windows. However, with the help of a friendly neighbouring policeman, a long ladder and some acrobatics, we were able to enter the house and snuggle down into our beds before long, warmed by hot-water bottles and secure for at least another night.

As the war finished, I passed the 'scholarship examination' to go to the Royal Liberty Grammar School at nearby Gidea Park. This school had a good academic reputation and I greatly enjoyed the wide range of subjects taught, excelling particularly at geography, art and languages. My physical frame was not a robust one and I was readily outstripped on the sport's field. However, I could produce a competitive breast-stroke, scored a few ready goals from 'inside right' and bowled some devilish off-spins, with an occasional Googly!

Perhaps the greatest thrill of those earlier school years was the development of an out-going camaraderie of up to ten very enthusiastic bird-watchers. One of the formative links of this group was my friendship with Rob, which began, somewhat tentatively, during our first term at the 'Liberty'. It was a classic example of C. S. Lewis's: 'What you too?'. The two of us began to talk one lunch hour as we strolled round the extensive school playing-fields. I soon discovered that he not only had some small, brown birds nesting in the gutter of his parents' house, but he *knew* that they were spotted flycatchers and, best of all, he watched them with keen interest.

In the first year or so, there was some perpetuation of a 'Swallows and Amazons' mentality amongst the growing nucleus of friends. This led to the formation of a small, exclusive 'in-group' with a 'secret' base deep in some thick mixed woodland, and with the password: 'Nidus' (Latin for 'Nest'), which evoked the reply: 'Sudin' from any true friend.

However, as the group grew, the business of bird-watching became too serious and absorbing for such a fantasy-world to persist. Our bicycles took us in an increasingly far ranging arc to the north and east away from our suburban homes. During the long arctic winter of 1946 and 1947, we trudged the frozen, iron-clad landscape watching birds the hard way, without a pair of binoculars between us and with nothing but a single copy of T. A. Coward's *Birds of the Wayside and Woodland* to aid us in identification. This book's tiny reproductions of Thorburn's beautiful, but stylised, paintings were little help in the face of the tantalisingly nondescript avian shapes that flitted through the winter countryside around us.

As we acquired more reliable bicycles, an assortment of binoculars and telescopes, and a better library of reference books, we began to push further afield to explore the estuaries of the Thames, Crouch and Blackwater, and the intervening coastlines. These cycling trips were memorable—long, arduous journeys against bitter winds, our saddle-bags laden with wellington boots, binoculars and food. Often the corned beef sandwiches of the outward ride were replaced by the corpse of an oiled or shot sea-bird on the return.

One favourite haunt was Leigh Point on Canvey Island, a remote spit of shingle pointing eastwards towards Southend pier, and approached across half a mile of salt-marsh. With the encouragement of a slightly older and more experienced ornithologist, we had once marooned ourselves on this crescent of mud and shingle. Lying flat and as hidden as possible by the rough shelters of stone erected by wild-fowlers, we waited for the rising tide to isolate us, along with the increasingly concentrated flocks of small waders, on the tiny island.

Having enjoyed the quicksilver proximity of dunlin, ringed plover, turnstone and, on this occasion, a few purple sandpiper. I attempted a similar exploit solo some weeks later. Carefully esconced within a modest wall of small boulders on an even more promising potential islet, I waited with relish for high tide and the panorama of bird-life it would surely bring. I had not consulted tide-tables and did not at first realise that my visit coincided with an exceptionally full spring-tide. As the waters rose and gradually penetrated my concealment, I began to notice that a number of usually exposed prominences were vanishing in the flood. Less intrigued now by the wheeling waders, I began to dismantle the encircling wall to erect a pyramid of stone, on the summit of which I was forced to sit by the rising waters. I had a vision of myself as seen from the sea-wall, a tiny speck merged with a tiny rock pinnacle half a mile away, and barely discernible in the grey sea beneath the grey sky.

Initially, I was amused by the slap-stick comedy of the situation—a sort of Charlie Chaplin against the elements—but as the waters lapped my dangling boots, the smile faded.

Even if a watery grave seemed a fairly remote possibility, there was no doubt about the realities of a very uncomfortably exposed few hours ahead. I remember perching there between sea and sky, praying the Lord's Prayer *most* fervently—and more than once. In time, the tide began to ebb, and, as the dusk gathered, I found my way cautiously across the diminishing channels to the path, the sea-wall and the bicycle, hidden in a bed of reeds.

During these early teen years, a sense of the reality of a personal God remained. As a result, although in a desultory way, I tried out a few Anglican churches in the vicinity, but did not feel compelled to attend any of them regularly. One Sunday, encouraged by the company of an older friend, I found my way to St. Peter's, Harold Wood.

The ministry and fellowship of this church were to have an enormous influence for good on our family over the next thirty years. We found the simplicity of that Morning Service attractive and the sermon not particularly memorable. What impressed me was the genuinely warm welcome of a young man in his twenties who shook our hands vigorously and enquired a little about us. This friendliness drew me back, and when he asked me some weeks later, 'Why don't you join our Boys' Bible Class?', I could think of no good reason why I should not.

That was a fateful step, for it exposed me for the first time to faithful and systematic teaching of the Scriptures. The vicar, the Rev. Hayman Johnson, was at that time leading the study of Mark's Gospel, and I was particularly impressed as he traced the Lord's inexorable journey to Jerusalem and certain death. I was stirred by the power and beauty of this Man's life and teaching, although there was much about His claim on our lives that I barely understood. I was asked whether I would like to consider Confirmation in the coming summer. I was fifteen and, although there was some uncertainty in my mind, my mother felt it was a reasonable age to be confirmed, and she seemed to be right.

Duly prepared with a group of other teenagers by the vicar, I was confirmed by Hugh Gough, then Bishop of Barking and later Archbishop of Sydney. The quiet dignity of the occasion, the simple spirituality of the bishop's address and the sense of a profound new beginning in life were memorable. My understanding of the step I had taken was limited, but there was no doubt about it being an important one of commitment to Jesus Christ.

There followed two very 'up and down' years where feelings ranged from peaceful exultation to miserable self-recrimination. I hung on rather grimly with assurances from others of: 'It's always harder swimming upstream' and 'You know you're a Christian, because the devil's only interested in you if you *are* one!' At times, I wished that the adversary was not so *very* interested. It was some years before this inner battle was assuaged by the Lord.

And so a family began to come to faith. My mother's adolescent commitment, although neglected through the years, the prayers and love of the neighbourly Mrs. Pugh and the seemingly fortuitous visit of two teenage lads to a local church were at least some of the links forged in the chain of a bondage that is freedom.

Some months after my Confirmation, Anne, now twelve, was shattered one evening by the death of a much loved kitten, a victim of the heavy arterial traffic that passed our house. Opportunistically, but with true 'philadelphia', I told her how she could find help from Jesus and how she could become a Christian. We knelt together by her bed, the air charged with a kitten's death.

The regular visits of Mum, Anne and me to church, the re-introduction of Grace at meal-times and some measure of a new love in the household gradually whittled down Dad's resistance to this strange new behaviour. Eventually, the *News of the World* was left behind of a Sunday evening and the four of us sat together in a pew, joining in the singing and listening to the preaching with varying degrees of enthusiasm. As the months slipped by, the influences of faithful biblical teaching and the caring friendships of local Christian people worked a deep work in the lives of our family unit. God's grace and love invaded the fabric of our existence and Dad could hold out no longer against the surge of the Holy Spirit's persuasiveness.

In 1950, during a local mission at which an up-and-coming young preacher called John Stott spoke, my father, responding with several other good friends, opened his good-humoured but temperamental life to God.

And so a family came to faith. No easy path was promised, and, for one member of the family, a seemingly life-long illness had already established itself as part of the pattern for the future.

CHAPTER FIVE

THE NOT SO LIGHT BLUES

Halts by me that footfall:
Is my gloom, after all,
Shade of His hand, outstretched caressingly?
'Ah, fondest, blindest, weakest.
I am He whom thou seekest!
Thou dravest love from thee, who dravest Me'.
Francis Thompson: *The Hound of Heaven*

'So this is the city of dreaming spires,' Sheila said. 'Theoretically that's Oxford,' Adam said. 'This is the city of perspiring dreams.'
Frederic Raphael: *The Glittering Prizes*

NINETEEN-FIFTY-TWO BEGAN WITH A NEW ENTHUSIASM FOR living. Diabetes had been diagnosed and was being treated by daily injections and by diet; health and some *joie de vivre* replaced the malaise and apathy of the previous year. I was thus able to return to the fold of our bird-watching côterie, enjoying our forays into the Essex countryside and our longer expeditions to the level horizons of the East Coast with a renewed zest.

The main nucleus of our happy band comprised, at this stage, three 'geologists' and three 'natural scientists'. It was a time of decision and readjustment concerning the future, and there was some shift in our prospective careers. Two of the latter had intended to be vets and one a doctor. In time, all three decided on a career in Medicine and I, as one of the trio of 'geologists', was also heading in the same direction.

My 'bargain with God' was honoured[1]; I gained good results in the 'Higher' exam, including Scholarship levels in Geography and Geology, and so, armed with a State Scholarship to read Medicine, I was able to switch to 1st MB subjects (Chemistry, Physics and Biology) for another year in the sixth form. In the middle of this transition, but fortunately one month or so after these crucial exams, I was 'laid aside' for another, though briefer, taste of hospital life.

Waking to a gnawing lower abdominal pain early on Sunday 20th July, I spent an agonising but hazily remembered day, while the discomfort increased and localised, and my temperature rose to 102.5°F. It required the doctor's second visit late that night to establish the diagnosis of appendicitis, and I was promptly admitted to one of the local hospitals. The welcome oblivion of general anaesthesia lasted until six the next morning, when I woke to the noisy bustle of a surgical ward, the soreness of my abdomen a tolerable contrast to the intense pain of the previous day.

Here, then, was another valuable experience for a would-be doctor, underlining the lessons of being 'on the receiving end', already tasted during the six weeks on a medical ward eight or nine months before. The exuberance of a visiting clergyman who *seemed* to treat the patients primarily as 'conversion fodder' and my own diffidence at talking too readily about Christ were counter-balanced by a refreshing time of meditation on the book of Isaiah and the reading of Mrs. Howard Taylor's *Pastor Hsi, One of China's Christians* and G. F. Dempster's *Finding Men for Christ*. At the end of a week, I emerged from the hospital, limping slightly because the severed and restitched muscles were pulled on, but, like Jacob, the better for a time of wrestling with the Lord and His loving interest in my life.

Although disappointed not to be able to accompany Rob and Dave on a long cycling trek around Scotland that summer, the adjustment to being a diabetic continued quite straightforwardly. I wanted to keep within any reasonable limits imposed by the need for regular injections of insulin and for predictable meal times, but I also wished to live life fully.

In order to keep fit, the diabetic needs to maintain the amount of sugar in the blood-stream between certain levels. This is done by balancing the quantity of insulin injected once or twice a day with the intake of carbohydrate at prescribed meal times. If a diabetic

1 See Chapter One, p.22.

overeats or neglects to take insulin, then the consequences of an unduly high blood sugar, including unquenchable thirst, malaise and lethargy, develop. Where this lack of management continues, the condition of untreated diabetes with the eventual dangers of coma and death may ensue.

If the insulin is injected but the intake of food is too little, the diabetic develops a 'low blood sugar' or hypoglycaemic attack. During this 'hypo', symptoms of dizziness, headache, hunger and cold sweats, and the appearance of pallor are common. If untreated by some glucose or other appropriate food, then there is a danger of a loss of consciousness. The improvement, to the onlooker, in a diabetic who is behaving more vaguely than usual, or even in a drunken manner, to one who is alert and attentive once more, following the nibbling or drinking of something sweet, can be dramatic.

If, on one of our protracted cycling trips, we continually debated just where we would stop for lunch, my rate of progress would diminish steadily as I became more dazed. When questioned, I found an inner resistance to declaring a drop in blood sugar. Somehow, the need to stop and eat did not fit in with our reckless pioneering spirit! Eventually, common sense, aided by the fall in my friends' blood sugars, prevailed.

One of the changes those around me noticed on such occasions was the loss of a sense of humour. Taking after my father in this respect, humour is a very important dimension of life to me. From my point of view, I would feel very vulnerable to find my sense of timing in repartee, or my grasp of innuendoes and witticisms, suddenly vanish. I suspect, at times, my friends found this lack of response quite a relief!

Perhaps the most venturesome thing attempted during the first year or so of diabetes, in terms of irregular hours, was to set the alarm clock for 2.00 a.m. one May morning and cycle four miles with Rob to a favourite coppice to listen to the dawn chorus. We waited in the sequestered gloom, the wood's silence penetrated by the occasional hoot of a tawny owl and the vibrant song of a nightingale. The first 'day-time' bird to venture its voice was a distant cuckoo at just before ten past three. It was another three quarters of an hour before true diurnal bird song was heard when a robin began its melancholy musings, followed by a blackbird's full-throated phrases five minutes later. Soon after 4.00 a.m. the wood resounded with the full dawn chorus. The impact of this rich and varied orchestration, building to its climax from the first few hesitant notes, was almost overwhelming. It really was worth the tussle with sleep and darkness to experience this prodigious beauty. Furthermore, it was helpful to find that I could cope with rising early, at least without undue problems developing with the diabetes.

Later that summer, the Young Peoples' Fellowship of St. Peter's, Harold Wood joined forces with a similar group from a church in Kent's 'Bible Belt', and spent a week's holiday at a large house in Langton Matravers, Dorset. It was there that I first met the Rev. Dick Lucas, his sonorous Oxford accent a source of wonder and amusement to some of us. Two aspects of our encounter stand out: one was the occasion when Rob and I were wedged under a couple of beds in the girls' dormitory with 'lights out' imminent, only to be prised out by the persistent ring of 'Loopy Lu's' stentorian voice, demanding: 'Come on out - you Bad Eggs!'; the other was a most helpful chat that he and I had on the last evening. My convoluted thinking had trapped me in a vicious circle wherein I questioned my own genuineness as a Christian. I told him that I was not sure whether I had been sincere when I committed my life to Christ. His reply: 'It isn't your sincerity but the *fact* of your commitment that matters' did a great deal to disentangle my muddled thinking.

In June 1953, I spent a few days in Cambridge taking exams in the three 1st MB subjects. On the eve of this exam, while spending the night in a room at one of Selwyn college's hostels, I had an unsettling experience of a hypnagogic nature.[2]. Feeling peaceful and reasonably relaxed about the morrow's papers, I undressed and lay on my back in bed waiting for the milk drink that the hostel-keeper had promised to bring me. Fully conscious, I surveyed the smallish room, noting its scanty furniture and studying the plastered ceiling above. I was suddenly aware of the pressure of what felt like another body on top of mine. The sensation of weight and mass appropriate to another human being, and the feeling of another's rate of breathing out of phase with mine were most frightening. I was aware of this 'presence' for a good half a minute and found it a great struggle to invoke the name of Jesus; when I did, the

2 Hypnagogic phenomena are thought to be hallucinations, which carry the conviction of reality, experienced on occasions by some people as they begin to fall asleep.

sensation faded.

Like others, I had had one or two similar experiences before, though these had usually been on waking in the night. I remember one windy night, at the age of seventeen or so, waking with my heart pounding at a fair gallop. My bedroom was dark but there seemed to be a particularly concentrated darkness at the bottom right corner of the double bed. There was an unnatural coldness in the room and a sensation of oppressive evil seemed to emanate from the gloom at the foot of the bed. Then, perhaps inevitably, I began to feel as if the bedclothes were being pulled steadily towards the unearthly shadow. Again, there had been the struggle to pray and, again, the feeling of dread was gradually replaced by the knowledge that the Lord was there and all was well.

Are such experiences completely explicable in terms of psychological insight? Was the episode at Cambridge simply the outcome of suppressed apprehension about the next day's exam? Or, are such events instigated, or capitalised on, at least on some occasions, by the Enemy? Either way, it is good to remember with the Psalmist that the Lord 'neither slumbers nor sleeps'![3]

In spite of the unsettlement of that first night at the college hostel, the exams were duly passed and, financed by the State Scholarship, I went up to Cambridge to study Medicine in October 1953.

Coming from an unprivileged and unbookish background, there were many adjustments to make to collegiate life. Many of my fellow students, straight from well known public schools or coming to university after their two years' National Service, seemed to be very much at home striding the courts and corridors, singing lustily at the daily worship in the chapel and jostling for a table amongst friends in the refectory.

I shall always be grateful to my Christian friends at Cambridge. Before I was barely unpacked on first arrival, Steve Houghton, the son of well known CIM[4] missionaries, swept into my room with a brother's welcome. He and others were big-hearted enough in their Christian love to receive me into their back-slapping, ex-public school and ex-Army côterie. We had a common bond in Christ, and the Holy Spirit broke down the walls of cultural distinction as we let Him.

My Christian commitment at least began to develop some

3 Psalm 121:4. 4 China Inland Mission, now the Overseas Missionary Fellowship.

substance as I attended the famous CICCU[5] Bible Readings on Saturday evenings with a small group of friends and began to live with words (and concepts) like justification, sanctification and glorification. Something of the thrill of beginning to discover eternal truths in fresh ways spilled over to my neighbours in the spartan little ground-floor corridor where we lived. I remember suggesting to Graham, an elegant first year student of History, that we read the Bible together; we started bravely with Habakkuk (where else?) but somehow foundered on reaching chapter two! The other room next to mine was occupied by a friend who is now the principal of a theological college. One Sunday evening, he was smitten in his mind and heart by what seemed to me to be an unhelpfully inconclusive sermon, delivered in the college chapel by a visiting preacher. My fellow-student and I talked into the small hours of the morning about sin, guilt and the open door to forgiveness and a new relationship with God through His Son.

The early 50's in Cambridge were the years of Frederic Raphael's *Glittering Prizes* and a great deal of inimitable talent in the area of undergraduate humour. Jonathan Miller, the actor, producer and broadcaster, was studying Medicine in my year. His appearance, with others, in the Footlights Revue at the Arts' Theatre, did a great deal to refresh my sometimes jaded spirits with the spice of humour. His zany, side-splitting perspective of life helped to prick the balloons of conformity and predictability—aspects of Man's existence which I have often found irksome.

Beyond the hearty singing and praying of the CICCU, and the world of *homo ludens*,[6] there was the heavier side of life where friends became depressed or were filled with anxiety. I remember listening to the needs of such and wondering why there was not more effective help for them, both through the medical profession and the Church. The grim reality of one of those notorious Oxbridge suicides, in a bedroom just above the Junior Common Room at Selwyn, shocked many of us into silence—at least for a few days. A massive overdose of injected insulin in a non-diabetic had been fatal, and the college flag at half-mast was a chilling reminder of harsher perspectives.

During my first and second years at Cambridge, there were times when I experienced the 'not so light blues'. There was still a considerable amount of inner conflict, particularly in the spiritual

5 Cambridge Inter-Collegiate Christian Union.

6 'Man (or woman!) at play'.

realm. At times, I was reasonably peaceful and confident, but much of this security came from achieving the daily 'quiet time' of personal devotion, and the regular attendance at prayer meetings and Bible studies. Although these disciplines were very valuable, I was too dependent on them. I rushed from one to the other to slake my spiritual thirst, without allowing their refreshment to work its good work quietly and thoroughly.

At this stage, a stilling influence on my feverishness was the gentle ministry of Mark Ruston, who had just been appointed as the vicar of the Round Church. Taking a series of Bible studies for the Christian Union at Selwyn, he led us patiently through John's first epistle, a feast of reassuring words to a troubled Christian. This minister's good sense and spiritual maturity began to draw me like a magnet to worship at the Round Church at a time when most of the evangelical Anglican students flocked to St. Paul's and Holy Trinity.

My hidden turmoil was further calmed through the friendship of an extraordinary Welshman, Raymond John Jones. This outgoing and good-humoured Christian had an acne-scarred face that shone like that of an unveiled Moses, hot foot from the holy mountain. He had been president of the Christian Union at Aberystwyth University and was now doing a post-graduate year in Agriculture at Cambridge. We shared the same landing for many months in one of the college's houses, a quarter of a mile from Selwyn. Our long discussions on points of doctrine did a great deal to strengthen my grasp of the revealed faith. His Open Brethren background in South Wales led to his frank astonishment at meeting an Anglican who was actually a Christian! There was a parallel incredulity, in those days, at coming across a student at Selwyn who was *not* a confirmed member of the Church of England.

My introduction, through Raymond, to the warm welcome of the assembly at Panton Hall and his own joyful and well informed faith have done much to make me feel at home in Open Brethren circles.

In spite of my ups and downs, Cambridge was a good place to be. The interlocking vista of collegiate buildings, mature trees, the mirroring Cam and the vast sky was a source of recurring delight. The dazzling splendour of autumn with limes and chestnuts glowing against the arching sky, the frost-gripped days of winter with the river frozen, the expectancy of spring with daffodils and crocuses bedecking the Backs, and the punting and May Ball days of summer, with the swifts screaming about the college towers, form an indelible memory.

In the summer of the second year an important crisis took place which brought a new stability into my life as a Christian.

I had taken a hesitant interest in a group of undergraduates who were involved in Christian work amongst eight- to thirteen-year-old boys in various parts of the country. That summer, they planned to take boys from as far apart as Liverpool and St. Leonard's in Sussex to Dolfriog Hall, a large house in the lovely wooded valley of Nantmor just south of Snowdon, for a fortnight's holiday. A medical officer was needed as some sort of insurance policy to cover their physical well-being; and so I was asked (as the nearest Christian medical student who looked gullible enough, or brave enough, to agree) to fill the post.

Money was difficult. The State Scholarship just covered each term's expenses with the most frugal of budgets. As a result, I spent most of the summer vacations working as an orderly amidst the blood and gore of the operating theatre in a local hospital at home in Essex. I decided that an economical way of extending the Welsh holiday was to cycle to Dolfriog, youth hostelling en route.

On the eve of this adventure, I attended the evening service at St. Peter's Harold Wood and heard the Rev. Don Churchman preach most powerfully on one of the briefest of texts : 'Remember Lot's wife.' (Luke 17 : 32). I can remember nothing of this sermon on Jesus' warning to His disciples, except for the three simple words of the theme. As I cycled the 120 miles through the Home Counties to my first overnight stay in the Cotswolds, the terse phrase : 'Remember Lot's wife' pounded in my head like hammer blows. I can still recall the twisting road ahead and the extraordinarily powerful sense of God's challenge beating down on me with the sun: 'Remember Lot's wife. She looked back . . . She did not obey . . . She gave up . . . What will you do?' I had begun to follow Christ at the age of fifteen and now, after five years of recurring uncertainty and vacillation, I was faced with a decision. I either had to turn my back on the Hound of Heaven once and for all or I had to follow Him wholeheartedly *wherever* He would lead.

A year or two before, a friend had bought me J. C. Ryle's *Holiness* and the challenge of the chapter 'A Woman to be Remembered' was now being reinforced, most persistently. Somehow along that long and beautiful road to North Wales, the Lord God spoke to me finally—or so it seemed. I could do no other than respond to this great Creator and Redeemer. Somewhere, between the surburban sprawl of Harold Wood and the hump-backed mountains south of Snowdon, the Rubicon was crossed—along with the Severn and the Wye! I arrived amidst the oak woods of Dolfriog, travel-weary and extremely chastened in spirit. The cost of following Christ had been counted some time before, prompted by J. C. Ryle's book, and there could be *no* looking back.

God's gracious communication continued throughout that rumbustious fortnight while I tried to help my Christian friends share His love with those lusty lads. God's grace broke through to me most significantly half way through the two weeks when, as medical officer, I was asked to give a 'sex talk' to the boys.

This was a crisis in its own right, and so I retreated with a well-thumbed copy of *Heirs Together* (once retitled by a friend *A Christian's Guide on How to Avoid Marriage*!) I took the book up the tumbling hill-stream to a safely remote spot, amidst the lichen-coated alders, to prepare the ultimate discourse on matters sexual. Already familiar with the book's cautious wisdom on relationships, I was transfixed by one of the later chapters on the death of Christ. I had always found the phrase, 'at the foot of the Cross' tantalisingly mystical, but now I was arrested by the horror and overwhelming compassion of His crucifixion. This was no vague sympathetic response on my part for, somehow, I saw deep down inside that this self-sacrifice was, mysteriously, not only for all mankind in a general sense but was also for *me* in particular. The risen Lord was there standing beside the turbulent river telling me of His love. The 'sex talk' forgotten, I knelt amongst the mosses and thanked Him for His death for me, gladly affirming that for the rest of my days I wanted His way. I was convinced intellectually and emotionally that He wanted nothing but good for me and that His will would always be the best in any situation.

After the fortnight at Dolfriog, I cycled on to meet a very special friend, Robin, a second-year geographer from Cambridge with a penchant for the wild places. We spent a memorable few days together, sleeping under the stars by Idwal Cottage at night and rock-climbing above Llyn Ogwen by day. This was my first taste of scaling the heights using rope and I found the working out of each hand- and foothold, while poised far above the lake, most exhilarating. Somehow, the trust placed in the other climber, the need to deal with the ascent one step at a time and the inadvisability of looking down and back seemed to form a powerful analogy of progress in following Christ. Lot's wife was being well remembered!

As always, the Lord was looking beyond the immediate to the next stage. And the next stage was the occasion of Billy Graham's first mission to the University of Cambridge. Another friend and I had been asked to be college representatives of the CICCU at Selwyn for the coming year and we would thus be in the midst of the fray.

While Robin and I were enjoying the mountain air, there was a brisk correspondence building up in *The Times* on the question of fundamentalism. Differences of opinion on the inspiration of the scriptures were freely expressed and a great deal of misunderstanding abounded. Along with this debate, the prospective mission to Cambridge led by Billy Graham was the subject of much controversy. Was the preaching of the 'simple gospel' quite appropriate in a city of such academic excellence? How would the American evangelist fare in debate with abrasive Cambridge theologians and philosophers?

Selwyn was a microcosm of these more general uncertainties. Having an Anglican foundation, this college attracted a disproportionate number of theological students. Many of these were of Anglo-Catholic or liberal persuasion and were understandably apprehensive at the advent of Billy Graham. Amongst my closer friends were a number of thoughtful Evangelical Christians who were also uneasy about the mission and its aftermath. They raised the perceptive query as to how suitable a 'nursery school' the CICCU would provide in the practical areas of living out the Christian life in a complex world. Their spokesman approached me, as one of the college representatives of the Christian Union, to express their concern and to gauge my support for their view. Although sympathetic to their dissension, I felt that I had to be loyal to the body I represented. These friends were consistent; they wrote to Billy Graham, sharing their anxiety and urging him not to confuse Cambridge by coming as its missioner.

However, he came. King's Parade was crowded every night as undergraduates queued outside Great St. Mary's to hear him; Cambridge dons were intrigued by the evangelist's sincerity and integrity, while profound issues were debated over lunch; and many young men and women found new life through faith in Christ.

During the first part of the mission, the number of known converts was negligible at Selwyn. We called a prayer meeting one lunch hour and locked ourselves in to call on the Lord. What was our motivation? Was it that we felt ashamed, at the level of inter-collegiate rivalry? Were we trapped by the 'counting heads' mentality? Or did we long that others should find abundant life through Christ? Although I suspect our motives were mixed, God answered our prayer most generously. Within a day or two eighteen young men from Selwyn had signed 'decision cards' to indicate their commitment to Christ.

God's message of reconciliation is for all and I was amused to find this borne out in the contrasting personalities of two new Christians I visited soon after. One was a most phlegmatic and intelligent student of Chemical Engineering, a keen ornithologist and botanist. I was greeted in a matter-of-fact way by this new, level-headed friend whose experience of Christ, although expressed so prosaically, was of a real and abiding quality. The other student, studying languages, was in his first year and welcomed me most warmly when I visited his rooms. As a medical student I was already reasonably unshockable, but the sheer multiplicity of bare breasts and buttocks that assailed the eyes from the magazine cuttings stuck to every vertical surface around this smiling, freckled young man, was distracting in the extreme. He talked freely of his hitherto sexually promiscuous life amongst the privileged of the West End of London. There was an extraordinary innocence in his newly realised sense of guilt as he said, 'I never knew there was anything wrong in sleeping around!' The Holy Spirit had made the point; I did not need to add to it.

By the time I had taken the Natural Sciences Tripos in the summer of 1956 and enjoyed the exquisite festivities of May Week —the frenetic clamour of the inter-collegiate 'Bumps' boat races, diminutive coxes hoarse with aggression; the champagne glamour of the May Balls; the limpid beauty of Elizabethan madrigals sung at night along the Backs at King's—I was ready to leave Cambridge —almost. By and large, I felt isolated and shut in from the everyday world of men and women, of family life, of people earning a living, of politics, of wars and rumours of wars. And yet, that last May Week held an element of the pain of separation from the beauty and culture of this delectable university city it had been my privilege to study at for three short years.

A week's mission in September with the Cambridge Pastorate at Hornchurch, only a few miles from our Essex home, was a maturing experience. It was good to work with and talk with

Christians of a variety of persuasions as we witnessed to the same Lord.

And so God had brought me from the 'not so light blues' of uncertainty and double-mindedness of my first two years at Cambridge, through the chastening and enriching experience of seeing something of His relentless love for me, to a preparedness for the hurly-burly life of a large London hospital.

Anne and I attend a May Ball at Selwyn College. *Right*: Myself on Graduation Day, Cambridge, 1956

CHAPTER SIX

THE BIG CITY

'In the suburb outside one of the gates there is a smooth field both in fact and in name . . . where there is a much frequented show of fine horses for sale.'

Fitzstephen on Smithfield (c. 1180)

'Look wise, say nothing, and grunt.'

Sir William Osler (1849-1919): Advice to medical students.

THE ROYAL HOSPITAL OF ST. BATHOLOMEW, POPULARLY CALLED Bart's was founded in 1123 by Rahere, a monk at the nearby St. Paul's Cathedral. Convinced that he had taken a wrong direction in life, Rahere had made a pilgrimage to Rome to seek forgiveness, only to fall ill during his stay in Italy. Fearing death, he struck a bargain with God that if he recovered he would build a hospital for the poor and sick of London. Perhaps he already had a heavy conscience concerning the needy inhabitants of the English capital and was thus primed to respond to their plight. Eventually restored to health, his journey back to London was interrupted by a vision of St. Bartholomew, who is said to have told the penitent monk to build this hospital in the marshy area of Smithfield. This 'smooth field', just north-west of the City, became the site of the annual Bartholomew Fair for the next 700 years and, in the sixteenth century, was the scene of many cruel martyrdoms carried out in the names of both Catholic and Reformed religion.

The 'Royal and Ancient' hospital of Bart's was granted a charter by Henry VIII for its bestowal to the City of London. In the same year, 1546, the hospital was created the parish of St. Bartholomew the Less and, to this day, the vicar and his curate are responsible for the spiritual welfare of the patients and all those who live on the premises. Life at Bart's, with its traditions deep in history, is studded with rather quaint official titles. There is a Steward, a Clerk to the Governors and a Hospitaller; and the medical students are designated Dressers while studying surgery and Clerks while working on a medical ward. Doctors who have brought fame to Bart's during the previous four centuries include Thomas Vicary, surgeon to Henry VIII, William Clowes, one of the surgeons to Elizabeth I, Percival Pott and John Abernethy, the distinguished eighteenth century lecturers in surgery, and James Paget, the Victorian writer, orator and surgeon. Perhaps the best known of all was William Harvey, the seventeenth century physician who was the first to demonstrate the circulation of the blood.

Arriving at this venerable institution in the autumn of 1956, I was eager to become immersed in a world where there was real need, a world of patients, ward rounds and intriguing operations. Of my year of 70 medical students, rather over half had studied at the Bart's Pre-Clinical School in Charterhouse Square and the remainder were graduates from Cambridge, like myself, with a sprinkling from the smaller medical faculty at Oxford. There were only half a dozen women medical students.

White-coated, our pockets crammed with pristine aids to diagnosis, we were let loose on the wards. We quickly needed to learn our place. Heady visions of being real doctors gave way to the awareness that we were ham-fisted medical students, our heads stuffed with comparatively useless knowledge of obscure anatomical and biochemical detail. We were marked out from the 'real doctors' by our youthful features, our readiness to blush and stammer when confronted by a ward sister and our well meaning ineptness at the bedside.

Each student was allotted, with another six to eight, to a particular 'firm', which comprised a team of surgeons or physicians caring for two wards, one for male and one for female patients. My first firm was surgical, studying under Basil Hume, a sturdy Yorkshireman and the Senior Surgeon of the hospital, and Alan Hunt, the *doyen* of liver surgeons, bow-tied and imposingly tall,

In those early months I would wait with the other Dressers in the corridor between the two wards for the arrival of the surgical team. Each of us had been delegated a few patients and needed to know their medical history, their present condition, findings at operation and the particular outlook for their illness. As we waited uneasily, each of us mulled over a series of anxious self-imposed questions: 'Did I take Mrs. B's blood pressure? If so, where did I write the result?'; 'Is Mr. A. due for operation today or tomorrow —or was he the one they fitted in as an emergency yesterday?'; 'Why is Miss C's serum bilirubin up again? How can I explain *that* if asked?'.

Thirty yards up the well polished corridor, the grating of the lift-door heralded the arrival of our superiors. The air stiffened as we grouped together, straightening ties, sweeping back unruly strands of hair to appear alert, attentive and intelligent to the advancing cluster of white-coated doctors.

The sense of a pecking order was paramount—the consultant, established enough to wear his white-coat unfastened, revealing dapper waistcoat and silver watch-chain, was a fraction of a step ahead of the registrars, confident in their amassed knowledge and accumulated experience and answering their chief's arrow-dart questions with precision as they swept towards us. Close to the heels of the registrars came the house-surgeons, heads held high, newly qualified—doctors at last! There might be others in attendance—a radiologist, a medical registrar researching a disease relevant to the ward round, a dietician, one or two physio-therapists . . .

As the armada of white sailed by in chevron formation, we clustered to fill the ranks at the rear of the hurried procession. The ordeal was under way. The ward with its waiting patients was entered

Joined now by a Sister and a Staff Nurse, the convoy decelerated to its first port of call, the bedside of Mr. A. The patient, his jaundice glowing tawny against the white of the bed-linen, raised tired eyes to the imposing array crowding around.

'Who is Mr. A's Dresser?', asked the chief of the firm.

'I am sir', replied X.

'Ah, Mr. X. What is Mr. A's pseudocholinesterase?'

'I didn't quite hear, sir!'

Silence followed as X racked his brain for an escape route.

After a pause, he added, 'I'm sorry, sir . . . I came to take blood yesterday afternoon and Mr. A wasn't there'.

'Where was he, Mr. X?'

'I really don't know, sir.'

'Could he have been in the operating theatre undergoing an emergency operation, Mr. X?'

X, clearing his throat: 'Possibly, sir.'

The thunder clouds were gathering. The rest of us, innocent at least of this culpable ignorance, tingled with excitement. We were disappointed. On this occasion the storm did not break. The consultant turned to the faintly grinning Mr. A to enquire about his first post-operative night, the registrars glanced helplessly heavenwards and the house-surgeons glared fixedly at the miscreant, who blushed deeply above his starched white coat, while the remaining students exchanged apprehensive smiles. It could be any one of us next.

Myself as a medical student, and fellow-students at Bart's on one of our first "firms"; *standing, l to r*: John Townsend (who has since worked with O.M.F. in Thailand and Tear Fund internationally), John Mercer, and Jim Williamson. *Seated*: Keith Durrant and David Parkes

We gradually came of age. Confidence grew as we became more expert at taking histories, examining patients, blood-letting, urine-testing and, specially important, anticipating the consultant's penetrating questions.

Encouragements came as difficult diagnoses were correctly made and understanding of the disease processes grew. On one of Mr. Hume's ward rounds, towards the end of the first three months on the surgical firm, I was singled out for an unexpected comment. This kindly Yorkshireman was instructing us in the need to care and to be seen to care as we tried to help our patients towards health. As we stood grouped around a bed attentively, his eyes caught mine. 'You've got a caring sort of face', he said, adding, 'You'll make the sort of doctor I'm talking about.' Vanity and diffidence struggled within for the ascendancy.

Discouragement came too. The tall and imposing Mr. Hunt carried out lengthy operations of a most difficult nature for a range of serious liver conditions. One particularly arduous procedure of his, in which a damaged liver could be by-passed by joining up two important venous systems, was nicknamed the Hunt Shunt. As Dressers we were committed to assisting operations on our 'own' patients. One day it was my turn to hold the retractor at a Hunt Shunt. Maintaining a steady pull with both hands on a large retractor is tiring work and, after an hour and a half, I began to develop the dizziness of a dropping blood sugar. One thing I had not learnt at that stage was the cultivation of a friendly nurse who could pop a cube of sugar behind my mask and into my mouth during a long operation.

As the faint feelings increased there seemed to be nothing for it but to mutter into the registrar's ear that I was a diabetic heading for a 'hypo'. Another student was asked to scrub up and take my place beside the preoccupied surgeon. Thus I was able to withdraw and eat something to right the symptoms. It was a minor episode but a salutary one and I was forbidden by the consultant to assist at any of the more protracted operations in future.

I was, of course, in the right sort of place for the appropriate care of the diabetes. Dr. Kenneth Black, the specialist in this condition at Bart's, was a wise and friendly adviser as he tried various changes in type and dosage of insulin in order to stabilize my rather 'labile' diabetes. He pointed out that the particular variety of this disorder that I had was specially susceptible to alterations in the timing of meals and its control was therefore the more difficult.

Bart's graduates had a strong tradition of overseas medical missionary work. A specially dominant influence on both fellow students and staff alike was the link with the Ruanda Revival. A particular range of surnames seemed to feature in conversation amongst Bart's Christian medics and nurses—names with strong missionary connections with Central and East Africa, including Buxtons, Churches, Guillebauds, Hindleys, Kitleys and Stanley-Smiths. Robin Church and Ted Cantrell were two particularly good friends in my year, both from Cambridge, both with missionary backgrounds and both brought up in Kenya. With their exilic desire to return to the uplands of East Africa, they whetted my appetite afresh for travel, and especially for things African.

But I had to be realistic. I discovered that missionary societies were extremely unlikely to accept diabetic candidates and that there could be serious problems with the supply and storage of insulin in tropical regions. The questioning of such Christian friends was a natural sequel to these considerations: 'Why not pray for, and expect, miraculous healing? *Then* you will be able to go out on the mission field!' I remember this question being asked as we sat and chatted together in the lecture theatre, awaiting a discourse on Pathology. Why not, indeed! As I thought the issue over, my conviction strengthened that the diabetes had come with divine permission and that its curtailing influence almost certainly meant a call to serve the Lord on the 'home front'. It was many years before the debate about miraculous healing became pressing once more in a personal way.

Another, rather amusing incident served to undergird the need to accept the diabetes and its consequences from the point of view of career. One result of instability in blood sugars can be dehydration, which in turn can lead to constipation. This was a modest but unpleasant problem which recurred a few times during the two and a half years at Bart's. On one occasion, bouts of intense abdominal colic brought me to the attention of Dr. John Coulson, who had the medical care of both nurses and students. A gentle and kindly Christian man, he had the knack of a word in season. As I writhed on his examination couch, his probing hand searching out the areas of greatest tenderness, he looked down at my puckered face and asked quizzically: 'What does the Lord require of you? Success?' Before my distracted mind could reach back to the appropriate biblical text, he answered for me: 'No! He only requires faithfulness.' It was a truth that I felt I had a fairly clear grasp of; and certainly thoughts of success, or failure, were a long way away from this constipated diabetic! At the time the comment seemed a *non sequitur*, albeit an important one, but its perspective has haunted me since.

There is no doubt that the Bart's years brought a stability to my Christian commitment and understanding. The contacts with fellow Christians in the Christian Union were invaluable as we prayed together in a draughty corner of the church of St. Bartholomew the Less in the lunch hours, studied the Bible (we always seemed to be half way through Hebrews!) and worked in our various corners of hospital life.

The CU had something of a reputation for narrowness—not only doctrinally but culturally. It was one thing to be shunned because of the 'offence of the Cross' but quite another to be seen as colourless due to a lack of appreciation of God's rich and complex world. Uneasy with such restricted views, I benefited greatly from a wide range of friends, including Christians of other persuasions. It was during this time that I found my way to the Art galleries, enjoyed the insights of Bernard Berenson's *The Italian Painters of the Renaissance*, frequented the Royal Festival Hall (rejoicing greatly to find my initials on all the doors!) and spent many blissful hours listening to Bach, Vivaldi and Mozart.

My awareness of the Lord's power and abiding presence increased. Aided by the continual need to keep blood sugars within certain limits, I had a straightforward sense of my weakness, both physical and spiritual. This led to an increasing realisation of the need to keep close to Christ and of the truth that without Him I could do nothing in terms of a fruitful, God-centred life.

Always having a certain diffidence in talking openly about Him, I was much encouraged in this respect over a few days during my first medical firm. Walking through the ward one day, I noticed a new patient, a middle-aged man lying in bed with a Bible at his side. I stopped to chat with him and soon discovered that he was a major in the Army who had been stationed in Egypt following the Second World War. He had now been admitted with a tumour of the pituitary gland, a small but vital area at the base of the brain which produces and controls many of the body's hormones. Fortunately, this particular growth was removable by operation and the major's health could be maintained thereafter by certain tablets taken regularly.

He talked freely of his former awareness of God's greatness as he witnessed the immensity of the desert and of the North African night skies. Through the prayers and love of a Christian nurse working on the same ward and through my involvement with him, he opened his life to the Lord a few days before his operation. Nearly twenty five years later we still correspond as two fellow Christians.

In the June of 1958, encouraged by a camping and walking holiday in North-West Scotland with another medic the year before, I resolved to take a fortnight's break in the Outer Hebrides alone. Life seemed to be working out well. I had recently acquired an intriguing new girl friend, my sister had just married my boyhood friend Rob, now newly qualified as a doctor, and the diabetes was being maintained satisfactorily. Along with a straightforward need for a holiday and the insatiable desire to revisit Scotland, I envisaged two weeks when I could prove the Lord's power to keep a diabetic camping solo in a remote area. I still hankered after the possibility of a pioneering career and needed to establish within myself that the Lord and I could cope together with some tricky situations!

The Lord, in His wisdom, arranged for another solitary camper, better equipped and more experienced that I was, to catch the same steamer bound for Lochdoisdale on South Uist. Mike, a geologist from Yorkshire and a devout Roman Catholic, was on leave from his National Service and was a godsend.

The previous summer, my fellow medical student and I had used dried out heather to fuel our fires while we camped on Skye and in Ross and Cromarty. The weather had been blisteringly hot. Now, Mike and I encountered weather more typical of the North-West and I was extremely grateful to him for the share of his portable Gaz stove as we camped together during the first week. Mercifully, he left me the stove for my second week while he returned south to the Army camp at Carlisle.

It was an exhilarating fortnight as the Lord proved his power to keep. Living on porridge—mixed with canned meat as a savoury and with dried fruit as a sweet course—I scoured much of the island for birds.

The prescription was a good one—walking the springy, flower-studded machair[1] along the west coast, assailed by the cries of nesting terns and waders; clambering down to the cliff-bound eastern side, having followed the spectacular spine of Ben Mhor, the island's highest mountain; running across the peat moors of North Uist later in the fortnight, to reach the higher ground of North Lee to escape the voracious cleg-flies; lying in the tent on the Thursdays, each of these days the centre of thirty-six hours of continuous rain; and finally, in the overnight steamer, returning to the mainland through a fitful night as forty Territorial Army soldiers from some of the main Highland regiments caroused and quarrelled, while their rather less drunken musicians skirled their bagpipes in the bowels of the boat.

I arrived back at Bart's a great deal fitter and with a firm

1 *Machair* is the grassy sward that fringes many of the sand and shell beaches in the Western Isles.

conviction that, diabetes or not, the Lord had a happy knack of keeping and sustaining the headstrong.

Like so many before and since, I was much exercised by certain teachings on a further, definitive Christian experience given such names as the Second Blessing, the Keswick Experience, the Baptism of the Spirit and the Filling of the Spirit. I had heard the late Tom Rees speak at a tea-party at Cambridge and it had seemed to me that he was stressing the need for 'something more' in one's walk with Christ.

Samuel Chadwick's *The Way to Pentecost* had been given to me by a saintly lady who emphasised the desirability of a 'second' experience. Unable to square up some elements in this approach with the scriptures, I eventually found a booklet by George Duncan on the subject most helpful. The key to the whole issue seemed to lie in the command: 'Be filled with the Spirit' (Ephesians 5:18), where the sense lay in the idea of continuous filling. I responded gladly and resolutely to this insight while eating a light lunch on a bench in the shadow of St. Paul's Cathedral. The prayer for a daily filling by His Spirit has been with me since.

It was another decade before Spirit-Baptism became, sadly, a rather divisive issue, not only between mainstream Pentecostalism (and various holiness movements) and other Evangelical emphases, but more widely through most branches of Christendom. I shall look at this debate and some encouraging elements in its resolution in a later chapter.

One of the most distracting features of life at Bart's was the nurses. Cambridge had been singularly marked by a scarcity of feminine company with its 10 : 1 ratio of male and female students. Amongst Bart's medical students the same disproportion held. And so the eyes, the thoughts and the feet wandered elsewhere.

Bart's nurses, trim in handkerchief caps, grey pin-stripe uniform dresses, starched white aprons and, while running the gauntlet of wolf-whistling meat porters as they hurried from nurses' home to hospital and back, mantled in heavy, navy-blue cloaks, the linings flashing a provocative scarlet, could be irresistible. A medical student's impressively regular appearance on the ward to attend his patients could be as influenced by the proximity of an attractive nurse as by the dedication to medical care.

This was the stage in life for a great deal of match-making and it was intriguing to observe the light in the eyes and the knowing half-grins of a number of friends as they became, one by one,

"One of the most distracting features of life at Bart's was the nurses." Bart's nurses singing carols outside St. Bartholomew's-the-Less, Christmas, 1956. *Inset*: "the other, a smiling and friendly person who was introduced as Joy"

bewitched by one particular nurse or another. Many of us battled with the illogical Evangelical taboo that you do not take a girl out regularly unless you are sure that she is the one God intends for you. Dire warnings of the wickedness of leaving a trail of broken hearts were given, as if the chase was a purely one-sided, male-inspired idea. I often wonder how much this 'all or nothing' mentality has led to incompatible or inappropriate marriages, made in good faith but seriously lacking in the maturer judgement born of experience with a wider range of friendships. The fear seems to have been that intentions were not honourable unless marriage was on the horizon. Imagine trying to make any other important decision in life without careful evaluation of the alternatives!

Perhaps influenced by this climate, I experienced the question from one girlfriend: 'Do you intend to marry me?' and, as the answer was 'No', we parted company. Another nurse with whom I queried the same prospect, fell about laughing, declaring, 'You need someone who will really love you!' The sheer logic of the statement carried the day.

During the last year of my clinical studies, rejoicing in the Lord and content with a vivacious Christian girlfriend, Jane, a most significant encounter took place. Working on a Midwifery firm at the time, I emerged from the Midder Block to carry a specimen of urine across the square to the Pathology laboratory. Bart's square is always a place to linger in, even with hands or pockets full of specimens for the lab! The fine, eighteenth century buildings of Portland stone, the cool sound of the central fountain and the dappled sunlight and shade beneath the plane trees were specially enticing on that particular Summer's day. Standing and chatting by the fountain were two uniformed nurses—the one the familiar figure of Jane, the other a smiling friendly person who was introduced as Joy. Clutching the specimen bottle, enamoured by Jane, I was oblivious of the fact that I had just shaken hands with my future wife.

CHAPTER SEVEN

THE HAPPY HOUSEMAN

'Happiness is like coke—something you get as a by-product in the process of making something else'.

Aldous Huxley: *Point Counter Point*

'It's the same with happiness—it doesn't depend on the actual number of blessings we manage to scratch from life, but only our attitude towards them.'

Alexander Solzhenitsyn: *The First Circle*

THE BREAK HAD TO COME WITH JANE, OR SO IT SEEMS IN retrospect. Although we had a great deal in common—our Christian commitment, a love of the open-air life, a deep interest in Natural History and a sense of humour that often tilted at the predictable and the conventional—our backgrounds were poles apart. Her more privileged world of fast sports cars, horse-riding and lawn tennis seemed a far cry from the push-bikes and neglected hard-courts of suburban Essex. A certain gaucheness on my part amidst the sparkling company of Jane's social life seemed to sound the death-knell of the relationship, and our ways parted.

However, the prospect of Finals six months away and the companionship of a few choice medical students, united by the faintly competitive atmosphere of pending exams, concentrated the mind and sense of direction.

Those of us from Bart's who were to sit the Final MB Examination at Cambridge were faced with a crisis of strategy. The results of the Part II of these exams were due disproportionately late and came a few days after the appointments, for our first jobs as qualified doctors, should have been taken up. There was some brisk competition to land an initial post at the teaching hospital with its promise of a select team within which to try out one's new responsibilities. In addition to the as yet unknown results of the examinations was the uncertainty, for the chosen few, of whether the much coveted posts could actually be embarked upon.

The failure rate for Cambridge graduates at Bart's was rather high that year and a number of excellent students who had been offered very good first house jobs failed to pass the exam at that stage. Naîvely, I had applied to be a house-physician in a firm that specialised in diabetes, ignoring the extremely strong likelihood of the post going to an older, more experienced candidate, who was also related to one of the team's consultants! However, the Lord honoured my simple (or, perhaps, simplistic) trust in Him and I was offered my second choice—sadly, at the expense of a good Christian friend who failed his finals at this point.

And so, with all the thrill and apprehension of being 'let loose' as a newly qualified doctor, I joined the more senior team of two Orthopaedic firms which were based at an extension of Bart's 'in the country' near St. Albans.

Hill End was designed as a Mental Hospital but, during World War II, a large section of it had been annexed by Bart's to continue to serve the community in an area safer from German bombing than the City of London. Nearly twenty years later found a continuance of this happy link between town and country. 'Happy' because the informal atmosphere at this provincial setting was a welcome contrast to the rigid authoritarianism of the parent hospital. The specialties of Ear, Nose and Throat, Thoracic Surgery, Neurosurgery and Orthopaedics continued to be housed at Hill End at that time.

Newly fledged doctors had (and perhaps still have) a reputation amongst the nursing staff of arrogance. A nervous, diffident and nail-biting medical student could become, overnight, an aloof or bombastic doctor whose mind teemed with partially digested medical facts. The years of study, of not getting it quite right on ward rounds, of recalcitrance or obsequy, were replaced by a dangerous (and often short-lived) sense of security. One had 'arrived' and the amazing complexity of the minds and bodies of one's patients was still barely appreciated. The need to make accurate diagnoses could preclude a sensitivity in handling the human condition. Recently qualified doctors sometimes rushed in where more seasoned medical men feared to tread.

Determined (like many others, I suspect) to avoid falling into this trap, I sought to establish good working relationships with both medical and nursing colleagues under the general maxim of 'the patient must come first'. However, the despotic streak surfaced from time to time.

Early during this first house job, I was woken at about 6.00 a.m. with the news that the Night Sister had found one of the patients, an overweight middle-aged woman, with an excessively high temperature. Annoyed at what seemed like an unnecessary wakening of a hard-pressed houseman, I dressed hurriedly and walked on to the ward to the bedside of the patient, who was sitting up and looked particularly unfeverish.

I turned to the attendant nurse and asked, 'How was the temperature taken?' 'Under the arm', she replied, a little offended at this rather impudent question. After all, taking temperatures was very much the nurses' domain.

Taking the thermometer from its bedside container I pulled back the bedclothes briskly to recheck the patient's temperature. Triumphantly, I extracted a freshly filled hot water bottle which had been lying suspiciously close to her right arm-pit. 'Here's the cause of the fever!' I exclaimed with dangerous confidence. My relief and sense of jubilation were profound when, on checking beneath the, by now, subdued patient's tongue (a thermometer placed beneath the tongue is rather subduing anyway), I found her temperature to be normal. The exultant 'Tell Sister that hot water bottles can give quite high temperatures' to the nurse felt good at the time.

My six months as an Orthopaedic house-surgeon were, essentially, happy ones. So much so that, quite quickly, I became known as the Happy Houseman. I enjoyed the process of getting to know the patients, many of whom, incapacitated for years with serious and often painful disorders of joint and bone, showed remarkable courage. I wondered at the resources within some who spent many long months almost immobilised by extensive plaster of Paris casts or who battled with the deep-seated pain of osteomyelitis or cancer of the bone. God's common grace given so generously to

The Happy Houseman with a mongoloid patient

mankind often showed through in the cheery good humour and resilience of such people.

Resolved to care and be seen to care for the patients, whether admitted for minor surgery or facing a huge crisis of incapacity, protracted pain or imminent death, I was fortunate to work with a like-minded Christian ward sister. Her far greater experience of orthopaedic conditions, her sharp mind and ready wit, and her genuine dedication to the comfort and well being of her charges were inspirational. Our relationship was a warm and affectionate one which, for my part, did a great deal to enliven my first six months as a doctor.

Apart from a minor complication of the diabetes, I kept very well during this period. The job was not especially onerous as there was comparatively little surgery of an urgent nature and so there were few disturbed nights. There was no recurrence of unsettling low blood sugars during long operations, although assisting in orthopaedic surgery, with its tendency to be a form of refined carpentry and metalwork, can be arduous. The secret was the cultivation of the excellent theatre nursing staff who kept a tin of boiled sweets by for their diabetic houseman. A drop in blood sugar could be quite welcome for its consequent attention by a nurse armed with sweet sustenance. My strictly private nickname amongst this select band was 'Sweety'.

I enjoyed, too, the stimulus of hard-working and colourful medical colleagues. Orthopaedic surgery appears to attract a certain range of personalities. The sometimes dramatic quality of bone-engineering and the sheer blood and sweat of the more massive procedures seem to invite some extroverted and cavalier characters.

James Donovan, a heavily built man and generally known as the Wild Irishman, was such a one. An activist inside and outside the operating theatre, he had been working hard to gain his pilot's licence and, about half way through my job at Hill End, he triumphantly achieved his aim.

'How abaht coming up with me on my first run, Roger?' he asked.

We fixed a date for the following Saturday, which proved to be a day of exceptionally strong and gusty winds. James phoned the private air-field to check the flying conditions and, receiving an equivocal reply, suggested we drove over there.

The bar of the Flying Club was crammed with grounded members. James tracked down the acknowledged expert on weather lore, a lean, tough-looking test pilot. His laconic response to James was: 'Well, *I* might risk going up.'

My large Irish friend turned to me with, 'Come on, Roger, let's jest go and look at the plane. She's a beauty, you know''. We did. She was.

Unfortunately, there was one other man abroad on the almost deserted air-field and he happened to be within hailing distance of the Auster mono-plane. 'Would you mind jest giving the prop a swing for us?', cried the indomitable James and, to me, 'Come on, Roger, into the cockpit with you. We'll just taxi out. If the wind drops, we're away. If it doesn't, well, we'll stay put'. As we gained speed, the wind dropped and we rose, a vision of anxious faces pressed to the window of the club-house.

'Where would you like to go, Roger? How do you fancy flying over London and the Thames?' 'Fine', I replied with limited conviction.

We headed south on a dizzy, leap-frogging course while the unpredictable winds waxed and waned.

Eight miles later, James became briefly informative: 'There's the Elstree Film Studios'. He jerked his head vaguely towards the sea of roof-tops way below. 'By the way, would you mind checking the fuel gauge for me? I should have done that before we left'.

The gauge was wedged between us but behind the pilot's field of vision. I craned my neck and blinked my disbelieving eyes. 'It reads "Empty", James'!

'Damn!' and, a few seconds later: 'Sorry abaht this—we'd better turn and see if we can land at Elstree'.

We radioed the aerodrome as we approached but, although they gave permission to land, they strongly advised against it as the viciously strong cross-winds would almost certainly tip us over as we followed the line of the homing runway.

James was unsinkable. 'We'll jest have to gain height and, if the engine cuts out, we might make Radlett or even home-base'.

I admired his sang-froid. 'See that bit o'pasture down there?' He pointed out a postage stamp of pale green on the vast chequer-board landscape. 'We could always land there'. I managed to return, feebly, his grin.

Radlett, its air-field crammed to capacity with huge jets, refused our radioed request to land. James, now visibly worried, make radio contact with our air-base, asking for permission to land without circling as we were virtually without fuel. And still the Auster's engine whirred unfalteringly.

The Flying Club's landing-strip now in sight, we dropped steeply down. As a clump of Scot's pines and the rooves of the town's suburbs rushed up to meet us, my suppressed anxiety and overtaxed vestibular system released an upsurge of vomit which spattered the front of the cockpit. This disgorge was accompanied by my fervent prayer for a safe landing.

Peering through the bile-stained windscreen, we touched down, miraculously without further incident, and taxied a little before the faithful engine cut out. Marooned far out on the air-field, the fuel tank was, finally, empty.

Back at the club-house, amidst the explanations and the recriminations, we were told how the experts were convinced we would crash. They had crowded the conning tower for a ringside view of the imminent disaster. No light craft could withstand the force of the cross-wind as it touched down, barring a miracle. As we came into land, they said, the wind mysteriously ceased for a few crucial seconds ...

Chastened and subdued, James and I drove back to Hill End feeling the force of the wind on the open road. As in the Outer

Hebrides, I was reminded of the Lord God's keeping of His children even when, as in this instance, hasty judgement had led to a contrary path through the air in a craft propelled by a small and unknown amount of fuel—just enough fuel to see us through but little enough to underline our folly, with a wind fierce enough to make our flight extremely hazardous but controlled enough to show His mercy at the vital moment.

Happy with a sense of the first house job successfully completed and enriched by a score of rewarding relationships with nursing and medical staff, I had kept a fortnight's holiday for the end of the appointment before launching out into further medical experience in the various hospitals of the City of Norwich.

One evening, during this brief respite, I played badminton long and hard with some friends at the old church hall of St. Peter's, Harold Wood. I felt on top of the world, the Happy Houseman Triumphant with the first hurdle of a medical career satisfactorily crossed. As I leapt and twisted and lunged to return the shuttlecock, I rejoiced in my comparative fitness—the diabetes was in its rightful place—a disorder harnessed, a servant rather than a master.

The next day, I woke to the agonies of an acute 'slipped disc'. Having looked after dozens of young men with this condition during the previous six months, the symptoms were only too clear —intense lumbar pain radiating down the line of the sciatic nerve into the ball of the foot. Some rapid conferring and brisk telephoning applied a friend's car to the situation, with the agreement to take me the thirty odd miles to my beloved Hill End. My thinking blurred by pain, it seemed that my Bart's colleagues must be the only ones who could deal with this emergency.

The journey was a long one, each bump in the road and each twist in the route intensifying the pain. Somewhere, amidst the agony, I sensed some sort of joke about the house-surgeon who, having just completed his job, is returned within a few days to lie in the open ward surrounded by his former patients.

At last we reached sanctuary with the confidence of being in hands of proven skill.

Following manipulation of the spine under general anaesthesia, there came three weeks of lying on my back at the tender mercy of the nurses, a cycle of back rubbing, bed baths and bed pans, interspersed with the challenge of eating in the horizontal position and of conversing with 'Doc's' erstwhile patients, while enduring a cricked neck. This experience was a levelling one in terms of both physical posture and of the doctor-patient relationship. I can still see the exultant faces of former patients, now ambulant, grinning down at me from the foot of the bed, asking such questions as: 'What's it like bein' on the receivin' end then, Doc?' It was survivable.

As I lay there during those three long weeks, I had ample opportunity to mull over the period of my coming appointment as a house-physician in Norwich. Although this sudden indisposition meant a delay in the commencement of the post, my main preoccupation was with matters potentially matrimonial rather than medical. I must leave the matter of the 'Short List' until the next chapter.

CHAPTER EIGHT

NORFOLK TURNIPS

'Norwich . . . is a monument to the north folk and it bears the marks of all their peculiarities—it has flint walls and is difficult to know at a glance!'
H.V. Morton: *In Search of England*

'Love is a universal migraine
A bright stain on the vision
Blotting out reason'.
Robert Graves: *Symptoms of Love*

THE *Son et Lumière* HELD AT NORWICH CATHEDRAL IN 1960 WAS a comparative novelty. A number of other key historical sites had received the treatment in the late 50's, their architecture and past illumined by a pageant of light and sound. And now, on a fine late summer evening, I shouldered my way through the crowded cloisters to witness this new form of entertainment, beneath the soaring 15th century spire.

As the dusk gathered, the crowd's excited chatter was suddenly swamped by the relayed opening chords of Bach's magnificent Toccata and Fugue in D minor. This was the dramatic entrée to a feast of visual and auditory impressions, spanning the cathedral's history from its foundation by Herbert de Losinga in 1094 to the Second World War. Sound and lighting combined to rivet our attention with visions of hammering stone-masons, the hustle and bustle of a neighbouring medieval market, thunderous cavalry charge, Cromwellian vandalism and a cascade of German bombs falling about our ears.

As I sat on the hard bench-seat, hemmed in by silent spectators, something else was falling about my ears, cascades of a different siren-music to that which preceded and followed the noise of bombardment. Not for the first, or the last time, I had fallen in love, and the symptoms of this distracting state seemed to charge the air as I sat and watched and listened.

Eight months before, the New Year of 1960 brought a crisis of strategy in the matrimonial stakes. Just finishing my first house job, I anticipated the move from Hill End Hospital, and its Bart's connections, to Norfolk as a journey into a conjugal wilderness. Twenty six years of age was hardly 'on the shelf' and yet, in my prejudice, I saw an unrelieved prospect of slow-witted East Anglian bumpkins as the sum-total of the marriage market. Over dramatically, the choice seemed to be between singleness for the foreseeable future, at least, and marriage to one of the less earthy and thick-skinned 'Norfolk Turnips'. This blinkered male vanity led to the rapid construction of the 'Short List'.

Who was there, amongst the delectable Bart's nurses, that was (a) Christian, (b) attractive, (c) available and (d) like my sister in certain respects?

At the time I barely conceded that I had, in Freudian terms, something of a sister-fixation. Who had I boldly invited to accompany me to my one Cambridge May Ball? My sister. With whom did I, at times quite consciously, compare potential girl-friends? My sister.

It would give the wrong impression to say that this was a blind obsession, for I was not uncritical of sister Anne. After all, I still had memories of relentless teasing and the ultimate ignominy of experiencing the flag-staff of a toy aerodrome being thrust up my seven-year-old nose as the climax of a heated exchange between us. However, she gave my psyche a rather generalised blue-print of what sort of wife I would look for. She would be of short to average height, brunette or black-haired, and of lively and engaging temperament. I would not be too purist about the details but the flavour must be decidedly 'Anneish'.

With these rather unspecific requirements in mind, I dutifully compiled the 'Short List' and found a tally of six potential candidates. Number One had already said 'No' and so I faced the conundrum of becoming better acquainted with Number Two on the eve of moving a hundred miles or so away from any straightforward contract.

Joy, the dark-haired nurse that Jane had introduced me to in Bart's Square that sunny day the previous summer, had materialised as Number Two. During the happy months of my friendship with Jane, Joy had been the intriguing 'girl next door'.

The room next to mine at the College Hall was occupied by a music-loving Christian student whose cup seemed full indeed with the spirited companionship of this attractive girl-friend. Life must be very good for these two, I mused, as peels of laughter, snatches of conversation and the grand swell of symphonies by Sibelius invaded my room through the thin dividing wall. A slightly envious interest was changed to a sense of impending possibility when I heard, long after my break with Jane, that Joy too was now unattached.

The vibrations were good but still ill-defined and there were only two weeks to go before the job to Norwich started. There was but one way, it seemed, to start the ball rolling and that was to invite this still rather mysterious person out. I knew she at least tolerated Sibelius and so a concert must be a safe proposition. Spurred on by a sighting during the recent Annual Nurses' Ball at the Grosvenor, two tickets were bought for a presumably safe mixture of Berlioz, Beethoven and Brahms at the Royal Festival Hall, and the first letter between us was written. A manoeuvre of the eleventh hour, the concert was to take place only two days before the move to Norfolk.

Whether this scheme was 'best laid' or not, it went astray. Joy's recent change of duties made the occasion impossible for her and, when the evening finally came round, I had been saved from trying to date Number Three, Four, Five, or Six by the prostrating inconvenience of an acutely slipped disc.

And so the land of 'Norfolk Turnips' was entered and I was absorbed into the fascinating work of a first-rate medical team. The satisfaction of relieving pain and distress at times, and the sorrow of losing patients to deterioration and death at other times, focussed my energies at many needy bedsides, while the spicy humour and professional rivalries of the residential medical quarters filled out those hours of waiting for news of yet another admission. The calculating perspective of the 'Short List' was set aside. The Lord had blocked the last-minute attempt to bid for a Bart's nurse. In cattle-market terms, the potential deal was off.

However, one last nod was made in the direction of the Divine Auctioneer. A carefully chosen postcard (nothing but the best—a J. Arthur Dixon of Stob Coire nan Lochan, in Glencoe) was written and sent from the wilds of West Scotland during an idyllic holiday in June with my parents, five months after our polite exchange of letters. Surely nothing could come from this most modest of gambits, but the image of the 'girl next door' would not quite go away.

A letter came from Joy in mid-July which seemed, ironically, to underline our geographical isolation. She, now a qualified staff nurse, had become joint-secretary of the Nurses' Christian Fellowship at Hill End Hospital, was 'always searching for speakers' and wondered whether I could manage to take one of the Thursday evening meetings. I was puzzled. Was this a ploy to encourage correspondence or did she really believe I could slip down to St. Albans and back after a heavy day on the wards? I wrote back a chatty letter explaining that I had one or two ward rounds on Thursday evenings but that I might make Hill End one weekend 'later on'. Inside, I felt that such a journey without a substantial pretext was most improbable. However, the Lord, with a teasing sense of timing, had prepared the way for this unlikely encounter.

Within the first month of my second house job in Norwich (paediatrics at the Jenny Lind Hospital), I developed monilial balanitis, an extremely irritating infection of the foreskin and a complication of diabetes. During a weekend off, I drove 'Kitty', a recently acquired, second-hand, white Ford Anglia, down to Bart's to seek advice. Admitted under the care of a very good Christian friend and contemporary, John Townsend, I suffered the indignity of a circumcision, followed by the inevitable discomfort, which gave me a gait like a saddle-sore cowboy for a week or so!

A trivial enough development in itself, this unanticipated surgery gave, during the brief convalescence, the seemingly impossible chance to visit Hill End on a Thursday evening! The sense of divine planning continued as I entered the hospital corridor close to the operating theatres to hear 'Number Two's' laughter echoing from a nearby room. We had met up at last.

Joy was leading the Christian Fellowship on that particular evening and so I stayed on to hear her talk about her recent trip to the famous decennial Passion Play at Oberammergau. Following this long awaited encounter, I drove down to Surbiton to spend the night at my sister's. As I played with Anne's eight-month-old daughter, Ruth, and later listened to a record of Mozart Flute concerti, my mind was filled with the prospect of further meetings with the 'girl next door'.

This whole episode was somehow underscored by a discerning friend who was doing a house job in Neurosurgery at Hill End. Tony, an Oxford graduate of disarming friendliness, assured me one day following my 'operation' that he had met 'just the girl' for me. 'She's a Christian and she's great stuff!' was his warm-hearted assessment of the dark-haired theatre staff nurse he had singled out. I knew she was a Christian; I was beginning to find out that she was also 'great stuff'.

And so, a fortnight later, as the broadcast bombardment of Norwich filled the night air, I rejoiced in the euphoria of a new relationship that promised well. The 'Short List' had been discarded —at least for the time being!

My eighteen months in Norwich, working at three different hospitals in three different specialties: Medicine (with Geriatrics), Paediatrics and Obstetrics with Gynaecology, offered a wide range of medical and surgical experience as well as, inevitably, the huge number of hours that housemen in busy jobs put in before there was at least some attempt to regulate the work-load in the 70's. In theory, the irregularity of the hours worked and the unpredictability of the amount of sleep achieved were likely to be disruptive of diabetic control. However, apart from the minor episode of the circumcision, this was a period when I kept well and, in fact, thrived on the challenges of diagnosis and the management of the ill. One memorable night up, trying to save the life of a baby with cardiac failure, was capped at about 6.00 a.m. by the admission of a toddler with acute meningitis. Facing another full day, I remember fighting to keep awake while explaining to the parents about the lumbar puncture I needed to do on their child. In one of my letters to Joy at that time I declared the special relevance to me of those encouraging words from the end of Isaiah 40 :

> 'Even youths shall faint and be weary, and young men shall fall exhausted;
> but they who wait for the Lord shall renew their strength,
> they shall mount up with wings like eagles,
> they shall run and not be weary,
> they shall walk and not faint.'

As well as the Lord's power to keep an exuberant and busy

diabetic doctor healthy, this time in Norwich also underlined His all-sufficiency during my long periods of isolation from Christian fellowship. At Bart's we had been repeatedly warned of the dangers of lapsing as a disciple amidst the demanding and time-consuming work of a house doctor. However, I found great spiritual refreshment throughout these three jobs from regular times of private Bible study and prayer. Further, there were times of encouragement through the few occasions I was able to join other Christians in worship in one or other of the many churches of Norwich; amongst these the godly Rev. Archibald Hay of St. Michael-at-Coslany was a great support through his prayerful interest. Again the small nucleus of the Graduates' Fellowship, meeting at the home of a Christian GP, Dr. Peter English, and his wife Rosemary, was a source of strength. Most of all, though, it was the strategically placed Christians of more advanced years who acted as pillars of stability in the midst of the relativism and materialism of the lives of many other colleagues. The Lord had placed one such in each of the units I worked in—a senior nursing sister of the 'old school', resolute in her devotion to her patients and severe in her censure of any lapse in nursing or medical commitment; a consultant paediatrician, kindly, good-humoured and an encourager; and a sister midwife, elderly, single and shy, but with a heart of gold and a deep love for the Lord. With friends like that and a Lord like theirs and mine, how could I fall away?

Into the melting-pot of these crucial years was mixed the essential ingredient of a career. From my earliest days as a medical student, I had foreseen a future life as a general practitioner. This was an unusual ambition at that time as so many saw General Practice as the cinderella of the profession. My conviction was that work in the community 'on the front-line of disease', so to speak, would be the most rewarding. The comparative independence of the lifestyle coupled with my desire to understand people in the context of their workaday lives gave the idea of General Practice a great attractiveness. The house jobs I was working through in Norwich were applied for with this end in view.

However, our training at Bart's had been singularly lacking in experience of General Practice and so I still awaited the next step of traineeship out in the community. There were a number of approaches from assistant-hunting GP's during my job at the Jenny Lind and the prospect of a life's work amidst the beauties of Norfolk's 'town and country' looked very appealing.

There were two other possible claimants for the future. Paediatrics, with its handling of young and tender lives, was, for me, a very fulfilling speciality. Furthermore, we were without a registrar for much of my six months in that post and so my experience and confidence in handling unwell children increased the more. The possibility of continuing in this discipline was a real one.

More prophetically, I was approached by a Christian psychiatrist, Bill Abel, over tea, following a medico-surgical meeting on school stress. We not only had Christianity in common but bird-watching too and so our conversation flowed happily. The next day, he phoned me to query my plans for the future. He put in a plea for more Christians in his specialty and urged me to think and pray about the possibility of an imminent post as a registrar in Psychiatry. My experience of traditional Psychiatry up to that point had not encouraged me to pursue this profession. So much of its diagnosis seemed to be too 'pigeon-holing' and restrictive of peoples' humanity, and so much of its treatment had an unimpressive arbitrariness. At that stage, I was unaware of the more dynamic approaches that were to emerge increasingly during the 60's. Dr. Abel's thoughtful enquiry was perspicacious because the psychological aspects of illness became my main interest within Medicine in the coming years.

And so, on every available weekend off from these busy jobs, I drove the 300 miles to Surrey and back in pursuit of my Joy-Bird. At the end of October 1960, she had left general nursing and was now training as a pupil midwife in the Guildford area. Some wag had summed up this frenetic, love-inspired journeying with a quotation from Blake that he sent to my sister:

> He who bends to himself a Joy
> Doth the wingèd life destroy;
> But he who kisses the Joy as it flies
> Lives in Eternity's sunrise.

The main problems of our courtship were the considerable mileage of sometimes very busy roadway between us and the tantalising way other commitments, both domestic and professional, prevented us from spending enough time together to understand and evaluate each other adequately. In spite of this, I became increasingly convinced that we could make a very happy marriage and that God's hand was shaping our destinies together.

How can one be so sure of such things?

My certainty grew out of a number of factors. The series of unexpected coincidences which linked our initial meetings played their part. Continuing prayer for guidance and clarification of issues seemed to unlock many doors of uncertainty. I remember grappling almost obsessively with the pro's and con's of our relationship and reading avidly the few books I could find which offered guidelines for such a momentous decision. There was no doubt we were head over heels in love and then, as always, this powerful state of heart and mind was exceedingly influential. I had one important reservation—in the area of our intellectual compatability. However, there were a number of circumstances which suggested this was an unnecesaary query and, in the last analysis, our match seemed so eminently suitable in all other respects that the die was cast.

There was no problem in the proposal. Joy's surname was Harding and so it was simply a question of phonetics. Meandering up a muddy Surrey lane in January 1961, I gently asked, 'Joy, will you change your 'a' for a 'u'?' Within a fortnight, a diamond ring of linear setting was flashing from a certain pupil midwife's left hand and readers of the Daily Telegraph who had our futures, apart or together, at heart were writing letters of congratulation.

"I knew she was a Christian; I was beginning to find out that she was also 'great stuff'" (see p.106): Joy in the summer of 1960, and myself on the day of our official engagement at Lavenham, Suffolk, January, 1961

CHAPTER NINE

THE SAP IS RISING

'There are three things that are too amazing for me, four that I do not understand: the way of an eagle in the sky, the way of a snake on a rock, the way of a ship on the high seas, and the way of a man with a maiden.'

Proverbs 30: 18, 19 (NIV)

'To-day has been very pleasant again—the weather that makes the blood tingle, the sap rise and fills the Rog-mind with Joy-thoughts!'.

From letter to Joy, 15th December, 1961

ON 2ND OCTOBER 1916 JOY'S FATHER, THEN A LAD OF FIFTEEN, 'took the King's shilling' and joined the Royal Navy. Albert Edward Harding (Bill to his mates), the third of a large family, had been brought up with his five brothers and five sisters in Wealdstone, Middlesex, where his father, Walter Robert, worked as an engineer.

The Great War was entering its third year and the heavy casualties inflicted by the Germans at the sea battle of Jutland were a sore and recent memory. Following his initial training as a boy sailor at Devonport, Bill was sent north with many others to join the British fleet in Scapa Flow. On the crowded train to Scotland he was accompanied by another fifteen-year-old, Frank Elliott, a country lad from Surrey who was bound for active service on the same battleship, HMS *Malaya.*

Bill and Frank soon became firm friends and it was established between them that, whenever shore-leave coincided, they would join forces and stay at the Elliotts' home near Wonersh, in the heart of rural Surrey. This arrangement suited Bill well. The Hardings' household at Wealdstone was bursting at the seams and so the lure of leafy lanes and deep woodland in the company of his ship-mate was doubly enticing.

Frank, along with his brother and two sisters, had spent his childhood roaming the woods and heathland of the western fringes of the great Lower Greensand ridge that culminates at Leith Hill seven miles to the east. His grandfather, Michael Elliott, had come over from Ireland and had joined the Royal Navy, working up to the rank of petty officer and serving in the Crimean War. In contrast, Frank's father George had trained in horticulture and was now the Head Gardener at Derry's Wood, the impressive country estate of John Michell Courage, the master organ-builder turned brewer. And so, George and his wife, Ada Elizabeth, brought up their four children in the brick, gardener's cottage flanking the big house's walled kitchen garden.

As the two young naval ratings grew into their early twenties, Bill Harding's interest in Derry's Wood developed beyond the rabbitting expeditions with Frank to a quarry of a different kind.

Marion Nancy Lucy was the third of the four Elliott progeny and, on leaving school, had served an apprenticeship to a Court dressmaker in Guildford. Spending many of her working hours making elaborate dresses for eager dèbutantes, this young seamstress keenly anticipated the regular visits of her nautical brother and his ship-mate. Interest deepened, love grew and, on 16th August 1930, Bill Harding, now a Warrant Officer, and Nancy Elliott married with full naval honours at the village church in nearby Shamley Green.

Inevitably, naval life meant a great deal of uprooting for the young couple. They spent the first two years of their married life moving from one naval station to another, eventually buying a house in Shamley Green at the end of 1932. After three years' service with the Mediterranean Fleet based on Malta, Bill was appointed as Master Boatswain of the Barracks at Chatham. In this capacity he became increasingly busy with the preparations for war during the crisis period of 1938. In the same year, Joy Elizabeth was born in the Royal Naval Nursing Home at Gillingham—on Mothers' Day. Her eldest brother Michael was then five; two years later the family was completed with the birth of Christopher.

Joy's father, Albert Edward Harding, at twenty-six, in the dress uniform of Warrant Officer, and her mother, Marion Nancy Lucy, at twenty-three

As an officer in the Royal Navy, Joy's father became increasingly involved in enemy action as World War II unfolded. Serving on the reconstructed veteran battleship HMS *Warspite*, Bill experienced something of the British fleet's attempt to stop the supply of Swedish iron ore to Germany by landing troops at the Norwegian port of Narvik. At the same time, bitter wrangling in the Home Government, a hopeless endeavour by inexperienced British territorials to help the Norwegians in their snow-covered mountains and the collapse of Norway to the German invaders, rendered the expedition to take Narvik superfluous. Following this débâcle the *Warspite* was ordered south to join the Mediterranean Fleet at Alexandria in May 1940.

For the next year, Bill served on his beloved *Warspite*, which was now commanded by none other than Admiral Cunningham. This fine battleship of the 'Queen Elizabeth' Class with her new engine and modernised 15-inch guns was the nerve-centre of the Fleet. As the Commander-in-Chief's flagship, she controlled the deployment of her sister battleships as well as that of the attendant cruisers, destroyers and aircraft carrier.

Following the declaration of War by Italy in June 1940, the Mediterranean Fleet operated a relentless strategy against the Italian warships under Cunningham's edict to 'seek out and destroy'. There was a presentiment amongst the crew that all would be well as long as the 'old man' was on board. In fact, his brilliant seamanship off Calabria, at Matapan and in the bombardment of Tripoli seemed to confirm this superstition.

However, in May 1941, the Fleet was to be deployed in an attempt to rescue thousands of British troops from Crete following the successful invasion of Greece by the Germans. Cunningham reluctantly decided he would control his ships best from the base in Alexandria, and so the sea force sailed north-west from the Egyptian coast with Rear-Admiral Rawlings replacing the 'old man' in the *Warspite*.

On 20th May the first wave of an airborne assault on Crete by the Germans broke upon the island. The augmented Fleet was ordered to close in but to keep out of sight of land during daylight. The *Warspite* with the *Valiant* and four attendant destroyers was to patrol a stretch of water to the west of Crete.

Thursday, 22nd May was a fateful day for the Royal Navy and for numerous British families back home. Rear-Admiral King's force was in the Aegean Sea to the north of Crete and was attacked incessantly by German bombers. He was compelled to withdraw westwards with his ammunition-depleted and damaged craft, and was met by Rear-Admiral Rawling's and Captain Rowley's combined forces. At that very moment of reunion (13.32 hours) the *Warspite* was dive-bombed by three Messerschmitts and her speed was considerably reduced. During this attack Boatswain Bill Harding, who also served as a gunning officer, was killed instantly by bomb blast, along with his gun crew. In all 1,838 men were lost by the Navy in the Battle of Crete, 17,000 soldiers were evacuated and 12,000 captured by the Germans.

The grim pattern of a telegram from the War Office, Air Ministry or the Admiralty received by the local Post Office, the locking up of the shop while the post-mistress crossed the green to deliver her heavy tidings, the breaking of the news, out of kindness, first to the widow's mother who lived nearby, and then the fateful knock at the door, must have been repeated many thousands of times in tiny villages up and down the country during the war years. The multiplicity of such messages did not lessen the blows for the individual women receiving them, and Joy's mother was no exception.

Hesitantly, she asked the anxious-faced post-mistress, 'Is it bad news?'. The reply needed no further explanation: 'Yes, the very worst'.

Joy at fifteen, with her brothers Michael and Christopher

Over the subsequent years, Nancy Harding struggled to maintain her family of three. She and her husband had agreed to give their children 'the best possible education' and, in the face of the limited facilities offered by local schools, this seemed to mean independent schooling. This, of course, was an enormous challenge for a war widow. Help came for Michael from a Merchant banker who provided a Governor's Presentation, enabling him to attend the Blue-coat school of Christ's Hospital. The Admiralty's pension contributed towards schooling for all three Harding children, although in Joy's case her mother needed to meet the fees from her own slender resources. As a result, Chris boarded at Reed's School, Oxshott while Joy bussed or cycled to and from St. Catherine's at nearby Bramley.

Joy recalls certain key incidents and perspectives which relate to childhood and adolescence without a father. The first relevant memory, which has been of deep significance to her ever since, is of a comment made by a Mrs. Emma B. Hallett who lived in a larger house a little way up the lane from the family home. This good lady had been a missionary in Nigeria, taught at the local Sunday School and, on most mornings of the week, before they reached the stage of Prep school, gave Joy and Chris reading lessons. One day she took the six-year-old Joy aside and said, 'You've got a beautiful name, Joy—Jesus, Others, Yourself. If you remember *that* all your life, you won't go wrong! It doesn't matter you having no earthly father; you have a Heavenly Father who loves you.'

Another important influence from outside the family on Joy's earlier years was the love and friendship of 'Auntie' Frances. The daughter of Arthur Dunford, the deceased headmaster of Shamley Green's village school, she was secretary to the local family doctor, Dr. J.T. Bell-Nicholl,[1] and became a life-long friend of Joy's mother. Both of these women, well instructed in the Catechism and Collects of the Church of England, helped to prepare the ground for Joy's growing Christian commitment.

The local church, where Auntie Frances was organist for fifty years, became the meeting ground of a number of friendly young people who joined the choir. Joy thrived in this environment and through it met the Thorpes. Their eldest son, Hilton, was a fellow choir-member and introduced Joy to wider horizons as she became absorbed into the Thorpes' family life. Living in a beautiful, half-timbered house set amidst apple orchards a few miles from Shamley Green, the Thorpes—including their three lusty sons—welcomed this unexpected 'daughter' in their midst. Tobogganing, tandem-riding, square dancing and sailing holidays were some of the breathless adjuncts of this enlarged circle of acquaintence.

At the centre of this vibrant household was the rock-like figure of Leonard Thorpe. A director of a large furnishing firm in London, his leadership qualities of strength, capability and dependability, laced with a great sense of fun, gave Joy a feeling of paternal stability which was crucial for her formative mid-teen years.

1 Dr. J.T. Bell-Nicholl later became a well-known speaker on the BBC's programme *Silver Lining*. In his autobiography *The Span of Time* he wrote of his conversion to Christ at Lee Abbey as well as his experiences in General Practice. See also Richard More: *Growing in Faith* (Hodder) 1982, pp. 55-58.

Joy's talent in the Crafts attracted her towards a career in Occupational Therapy. Funds, however, were inadequate for the training and so, pursuing the idea of another of the caring professions, she applied to St. Bartholomew's Hospital for the three year course in General Nursing. On the whole, she had not enjoyed rubbing shoulders with the privileged at school and had found very little encouragement from the establishment. The head-mistress's parting comment to her, 'You're too soft to make a nurse' seemed to spur her resolve to succeed. Accepted at Bart's, she filled in the intervening year at Guildford Technical College to achieve the City and Guild's Certificate in Homecraft and Catering. And then, two-thirds of the way through her hospital training, she came second in her year for both ward work and exam results.

In that same year, while lingering in the square at Bart's on a hot, summer's day, she was introduced by a fellow-nurse to a fair-haired medical student who clutched an unprepossessing specimen jar of urine, and who seemed to have eyes only for her female companion.

During my last six months in Norwich, a great deal of time was spent in praying, thinking and following up leads about the next step on the ladder of a career. A letter was written enquiring about the possibility of a Registrar post in Paediatrics at the Jenny Lind Hospital but the timing did not seem right for this development. Dr. Abel's query of pursuing the profession of Psychiatry lay fallow, and so most of my energies went into finding a suitable opening in General Practice.

Although this branch of Medicine had been my central ambition throughout training, I still needed to work in the community for a reasonable length of time before committing the future. At that stage, fresh from a job in Obstetrics and Gynaecology, I was keen to find a practice with plenty of experience in Midwifery, ideally based in that increasingly rare phenomenon, the G. P. Hospital. I had visions of working in a group practice set in a delectable market town somewhere in the southern half of England—preferably in East Anglia with its cheap, historic property and its access to the sea, the Broads and to family in the London area. Possibilities came up in North Walsham, Burnham Market, Bury St. Edmunds and on the outskirts of Norwich itself, but none of these seemed either suitable or were finally available.

I had been a member of the Christian Medical Fellowship since qualifying and one or two helpful contacts came my way through their mediation. Late in May 1961 a letter arrived in a neat, precise hand from a Doctor Arthur Casson who had a practice in a Cotswolds' town with the unlikely name of Chipping Sodbury. He and his partner, Gerry Davies, were both Christians and were looking for a like-minded Trainee Assistant for one year. The prospect seemed an attractive one as it would give both General Practice and me a trial period before I took the far-reaching step of entering a partnership. The possibility of working with Christian colleagues in a beautiful part of Gloucestershire was worth looking into and so, in July, Joy and I drove westwards to inspect and to be inspected.

Once more the Lord was guiding through a number of circumstances which narrowed down the choices. The Cassons and Davieses were most welcoming and offered me the post within a week or so. The appointment was available under the new scheme for trainees sponsored by the Government and seemed an excellent one for learning the art of General Practice. And, so, on 28th August, I arrived in the West Country to begin a most memorable year.

Yate Cottage belies its name as it is in fact a fine period house with an extensive walled garden. It now looks out on the supermarkets and roof-tops of a vast development and yet, in 1961, the view to the south was an uninterrupted one of hedgerows, trees and fields, the nearest of which was occupied by a small group of Shetland ponies. Although the house faced on to a busy thoroughfare, a few minutes walk past the tall, Perpendicular tower of the church would bring me to the sequestered beauties of Goose Green—a cluster of small cottages, and occasional grander house—hemmed in by the verdant Gloucestershire countryside. Yate Cottage, the home of the Davieses, was to become an idyllic haven of retreat during the coming months. This was not the treat of escapism but a withdrawal into a real home—a place where I could be myself.

Gerry and Helen were a marriage of opposites. He, a sturdy Welshman whose father farmed in Glamorganshire, had a shyness and diffidence which, on further acquaintence, melted away to reveal a warm and reassuring personality. Although he worked hard to avoid the limelight of public speaking engagements, he was excellent with people individually and was much loved by his ever increasing number of patients. Helen, a little taller, had expressionful blue eyes and was a force to be reckoned with. She was a person of great compassion who keenly felt the sorrows and follies of those around her. Her soulful eyes reflected very precisely her thoughts and emotions. They would melt with concern over the troubled, flash with hot indignation at injustice or set with steely determination when her mind was made up. You knew where you were with Helen.

This happy household was completed by three delightful daughters, two of whom were still at the pre-school stage, and a very tolerant Labrador called Honey. The over-all welcome to my stay at Yate Cottage for the initial week was made tangible by the luxury of a huge, recently decorated bedroom, its double-bed spread with ice-blue and cream Candlewick. A tiny fistful of hand-picked flower buds, peeping from a bedside cup, was heralded by the cry of an excited four-year-old Nicola Davies—'for Doctor Hurding!'

While Joy began the second part of her training as a midwife at the Jarvis Maternity Home, Guildford, I was launched into the bewildering diversity of my first weeks in General Practice.

These were the days when dark suits and white shirts were obligatory for the doctor on duty, and yet this 'uniform' did not identify me on one of my first visits. Called to see a sick child on a nearby housing estate, I thought I would arrive on foot as my destination was within walking distance. The door was opened by a distraught mother who hesitated a moment at the sight of this unfamiliar figure clutching a bulky, dark brown case. Her indecision overcome, she turned towards the stairs and her crying child and said, 'This way'. I followed promptly, eager with incipient diagnosis and advice, only to walk into her as she stopped, turned and stooped to open a cupboard under the stairs. 'It's in here' she said. Wondering at the impersonal pronoun used and conjecturing a possible case of cruelty to children, I peered into the shadows. It took another second or two of mystification to realise that she was also expecting the Gas man to come and read the meter. My budding professionalism considerably chastened, I mounted the stairs to the challenge of a crying child.

General Practice is, of course, general in the sense of comprehensive and this necessitates the doctor's involvement in the 'front line' of Medicine. Someone needs to be available when people are first afflicted by illness and accident; someone needs to be able to answer the pressing questions: 'What's wrong with me?', 'Is it serious?', 'When will I get better?', 'Will I get better?'; someone has to decide what needs to be done, if anything, in this or that medical situation in the home; someone has to sort out, within the immense range of human suffering that the doctor may be called out to, which channel of help is most appropriate. And this someone needs to be a generalist—albeit a competent and compassionate one—to succeed.

This generalism obviously encompasses great diversity. My experience of this variety during the first few months at Yate and Chipping Sodbury was not exceptional because the variety is always there for every general practitioner. However, every new encounter helped to consolidate the need to be ready for *any* eventuality as a doctor. Within the first day or two I was called to see a farmer's pregnant wife who had been badly kicked by a frisky heifer; it was a great relief to listen in to a steady foetal heart and so reassure a frightened woman. On another occasion, an elderly man with high blood pressure had collapsed in the loo of his house and the toilet door had to be prised open with an axe to reach his dead body. Specially tragic was the outcome of a fire which swept through the home of one of our patients one morning after the father had left for work and while the mother was visiting her own mother across the road. Gerry was called in to confirm the deaths of their three small children, and the aura of this tragedy stayed with us for many weeks.

However, the distinctiveness of General Practice for me lay less in the rich variety of 'all sorts and conditions of men' that came our way than in the matter of responding to that variety—the art of being a family doctor. This new perspective contrasted with hospital medicine in at least two ways.

Working in a hospital environment, an accurate scientific approach had been the order of the day. Although I had striven to see the patient on the ward as a whole person, the disease process had seemed to command the most attention and questions of the interpretation of biochemical tests, of whether or not a cardiac murmur was present, of the careful calibration of medicaments and of the timing of when the patient was sufficiently improved to be discharged had been paramount. Now, I was being confronted by statements such as: 'No, doctor. Oi'm not gonna take moi shirt off fer you nor nobody. Just give me the medicine an' Oi'll be off!' and requests like this one made over the phone on a Sunday by a young man: 'Doc, come straight away will you? I think I've got another stye coming'. I soon realised that many people in the community did not fit at all readily into the orderly world of examination, investigation, diagnosis, treatment and prognosis that marked out their lives once through the hospital doors. In many ways the common, everyday troubles that people brought into the surgery would not be straight-jacketed into a regimen designed more for the ward than the workaday world. A new art, where intuition, reading between the lines, knowledge of a particular family's problems or a certain individual's propensities, needed to flesh out one's carefully acquired training, experience and skill from hospital days. Within the first few days of traineeship at Yate I wrote to Joy: 'It's amazing how ignorant one is of the really basic things whereas Disseminated Lupus Erythematosis or Acromegaly are much more familiar'.

As well as the need to become acquainted with the 'everyday' and 'down to earth' aspects of peoples' illness, there was the enthralling perspective of the doctor-patient relationship to explore in this 'art of General Practice'. In the same letter to Joy, I wrote: 'The work is . . . so different to the hospital world—it's much more a series of relationships with people, reassuring, encouraging and perhaps rebuking'.

It was the profound importance and desirability of developing rapport with my patients and their families that captivated me in General Practice and, in turn, stimulated my growing interest in medical counselling and psychotherapy. Encouraged by Gerry's perceptivity and by his introduction to the writings of Michael Balint who, at that time, was pioneering the concept of psychotherapy in General Practice through his work at the Tavistock Clinic, I increasingly employed the 'long interview' in trying to help certain patients. In this way more time was offered to the depressed and the over-anxious in an attempt to help them cope better with themselves and others. One of my first patients in this field was a tearful man in his early thirties who had withdrawn into his shell since school days. Somehow he had emerged enough to marry, but his wife was by now driven to distraction by his melancholia and was threatening separation. In my comparative inexperience I listened carefully throughout a lengthy appointment and then prescribed a course of anti-depressants laced with John's gospel and an arrangement to see him again the following week.

The year in Gloucestershire provided a rich experience in other ways than the purely medical. The love and friendship of my Christian colleagues were a great stimulus to a deepening commitment to Christ. One of the highlights of the week was the Practice meeting held on Monday evenings when Arthur, the senior partner, and his wife Clarice joined Gerry, Helen and me at Yate Cottage. The time together was often hilarious while the anecdotes of the previous week were being shared. The signal for the evening to close was frequently a firm, 'We must pray, Arthur,' from Clarice. This injunction would brook no delay and so the five of us would kneel about the comfortable sitting room while Honey dozed before the open fire. The time of prayer was full of praise to a loving Father and was also exemplary in the specific nature of the requests for patients and family alike. These evenings of mirthful fellowship imprinted deeply something of the joy of the Lord in my heart and mind.

Arthur was a G.P. of the old school. Tall and imposing, he was a tower of strength both physically and spiritually. His care of the genuinely sick was meticulous, but woe betide the malingerer. Many a patient staggered into his capacious surgery with the countenance and posture of the afflicted only to re-emerge seconds later with a flea in the ear, a final certificate in the hand and a surprising spring in the step.

Arthur, a Diocesan Reader based at the local Anglican church and a member of the House of Laity, was also deeply involved in the lives of the young people of Chipping Sodbury. He and Clarice, the wise and gentle sister of the Bristol surgeon Melville Capper, ran both boys' and girls' bible classes in their beautiful, 18th century home, Hill House. This loving ministry continued during the week, when 'Doc' would take a dozen or so lads, squeezed into his estate car ('Heads down if you see a policeman!'), the seven miles to Downend for an evening's swim. In these ways, and through the summer camps the Cassons ran, many a local teenager began his or her discipleship as a Christian.

Of their three children, James was still at school at Marlborough. Like his parents, James was a great original for the Lord. His gallant spirit as he faced death from malignant disease nearly twenty years later (so movingly described in his booklet *Dying — The Greatest Adventure of My Life*) was a tribute to the inspiration of this very special family.

The New Year of 1962 dawned, and thoughts and feelings focussed more and more on our coming marriage planned for

"Joy and I joined hands to clasp the hilt of her father's highly-polished naval sword ..." At our wedding breakfast, Shamley Green, 21st April, 1962

Easter. Helen entered into the atmosphere of starry-eyed anticipation with great relish. In my early days at Yate she had sought out a meeting with Joy 'to make quite sure she's the right one'. Her imprimatur given, many a knowing look and long conversation about the delights of marriage followed, culminating in a particularly memorable, lingering encounter over lunch at the beginning of February. Through the main window of the dining area at Yate Cottage could be seen a magnificent weeping willow. That day the tree was resplendent in the soft winter sunshine, its branches glowing orange with the anticipation of spring. Helen, the observer of thoughts, caught my eye and, with a metaphorical squeeze of the hand, declared, 'The sap's rising, Rog'. It is impossible now to look at the blaze of Spring twigs without thinking of Helen and the heralding of marriage.

And so, on 21st April 1962, while a soft drizzle filled the Surrey sky, Joy and I plighted our troths before friends and family in the small, stone Victorian church of Shamley Green. The neo-Geothic interior was festooned with hedgerow flowers—primroses, daffodils and pussy willow. Spring was upon us and the sap had truly risen!

Their whiteness glowing above the altar, a group of arum lilies arrested the gaze and prompted memory. The display of these sophisticated blooms in the sanctuary was a village tradition — a call to remember the dead, including those of two world wars.

This blend of eager anticipation and wistful reminiscence was further captured during the wedding breakfast in the church hall nearby. Joy and I, walking on air amidst the festivities, joined hands to clasp the hilt of her father's highly polished naval sword as we directed the point of its blade down through the two-tiered wedding cake. The symbol of the lily and the memento of steel linked us with another marriage celebrated in the same church thirty-two years before.

CHAPTER TEN

GENERAL PRACTICE

'To write prescriptions is easy, but to come to an understanding with people is hard'.

Franz Kafka: *A Country Doctor*

'The more one learns of the problems of general practice, the more impressed one becomes with the immense need for psychotherapy'.

Michael Balint: *The Doctor, His Patient and the Illness*

'Honour the doctor with the honour that is his due in return for his services;
for he too has been created by the Lord'.

Ecclesiasticus 38:1 (The Jerusalem Bible)

CROWTHER'S FARM WAS A SOLID, STONE CONSTRUCTION OF TWO storeys sitting four square to the lane which ran from Goose Green to the grander Rectory Farm. Behind the farm-house and its muck-spattered yard rose an assemblage of out-buildings which included the milking shed, whence a herd of Friesians gravitated twice daily. Beyond these outhouses the farm pastures ran in a series of consecutive fields, flanked to the west by a ditch and thorn hedge and to the east by the gardens and roof-tops of Goose Green.

Crowther's was farmed by Tony and Moreen Marsh, both born and bred locally, and was to provide the rented accommodation of our first home. I had moved in two months before the wedding and

Crowther's Farm, where we spent the first months of our marriage

had grown to love the rural setting. The thick walls of the house muffled any noise from outside; those sounds that penetrated were the acceptable sounds of the country: at night the 'keewicking' of a tawny owl, the sharp bark of a dog fox or the strangled scream of a vixen; and in the early morning, before I had left to take a surgery, the lowing and hoof-scraping of the cattle as they filed through the yard to be milked, the ring of pail and churn, and the urgent cries of the farmer to check a wandering cow or to hasten his loitering son, the four-year-old Andrew 'Tomall' Marsh.

There was a thrill, too, at night, curling into the cold sheets of the generous double bed anticipating the delights of sharing bed and board with Joy Elizabeth. And all this for only £4.4s a week!

We returned from the ecstasies of a honeymoon in North-West Scotland to the realities and readjustments of life together. We survived the exceedingly chilly bathroom which was housed in an extension jutting out into the farm-yard and exposed to three of the four winds; Joy worked wonders in the cramped end of a short corridor which served as a kitchen, producing steaming, tasty sustenance from the minute stove which sported the misnomer of

'Jackson Giant'; and we enjoyed the farm atmosphere with its fresh milk and eggs, the soft cheeping of scores of incubating chicks (just the other side of a door into our cubby-hole kitchen) and the bantering companionship of our farmer friend, Tony Marsh.

Tony was a strongly built man of average height whose lined and weathered facial features were crowned by a shock of unruly, black hair. He spoke with a fruity Gloucestershire twang and always seemed ready to engage in conversation on a wide range of topics. A lay reader at Yate church, his sympathies were Anglo-Catholic and, as such, he would bemoan the historical fact of the Reformation with great verve. This enthusiastic dairy farmer was to become, some years later, an equally enthusiastic Anglican vicar whose knowledge of country ways and whose love for the Lord won the hearts of many parishioners.

Crowther's Farm lay on the edge of 'Beaufort' country, that extensive tract of land centred on the estate of Badminton and quartered regularly by the Beaufort Hunt. Paradoxically, this was a kingdom in which the fox ruled because farmers in the district were dissuaded strongly from shooting Reynard. It was even rumoured that an advert in the local paper had invited those interested in shooting foxes to write in to a certain box number. At a subsequent meeting of the farming fraternity, so the tale continued, the Duke of Beaufort declared, 'Now we know who our enemies are'! As a result of influences like this, foxes trotted quite freely across our farmyard to inspect the chicken-runs.

One day in high summer, while the Marshes were away, Joy and I were summoned to the front door by two serious-faced boys, aged eleven or twelve. The spokesman was a bespectacled, Billy Bunter figure. 'Have you got a humane-killer we could borrow, Doc?' was his rather sinister query. My visions of an ailing relative crying out for a knock-out injection of morphine were dispelled when he added, 'It's for a fox'.

I followed the two eager lads across the Marshes' fields to a boundary line bordering a deep ditch and a thorn hedge. There, suspended over the dyke, hung a vixen. She had tried to jump the fence to reach a blackbirds' nest in the thicket beyond but one of her hind legs had been impaled by the barbed wire. The fence leaned out over the ditch and so she swung there in her agony. The rake of the boundary posts was such that all I could do was to lean out and stretch to lift the injured leg free of the barb and so drop the fox into the ditch below. She seemed little impaired and, after a moment's hesitation, streaked up the bank on the far side and away through the hedge.

That night one of a neighbour's domestic geese disappeared leaving a tell-tale flurry of blooded feathers. Word soon got round that the doctor and his freed fox might well be guilty!

By the autumn of 1962, the sights, smells and sounds of young calves and innumerable cheeping chickens may have worked a deep work in our own body chemistry. In November, at the death of Gerry's father, we were asked whether we would move into Yate Cottage for a week or so to look after the Davies's older daughters, Christine and Nicola, as well as their sundry pets. We gladly assented.

Nicola, at the compelling age of five, we found especially endearing. Her outgoing enthusiasms and wide-eyed questions stirred deep, broody feelings in Joy. Our mutual desire for parenthood reached a climax (in both the general and sexual senses of the word) on the night of 5th November. With such disarming company as the Davies's daughters and some of their friends, Guy Fawkes' demise had to be celebrated with a generous burst of noise and colour. As a cluster of rockets bored their way into the leaden, wintry sky, Nicola asked with a lisping intensity: 'Won't the rockets hurt the Lord Jesus?'.

The magic was too much for us. That night our first-born was conceived.

As the charmed year at Yate drew to a close, we did all we could to find an opening in General Practice in the area. Arthur and Gerry expressed the wish that I should continue to work with them but, at that stage, they could not afford a third partner. From September to November I was able to work as a locum in a single-handed practice on the outskirts of Bristol. A woman doctor was exhausted by seven years of working alone and was seeking an alternative career with her husband. There was understandable pressure from them for us to buy their house and take over the practice. However, we could not afford the transaction and the prospect of a single-handed General Practice did not seem too inviting to a diabetic doctor.

During the month or so before our wedding, we had visited two practices, each run by Christian doctors looking for an additional partner. Both teams responded favourably to us and so a decision between them was not easy. Our experience working with Christian colleagues had been so encouraging that we felt it right to look for an opening in a similar partnership. After due prayer and thought, and attracted by the prospect of a new, purpose-built health centre (the 'New Jerusalem') planned for completion in 1965, we took the offer to join a practice in Chelmsford, Essex.

Leaving our beloved West Country friends, we drove east amidst the blizzards of the 1962/1963 winter. Within a week of our departure, Crowther's Farm and Goose Green were cut off by deep snow, the corner of the yard where we had parked our Mini being obliterated by a huge drift that rose up to meet the eaves of the house. Throughout the Cotswolds GPs with experience in Winter Sports were out on skis visiting their more isolated patients. These arctic conditions complicated the early weeks of my map-reading in Chelmsford and so many a needy person had an excessive wait for the new doctor during this period, because the road signs and street names were obscured by ice and snow.

Following the three months of mutual probation, I was offered a partnership to work alongside three other principals: Dr. Cyril Politeyan, a shy and gentle man who had been a missionary in Palestine, Dr. Robin Catlin, extroverted, ambitious and an excellent administrator, and Dr. Hedley Missen, a caring and conscientious GP who had inherited many problematic patients from his predecessor.

I had the great privilege of taking over the list of Sir Ivor Beauchamp, an ex-CIM missionary whose loving identification with the Chinese seemed to be mapped out in the somewhat oriental lines of his kindly face. Sir Ivor's Christian commitment had led to his disinheritance as the elder son when he obeyed God's call to China. However, in time he was restored to favour and, at the death of his father in 1939, he inherited the estate after all, becoming the 8th Baronet in the family of Proctor-Beauchamp. He then bought a large Victorian mansion to house the priceless treasures of paintings, books and antique furniture he had acquired. It was a delight to know this humble and trustworthy man whose life seemed completely unfettered by these valuable possessions. It was a measure of his graciousness that, although he had relinquished the partnership and was continuing as a part-time assistant for a while, I never felt oppressed by his presence while I tried to win the confidence of his former patients. He was a living testimony to his family motto: *Toujours fidèle.*

The responsibility of having my own patients was most welcome. At last, I felt, I could work at continuing relationships with the families under my medical charge and so be in a better position to understand the context of illness and accident. I found, too, that my interest in the psychological roots of and links with physical illness continued to develop. As this understanding grew so did the frustration of trying to help so many needy people with only limited time available. Particularly prevalent were anxious or depressed women, often with small children and often, it seemed, ill understood by their husbands. Many were faced with an apparently endless cycle of loneliness and stagnation where the only company was the continuous demands of their attention-seeking babies and toddlers. Of the many families in need under my care, I could only select a handful at any point for the more time-consuming help I wanted to give. For the others, I could only offer a listening ear for a brief appointment or two together with some symptomatic relief for anxiety or depression.

However, the fact that someone was prepared to listen with complete attention, even for a limited period of time, was a luxury to many patients. One of our trainee assistants, Dr. Rachel Anstead, was particularly generous in the time she gave to some. One middle-aged lady emerged from the surgery after half an hour with Rachel, her face radiant as she exclaimed to her companion, 'I've forgotten quite why I visited the doctor ... but she listened so well that I feel *much* better!'.

The psychiatric services were similarly hide-bound by the exigencies of the time factor. A psychiatrist whose approach I particularly respected, Dr. Kenneth Marshall, declared that he was no better placed in the setting of a hospital's Out Patients than I was in a GP's surgery for the vast majority of our patients.

However, there were some whose psychological illnesses were too severe or too disruptive for them to be contained in the community during their more disturbed periods. One gusty winter evening, I was phoned by the police to say that one of our patients, a schizophrenic in his early 30's, had run away from the Maudsley Hospital, was heading for Chelmsford to get in touch with his wife and was known to be carrying a loaded pistol. The voice of Law and Order at the other end of the phone assured me that, as the family doctor, I would be less likely than the police to provoke attack and asked me whether I would therefore visit the patient's address to persuade him to hand over the weapon and return peaceably to hospital. In turn, I phoned the Mental Health Officer, whose presence would probably be needed to effect re-admission, and we arranged a rendezvous at one end of the short street in which the patient's wife lived. My own tenuous confidence was not strengthened by the MHO in whose parked car we discussed a plan of procedure. Chain-smoking with tremulous fingers, his understandable agitation at the prospect of meeting an armed schizophrenic was plain to see. The atmosphere of impending danger was further enhanced by the unobtrusive presence of the police guarding each end of the road.

As my nervous companion and I approached our destination and knocked at the door, he urged me to enter the terraced house first as a patient would hardly shoot a general practitioner! A woman aged about thirty answered the door and, on learning our identity, invited us into her sitting room. The MHO, groping for his cigarettes once more, asked, 'Is he here?' and then collapsed with relief on the sofa when she replied, 'No! He's been, but he's gone again. Don't worry ... he's left the gun with me.' Cool, resigned, even a little bored with the proceedings, our patient's wife put to shame the MHO's swinging agitation and my own quieter trepidation.

More generally, the experience of these years in Chelmsford underlined for me that most people in need seemed to gravitate, at some stage or other, to their GP. He or she, in turn, could only offer limited time and was often tempted thereby to refer the patient unnecessarily on to the psychiatric services where another time-barrier was often met. There appeared to be an enormous need for people who not only cared but could also offer the time that adequate caring often requires. Compassionate friends and neighbours can help in ways that are sometimes more appropriate to the lonely, anxious and depressed than those offered by the medical profession. The Christian church should be in the vanguard of such practical love for the needy.

In many ways great strides have been made to fill this vacuum of caring through the extension of the Social Services and the development of numerous self-help agencies, such as Alcoholics Anonymous, the Phobic Society, Gingerbread (for single parents) and Cruse (for widows). Christians, too, during the second half of the 20th Century, have allowed themselves to rediscover the story of the Good Samaritan and Our Lord's command to 'Go and do likewise.'

There were both privileges and problems in working in this particular Christian practice. At that stage we looked after about 12,000 patients and provided the care and attention of four partners, a trainee assistant and a splendid team of receptionists and secretaries. Being a Christian group was, obviously, no guarantee of openness and harmony and the undercurrents of what we lightly dismiss as 'personality clashes' were a force that could not be ignored. At interview, Joy and I had sensed the possibility of conflict when we were told that release from the partnership was of the order of seeking a divorce from marriage! I had been uneasy at so sweeping a commitment and yet could see, up to a point, the need for loyalty and mutual submission for effective teamwork.

My own individualism and tendency to submerge feelings of anger and resentment did little to take the lid off the situation in a constructive way. One attempt to come clean with one of the partners proved abortive and the ranks closed together once more. However, relationships *did* improve after this in that there seemed to be a deeper level of mutual understanding. Perhaps the most stabilising influence amongst us was our chief receptionist, Betty. Caring and cheerful with patients, doctors and the other staff, she soothed the most jangled nerves with her sensitivity and equability.

For the first year or so we lived in the first floor of 37 Baddow Road. The suite of consulting rooms and the caretaker's flat occupied the ground floor while, at the front, we looked down on the busy thoroughfare through which both patients and doctors came and went. To the rear, we could see across a large, walled garden to the sluggish River Chelmer and the gas-works beyond. The garden was endowed with a magnificent, ancient mulberry tree which, when fruiting, attracted swarms of rats from the river into its branches. Mr. Felton, the caretaker, shot seven of these voracious rodents out of the tree at one sitting. We had something of a beleaguered feeling in our upstairs flat!

During the first eight months of 1963, Joy steadily increased in girth as the precious new life was formed and grew within. We had assured Nicola that the rockets could not hurt the Lord Jesus and our conviction was confirmed in the strong sense of His presence as the 'Expected Date of Delivery' approached.

Waking in the small hours of 26th August, Joy declared that she was feeling contractions at the rate of one every fifteen minutes. Ingrained with obstetric 'know-how' that, with a *primigravida*,[1]

1 A primigravida is a woman who is pregnant for the first time.

there would be plenty of time ahead before delivery, I sleepily replied to Joy's statement of fact with: 'Fine, dear; I'll just go and shave.' While I gazed blearily at the familiar features in the mirror, the cool appraisal of the doctor wrestled with the mounting excitement of the expectant father. A smooth-jawed decision was made, the midwifery unit was phoned and I drove my labouring beloved to an experienced reception at St. John's Hospital. Joy was ushered into a side ward by a rather brusque Sister, given an injection of Pethidine and left while she vomited into the sink. My husbandly concern and medical competence received a jolt when the Sister returned and, using a voice that brooked no contradiction, commanded, 'You run along, now, and get some more sleep. Your wife will be some time yet'.

The surgeries and visits of that day seemed interminable although they were punctuated by frequent phone calls to the unit. At last the evening came with news of progress in labour. Joy and I joined forces in the 'Second Stage' Room to push out our first-born, while the midwife's skilled hands directed the baby into the environmental shock of bright lights and human voices. My exclamation as the moist bundle of new humanity was extruded, severed from the cord and held aloft was one of surprise: 'It's a girl!' This objective clinician, knowing full well that we might have a Simon *or* Sarah first was caught out by some unconscious presentiment. However, there was no disappointment—merely a surprising surprise.

After six long days, Joy and I were reunited at Baddow Road to begin the lifelong, parental commitment of nurture and release—of holding close and of letting go.

In April 1964, when Sarah was eight months old, we moved from the siege conditions of the centre of Chelmsford to a modern chalet set in a large garden amidst open fields and orchards near the bottom of a gravelly, unmade road that ran from the common land of Galleywood down to a narrow bridge across the River Wid. The purchase of this property arose from a seemingly chance scanning of the local paper one afternoon when we were specially disenchanted with our cramped environment at Baddow Road. The sea of apple blossom viewed through Scots pines to the south and the sweep of hedge-lined arable land and coppice to the north rejoiced our hearts as we set about imprinting our tastes on house and garden. One of the first jobs to establish the change of ownership was the removal of the name-sign, pretentiously blazoned 'Chateau Lugano', and the carving of the more appropriate honeymoon destination 'Torridon' on a piece of cedar to welcome visitors.

Having decorated the outside of the house to obliterate the pinks and blues of its former identity, we set to to transform the garden. I spent most of my half-days and Saturdays double-digging the heavy London clay to prepare a series of curved borders. Inspired by the ideas in Michael Haworth-Booth's *Effective Flowering Shrubs*, I worked out a seven year plan to establish that elusive goal—the trouble-free garden! This was to be planted mostly with low growing shrubs backed by taller specimens, the whole planting giving an over-all effect of varied shapes, textures, scents and colours in both flower and foliage. The Scottish flavour given by a pair of pine trees and the house's new name was reinforced by an underplanting of rhodedendrons, azaleas, brooms, heathers and heaths in the front garden. At the back, a small, tiered rock garden planted with alpines ran down to the sloping lawn which in turn was flanked by a sweeping, curved border of shrubs framed by climbing roses. The eye was thus carried down the tilt of the garden to a series of island borders running diagonally towards the bottom left and, on the right, to the more informal plantings of a small, woodland area which merged with the hedge line and rivulet at the lower boundary.

This new passion for gardening became dangerously all absorbing in terms of time and money. My preoccupation was tantalisingly challenged through the intervention of certain of God's creatures. The open plan of the site leading out into the lane and orchard beyond was a sore temptation to a particularly obstinate doe-rabbit, who finally succeeded in raising a litter of four young in the improved soil of a choice border close to the front door. My attempts to chase this family back towards the orchard and away from its freshly imprinted homeland were frenzied and completely lacking in humour; these determined acrobatics left Joy feeling puzzled and angry.

A further trial was in store in the back garden when, some time later, two or three moles burrowed their tortuous ways amidst the sandstone strata of the rock garden threatening the root systems of a score of treasured miniatures.

Yet more hazard struck through Sarah's pram which Joy, blinded perhaps by her husband's new compulsion, pushed several times at a lawn specimen of *Magnolia stellata* whose proportions were steadily diminished.

These attacks on what had almost become an idolatrous obsession were salutary and I gradually began to find a more detached and less possessive attitude towards the garden's flora. Enthusiasm can become fanaticism and this is a development that some of us are more prone to than others. It has always been my particular temptation—whether bird-watching, fell-walking and the pursuit of lonely places, gardening or, some years later, local history and genealogy. I suspect that God, in creating Man, has put into our hearts the capacity to revel in this or that aspect of the Created Order. This capacity for enjoyment for what is derivative may express itself through the pioneering spirit, the love of adventure, the desire to achieve and in sheer delight at the beauty or rarity of what is observed, acquired or nurtured. Sadly and perversely, Man muddies the waters of unsullied appreciation of God's world. What should be a worshipful celebration of a wise and ingenious Creator for 'making all things well' is invariably contaminated, to some extent at least, by our rivalries, selfish ambitions, acquisitiveness, our vanity, exclusivism and obsessive fixation on things created. Thank God that, in spite of Man's contrariness, His common grace has led to many admirable achievements throughout history, reaching their zenith in the lives of such single-minded enthusiasts as Leonardo da Vinci, Michaelangelo, Shakespeare, Galileo, Newton, Beethoven, the Brönte sisters, Lister, Madame Curie and Einstein. Thank God that, through Christ, idolatry can be defeated, motives be purified and something of the unalloyed pleasure of Eden be restored. The Lordship of Christ over our enthusiasms can make sense of them once more. And this gradually became true of my delight in gardening!

In spite of my excesses and all the mistakes we made in the handling of our lives at Torridon, we had an increasing sense of God's hand upon us to protect and to lead forward. One curious telephone call seemed to put the seal on our awareness of His guardianship.

It was a cold February night in 1965 and Joy and I were soundly asleep in the snugness of our double bed. Although I was not on duty that night, the phone rang at the merciless hour of 1.00 a.m. My head full of sleep, I mumbled our number into the mouth-piece to hear the familiar voice of one of my more 'difficult' patients. A young and attractive married woman, she had been a frequent attender at the surgery for a host of difficult problems. Her simple statement of fact over the phone took some assimilating and, in turn, some handling. 'I'm cold' she said. A bewilderment of thoughts assailed my mind: 'Not unreasonable on a cold night', 'Is she really phoning her off-duty doctor at 1.00 a.m. for a discussion on weather conditions?', 'What does she really want?', 'Does she expect a visit for hypothermia?'. Struggling for sensible ideas, I asked her, 'Is your husband with you?'

'Yes!'

'Can't you get him to rub you down to warm you?'

'He's done that!'

'Ask him to try again!'

'All right.'

Not the most brilliantly executed medical advice, but she rang off with seeming contentment.

Woken by the phone and my inane comments into it, Joy visited the loo along the landing. My conversation completed, she returned to the bedroom wide-eyed and tense. 'I can smell smoke' she said, 'it must be the kitchen!'

Rushing down the stairs to the kitchen's inner door, I was met by a pall of smoke and a wave of intense heat. Unthinkingly, I opened the rear door out into the garden to release the fumes. Fortunately, this foolish manoeuvre and its consequent inrush of night air did not provoke a fire. As the smoke cleared we could see that the kitchen was devastated. A line of Sarah's nappies suspended above the solid fuel stove had ignited, involving the woodwork of the surrounding shelving. This panoply of charred wood had filled the area with dense smoke which in turn had penetrated every cupboard and every interface of the crockery and aluminium-ware within. The plastic curtain-rails above the garden windows had melted in the heat so that they now ran in a scalloped design, each segment curving limply down from its wall fixtures. The firemen called later and were quite astounded that the kitchen had not burst into flames when the back door was opened.

This story does not have the drama of John Wesley's boyhood escape from the flames of his blazing family home—'a brand plucked from the burning'—yet Joy and I had a truly Wesleyan sense of divine protection following this incident. What a God to stimulate a particular patient to phone her doctor out of hours (the only time she phoned me at home over six years!) with a seemingly nonsensical but exquisitely timed request which stirred the doomed slumberers into action!

In spite of the ravages of rabbit, mole and fire, the years at

Torridon were happy ones. It was during this time that our family unit was completed with the births of Simon Bartholomew and Rachel Emma Louise, both home confinements and both born in May—in 1965 and 1968 respectively. Each of our three children was baptised at St. Michael's, Galleywood, during the main Morning Service. It is in the context of a believing family set in the fellowship of God's people that infant baptism can make theological sense and, moreover, these three occasions seemed to be highlights in the life of the expanding local church.

Our involvement in the Lord's work at and through the parish church was considerable. While at Baddow Road I had prepared for the Diocesan Board's examination for Lay Readership by battling with Old and New Testaments, Church History and the Book of Common Prayer in an attic room during the small hours, before the busy day of family life and General Practice was under way. Somehow achieving distinctions in the four papers taken, I was launched into the privileged commitment of leading services and preaching at St. Michael's, along with the vicar, the Rev. Eddie Lendon, and my fellow reader, Frank Sprange, the headmaster of the local church school.

Further, Joy and I started a young people's group, affiliated to CYFA, sending invitations to sixty potential members to come to Torridon on Sunday afternoons for Bible study and discussion. Six turned up the first week and formed the nucleus of a splendid band of 14-18-year-olds who grew in commitment and Christian maturity through the years and gave us, in several instances, some lifelong friendships. The climax of our involvement in their collective lives was a holiday in September 1968 when we took fourteen of them, along with the four-month-old Rachel, for a week on the Thames in two aggressive motor cruisers. The splayed bollards just above Folly Bridge at Oxford are symbolic of the riotous time we had.

Beneath the joys and trials of our family life and our work for the Lord lay the continuing questions of my health. During 1964, I developed recurring headaches whcih centred behind the left eye and radiated into the forehead, cheek and ear—all on the left side. The pain was a dull aching and burning one and was accompanied by difficulty in breathing through the left nasal passage. The headaches were stimulated by a fall in blood sugar and were alleviated by an ice-pack held over the left eye. In time, these symptoms were gathered up under the rather grand title of Atypical Migrainous

Neuralgia. Their persistance over the next ten years or so was a source of distraction and frustration for us all.

Further, both Joy and I became afflicted with chronic laryngitis, which robbed Joy of the delights of sustained singing—an ability she had previously enjoyed—and led me to some difficult communication problems with demanding patients (giving complex advice to deaf or obtuse people is not easy with a barely existent voice!).

Most disruptive of these physical afflictions was the increased difficulty of keeping the diabetes stable within a busy general practice. In the autumn of 1967 the frequency of night calls had an adverse affect on my health. I found it difficult to estimate how much extra food I would need in visiting patients in the small hours. Anticipating a protracted time of involvement, I might stoke up considerably. The situation might then prove less arduous than predicted and so the next day I might be contending with unpleasant symptoms of hyperglycaemia. Having a 'labile' form of diabetes, I could then be troubled for many days with swinging blood sugars.

This debilitating cycle continued during the winter months and so it came about that, in February 1968, the partnership offered me the possibility of relief from night and Sunday duties. As this meant a proportionate drop in salary from £3,000 to £2,800 a year, we had to consider the idea carefully. Health, however, was at a premium and so we opted for a less disturbed life. The arrangement worked wonders and by the end of the year I was feeling much stronger.

However, there were problems in this 'solution'. Financially, we were worse off but, more significantly, we also faced the prospect of a progressive *drop* in income over a number of years while the practice expanded and took on new partners. Further, there was the psychological difficulty of being a partner and yet knowing that I was being carried to some extent by the others; inevitably this began to colour the decision-making discussions of the practice. Although these restrictions were surmountable, they seemed to indicate that we should consider alternatives for the future.

What could I turn my hand to as a diabetic doctor after nearly eight years in General Practice? I had enjoyed the diversity and challenge of this branch of Medicine greatly and was loath to discard it too readily. Ideally, I needed work with hours that were predictable enough to keep the diabetes stable and with sufficient contact with needy people to exercise my skills and aptitudes in listening and communicating. A year previously, when the writing on the wall was first glimpsed, I had responded to an advert for a post in Industrial Medicine at Hoffman's—the local ball-bearing factory! Although the job had excellent medical and nursing facilities there were two snags: I would have no patients of my own and so, for example, many of the surgical procedures would need the go-ahead from the relevant GP before applying scalpel to tissue; and, also, I would have great difficulty in surviving the ear-splitting din of the assembly lines—not an environment for a silence-loving doctor with headaches!

Psychiatry was once again considered and looked to be the most attractive solution. However, the thought of a return to the hospital setting and the disruption of night duties did not seem to make sense at that stage.

At the beginning of November 1968, ironically during a more settled time when an extension on the house had been completed, new curtains and carpet had been purchased and my health had improved, one of the partners pointed out an enticing advert in the British Medical Journal asking for a Medical Officer in the Student Health Service at the University of Bristol. 'Are you interested?' he asked. There seemed to be two messages in the query. My colleagues were also thinking that perhaps I should leave and, secondly, here was an open door through which the view was not only attractive but, on further scrutiny, was actually beckoning.

CHAPTER ELEVEN

WE GO WEST

'I do believe an alternative society is emerging in the West, based on an alternative morality.' Ranged against this is 'the greyworld : the world of straights, of the boxed-in mind, the boxed-in soul, society, glitter, anf false values, factories and smog, the business-world, bureaucrats, uncivil servants, repressions, wars, silent screams and suicides.'

Richard Neville: The *Guardian*, 1971.

'The new generation insists upon being open to all experience. It will experiment with anything, even though the new "trip" does not fit into any preconceived notion of the individual's personality'.

Charles A. Reich: *The Greening of America*, 1970

I DROVE TO BRISTOL TO SPY OUT THE LAND GLIMPSED THROUGH this new open door of opportunity. I met Dr. Derek Sylvester and was immediately taken by the quiet courtesy and gentle manner of this cultured man who headed up the Student Health Service—two women doctors, two nursing sisters and an excellent team of receptionists and secretaries. A fourth doctor was needed to replace a former member of the service who had recently made the opposite journey—from Student Health to General Practice.

The group of four doctors provided full-time cover for the medical needs of over 6,000 students (both undergraduates and post-graduates) and of approximately 700 nurses at the Britol United Hospitals. The work included a great deal that was routine in the way of immunisations and medicals but also embraced the wide diversity of physical, emotional, psychological and social problems that these young adults might bring to their doctors. This variety was further increased in the care for families of married students and nurses who registered with the team as well as in the commitment to many overseas students.

Although I felt I would miss the wider age range and the full social spectrum of General Practice, I knew, from my experience with students from the Mid-Essex Technical College in Chelmsford, that I would find intelligent late adolescents and young adults a most rewarding group of patients to care for. Further, I was encouraged in my interest in the post by the importance of psychological insight in Student Health. I believed that most people with disturbances of personality, mood or behaviour needed, at least at some stage, the offer of time and the listening ear. I was delighted to find that, with a ratio of one doctor to 1,500 patients, the provision of unhurried time could be made when necessary.

Apart from the intrinsic fascination of the job, the structure of the working day looked ideal from the point of view of my health. An average day consisted of seeing patients by appointment during 'office' hours. Although the medical team worked a one in four rota to cover nights and weekends, there were comparatively few visits, it seemed, requested by this relatively fit population. All in all, this blend of regular hours, clinical interest and intellectual stimulus appeared to be tailor-made.

In spite of these encouraging considerations, the decision to leave Chelmsford was not an easy one. The diabetes had stabilised well on my gentler duties and, after six years as a principal in General Practice, I was now enjoying a good rapport with many of my patients. Our Christian work at Galleywood seemed to be thriving and the 'Young People' (as we called our CYFA group) had become a much loved part of our lives. I was looking forward, too, to continuing my readership with our new vicar, the Rev. Allen Willett, who, paradoxically, had just arrived from Bristol. Some time before the crisis in my health, Joy and I had planned an extension at Torridon to provide a third bedroom for our expanding family; this had just been completed when the substantial queries about a move arose. Further, we had the rare advantage of a *fixed* mortgage (of only 6%!) and this most desirable asset would have to be given up if we were to leave for the West Country. Finally, the garden was in the fifth year of its seven year plan and a new plant order had just arrived.

During November 1968 we talked and thought and prayed daily about this potential uprooting. It was a time when we had a powerful sense of God's nearness. He seemed to be saying, 'Trust Me. I know this is a difficult decision for you but I am much bigger than your circumstances. You can think about the issues as much as you like—and you must. However, I will show you what to do at the right time—no sooner and no later'. We were reading through the Psalms during this period and found great assurance of His loving sovereignty as the Spirit spoke to us. Psalms 23 to 37 seemed specially relevant and phrases such as : 'Good and upright is the Lord; therefore he instructs sinners in his ways' and 'Be still before the Lord and wait patiently for him' (Ps 25:8; Ps 37:7) reverberated in our minds and hearts.

We did our thinking. We wrote out a list of the pro's and con's of the situation and produced fourteen reasons for going and an equal number for staying. Rationality alone could not settle the issue. I applied for the job, and was short-listed. Still undecided, we rested in the fact that the Lord would be the Lord of the interview and its outcome.

And so, on Wednesday 4th December, four interviewee doctors rendezvoused, one by one, with an imposing panel of interviewers ranged around a large, polished oak table in one of the grander committee rooms at the University's Senate House in Bristol. As I sat there, scrutinised by seven or eight pairs of enquiring eyes and plied with a series of probing questions, I was specially conscious of the presence of the Master Chairman, the Divine Interviewer, and the power of His casting vote. He said 'Yes' to the post, it seemed, for the verdict was unanimously favourable.

Joy and I had planned two days in Bristol in the event of the job being offered. We now spent the second of these in the hands of a friendly and informative estate agent, looking at a wide range of properties within a ten mile radius of the city centre. It was fun peering into the privacy of houses old and new, including a converted Old Bakery, a Georgian merchant's house and a 17th Century cottage with a well in its garden. However, during the following weeks, good sense and a limited bank balance cut us down to size and the choice narrowed eventually to a half-finished, split-level house in Portishead with a sweeping view of the Gordano valley to the south and east.

There remained two major bridges to cross in our disengagement from Chelmsford. The first was the matter of informing my patients of our apparently sudden departure. The official notification would be handled by a letter from the Executive Council giving them the chance of either transferring to a colleague or remaining on my list until taken on by my successor. The complexity of enquiries and solicitations that might arise during the surgeries of the last few weeks was not something that I looked forward to. There were, of course, many patients that I wished to say goodbye to in an appropriate way but this option was not to be available. One month before I was due to start in Bristol I contracted a viral pneumonia and so spent my last weeks of General Practice on the receiving end of Hedley Missen's kindly attention. Again, the Division Interviewer appeared to be several steps ahead of us.

While sitting in the Senate House in December, I had been asked by one of the panel members: 'Tell me, Doctor Hurding, if you were on your back for, say, a fortnight, what would you do with yourself?' I replied, 'Read *War and Peace*'. And so there I was, four months later, propped up in bed reading Tolstoy's masterpiece between bouts of fever and coughing. However we understand illness (and I will look at the subject more thoroughly in the later chapters), God seems to allow its infliction, in at least some instances, either to bring about a change of direction in our lives or to soften the impact of that change.

The second, and longer, bridge that we had to cross before leaving Essex was the sale of our beloved Torridon. This property was a house of great individuality with amenities of equally great individuality, all set in an area of considerable isolation as well as beauty. The rather impressive extension, which incorporated the third bedroom over a new porch, gave the chalet-bungalow a slightly top-heavy look on first acquaintance. Built on the brow of an incline of London Clay, closer inspection revealed the inevitable settlement cracks in the concrete surrounds. Another dubious feature was the private drainage (described on one estate agent's blurb as 'modern') which ran to a large cesspool sunk at the lower end of the rear lawn. A tell-tale line of lusher grass bridged the last fifteen yards between the man-hole cover and the boundary brook. This overflow was an open secret.

Further, the picturesqueness of Torridon's setting was approached by a one mile stretch of private road which wound its way down from Galleywood. Its surface was kept in some repair by the collective efforts of local house owners but, by and large, its loose gravel and gouged out pot-holes were a source of irritation to car-drivers, cyclists, equestrians and pedestrians alike. Added to all these endearing but troublesome characteristics, we were trying to sell throughout the bitter weather of February 1969 when the state of the access road alternated between an ice-rink and a watershoot!

Surely no-one—save perhaps a family of hermits (if there was such a thing) or a group of backwoodsmen—would venture to buy the property. Joy kept the house in apple-pie order week after week and showed the very few would-be purchasers round with enthusiastic style but with a sinking heart. Time was running out as I was due to begin work in Bristol on the 1st April. (All Fools' Day seemed specially significant—I had been baptised on it and was now about to start a vital new phase of life on the same date).

The deadline came and I left the family for an indefinite period, during which Joy was trying to sell Torridon, our new house in Portishead was being finished and I was adjusting to my job with the students. When we were at our most despairing of a solution, my mother mentioned the attempted sale to some Christian friends in Harold Wood who were looking for somewhere to house their family of six. She added, 'But no-one would want *their* house. Roger and Joy love it, but it's much too cut off for most people!' However, these friends were interested in the details my mother gave; they visited Torridon and soon fell in love with it and its possibilities. This family, the Attenboroughs, envisaged yet another extension—this one incorporating a garage—to provide a 'granny flat' for Ruth's mother, Mrs. Hartley Brook. Joy was jubilant on the phone to Bristol, and, eventually, the sale went through. We were doubly thankful to God for His keeping through the taxing experience of selling a difficult property and for the bonus of selling to Christian friends who would continue the Lord's work amongst the much loved 'Young People' of Galleywood.

And so, on 19th May, after a long six weeks of separation, we drove west once more to spend a night with the Davieses of Yate Cottage before moving into our completed house at Portishead the next day.

The new situation was a delightful novelty to us. Our sturdily built house was perched on the steep southern slope of Wood Hill, a sycamore-studded eminence which was once crowned by a pre-Roman camp. A large, stone Victorian house, distinguished by step-gables in the Scottish style, had been bought by a local builder and its land parcelled out for a so-called 'superior development for the higher income bracket'. A number of individually distinct chalets and bungalows were being built on modest sized plots to make up a new community of people—mostly immigrants, like ourselves, from the North, the Midlands and the Home Counties.

We named the new house Conifers—a title of faith in that the slow-growing shrubs planted would take at least ten years before they were seen by strangers as the source of the property's name. They were 'the substance of things hoped for'.

From the sitting room's picture window our view to the south-east, although partially obscured by a clump of sycamores, embraced a wide sweep of the Gordano valley. This valley, bounded to the north-west and the south by two converging ridges of limestone and open to the Severn estuary and mouth of the Avon to the north-east, is said to give the district its Italian sounding name. There is a theory that 'Gordano' derives from the Anglo-Saxon words: *gore*—a spearhead or triangle, and *dene*—a flat place or valley. This explanation exactly fits the moor's topography.

Between the sycamores and a solitary ash tree at the foot of the garden, we looked across the roof-tops of Portishead to the ornately pinnacled 15th Century tower of the parish church. To the east, beyond the local docks, could be seen Shirehampton, Sneyd Park and Stoke Bishop, western suburbs of Bristol, which merged on the sky-line with the extensive beech woods of Abbots Leigh and Leigh Woods. On a clear day, pricking the horizon above these trees, the long-sighted could see the elegant spire of Christ Church, Clifton—a centre of worship that was to become our new spiritual home in the coming years.

In terms of schooling, church attendance and accessibility to my work, Portishead seemed to be well placed. The local primary schools had a very good name for their level of teaching and, looking into the future, we had heard favourable comments on the Gordano School—one of the first purpose-built comprehensives in the country, whose headmaster, Dr. Fred Lorenz, was contributing a great deal to its high reputation.

While in Essex, some friends had specially urged us to try to attend Christ Church, Clevedon, where the Rev. Michael Rees was vicar. We did so initially and were soon involved in the life of the church—Joy helped with the Young Wives' Group, Simon and Sarah attended Bible classes on Sundays and I was speedily prevailed upon by the persuasive Michael to be his Reader.

The twisting eight or nine miles between Conifers and the Student Health Service in Clifton soon became a familiar part of the day (and sometimes of the night). By the time the rest of the family joined me in the West Country, I had become acclimatised to the distinctive flavour of medical work amongst students. On my first day at the university, while taking some blood for diagnostic purposes from a male student, I was asked by him, 'Now, which particular biochemical test are you going to use?'—and he expected an answer! In General Practice, I had been accustomed to explaining much to patients but not at the technical level demanded by this undergraduate. This sudden exposure to more intellectual—though not necessarily more intelligent—conversation with patients was a great stimulus to my thinking and reading, not only in Medicine, but increasingly in the realms of literature, history and the Social Sciences.

Entering the student world in 1969, I found many of my patients revelling in the hey-day of the Counter Culture and, as a Christian, I needed to think long and hard about a number of the ethical issues which became specially pressing in and through the mores of the Alternative Society. This movement, given initial impetus by figures like Jack Kerouac and Allen Ginsberg in America back in the 50's, had gained momentum through the 60's as a challenge to the technological and institutional aspects of society in the West. I found many of the students' views at Bristol refreshing in the questioning of the postures and prejudices of officialdom. They shared the optimistic, if not heady, opinions of Charles Reich who wrote in his *Greening of America* (1970) of Consciousness III as a protest of hope against the meritocracy of the affluent and materialistic American middle-class.

Nevertheless, behind this idealism and its laudable desire for a more open and just society, there were a great number of moral questions. Freedom was the watch-word, but the bid for freedom from hypocrisy and manipulation in private and public life was inextricably bound up, it seemed, with the desire to be free of all restraints—not the least from those limitations to conduct which the Lord God has given as the basis for responsible freedom—the Ten Commandments. Richard Neville, in a letter to the *Guardian* in 1971, pointed to the radical nature of the Counter Culture: 'I do believe an alternative society is emerging in the West, based on an alternative morality'. In our work with the students in the early 70's some of the less happy repercussions of the 'alternative morality', in the areas of sexual freedom and drug-taking, kept us busy.

One of the basic predicaments in the medical care of young people is between, on the one hand, the increasingly pressing requests for effective contraception and, on the other hand, the demands for abortion where contraception has failed. Behind these two horns of the dilemma is, of course, the fact of widespread pre-marital sexual intercourse. Although my study of parish registers has indicated high rates of illegitimate births and shot-gun marriages through the last century and earlier, it is difficult to avoid the conclusion that the 'alternative morality' of the 60's and the 70's has set the pace for a great tide of sexual liberalism with its concomitants of disillusioned liaisons, betrayed relationships, emotional instability and venereal disease.

In taking the job at the University I had to make a decision about my role as a Christian doctor when faced with requests for contraception by the unmarried and for terminations of pregnancy. I knew of others, in a similar position, who had opted for either agreeing with virtually every appeal on the grounds that it would be wrong to arbitrate between one request and another, or refusing to discuss the pro's and con's of the enquiry on the basis that it would always be morally indefensible to comply. On reflection I was not happy to adopt either absolutist approach as they both seemed to rob the doctor of enormous opportunities for counselling.

There were, of course, many difficulties in my middle course. I often asked myself 'Who am I to judge in such matters of private morality?' Nonetheless, many young women seeking a prescription for the Pill expressed gratitude for the chance to discuss their thoughts and feelings about sexuality as well as the particular relationship which had prompted their query. Where a final-year student was in a 'stable relationship' with marriage on the horizon and was already risking pregnancy, it seemed churlish and impractical to decline contraception where the patient's world view was not at variance with her degree of involvement. Where the Pill, or other contraceptive method, was requested 'just in case I meet someone on holiday' I had no compunction in refusing. Some of my theological friends would cry 'Situation Ethics!' and reach for their

Bibles. However, those working in the consulting room know that they often have to advise between two courses, which *per se* are both wrong. In a fallen world, within such dilemmas, one strives as a Christian to guide in the direction of 'the whitest bit of grey' in the grey areas of peoples' lives.

Let me give an example of the more constructive side of counselling in this realm of sexual morality. I was visited by a second year student of Psychology (let us call her Mary) who had developed a growing friendship with John, another student of the same year. Ostensibly, she came to see me to ask for the Pill but, on questioning her, the following story emerged. John had made sexual advances but had not persisted on discovering Mary's negative reaction and feelings of guilt about sex. 'Go and see the doctor', John suggested. 'He'll sort you out and then tell you how to sleep with your boy-friend'.

I discovered that Mary's parents were Christian and that she got on well with them. At university she had felt the conflict between her parents' views on sex outside of marriage and those of her flatmates who had 'gone all the way' with their boy-friends. Who was right? We discussed different attitudes towards sexuality and she seemed to leave with her mind clearer on the issues involved. She was at least moving in the direction of making up her own mind on the matter.

A few days later, Mary returned—this time with John. It became obvious that he greatly respected her dilemma and he shared that he had decided it would be quite wrong to insist on intercourse. Interestingly, he too was undecided about the claims of Christianity and commented with mathematical precision: 'I find only 2% of Christians attractive as people!' It appeared that his parents also had some degree of Christian commitment. I like to think that the prayers of the parents of this likeable couple had kept them from folly.

I found the issue of abortion even more nail-biting. It seemed bad enough to appear to condone love-making outside marriage by providing the means to prevent conception; it seemed a great deal worse to be instrumental in the taking of foetal life once that conception had taken place. In trying to walk through the mine-field of ethical considerations in this area, my thinking was influenced by the arguments in R. F. R. Gardner's book *Abortion: the personal dilemma* (1972). I respected greatly his cautious approach to the subject in the controversial spheres of the principle of the sanctity of life, of the exact nature of the foetus in human terms and of the interpretation of the vast numbers of conceptions that are shed as 'natural wastage'. A decade later the debate goes on with the views of Francis Schaeffer and others inviting a more conservative approach.

Again, I sought to counsel the student seeking abortion along certain lines. I gave ample time to encourage a thorough appraisal of the alternatives of a continued pregnancy, with or without adoption. Where appropriate I asked to see both the student and the putative father to help them see their combined responsibility. I urged them to consider that whatever decision they made, it must be one that they could live with thereafter. I declined to support requests where there was an established relationship between the couple involved. I would say, 'I cannot agree to a termination of a life that is, however mistakenly, a product of your love for each other.' I was, of course, bound by the law to suggest another doctor who might comply where a request for abortion was pursued.

More heart-rendering were the situations where a student had become pregnant following some fellow's opportunism at a party where the drink had flowed too freely or where, more generally, there was no love relationship between the individuals concerned.

It is in this area of student pregnancy that some of the most heart-searching counselling has to take place in terms of, for example, the unpromising future for a pregnancy which is deeply resented, the state of mind of a young woman who is depressed and even suicidal about her new condition, the suitability for motherhood of an immature and unstable eighteen-year-old, as well as a student's training for a career.

During 1971 to 1974, I conducted a survey, with the help of my colleagues, to look at the backgrounds, circumstances, behaviour and attitudes of single students who became pregnant. Seventy-five students in this category came to the Student Health Service within these four years and were compared in many details with 239 non-pregnant women students who attended my consulting room during the Summer Term of 1973.

Many interesting observations came out of this review. Of the seventy-five students who were pregnant only six continued to term and all of these married the putative fathers. Sixty four (85%) of this group had terminations under the Abortion Act of 1967. An attempt was made to assess attitudes to the outcome of the pregnancy six months after that event. Something like 30% of these students were either equivocal or regretted the outcome of termination. Further, this survey showed that it is extremely difficult to predict which students will be the most vulnerable following abortion. All in all, this piece of research underlined that advice to terminate pregnancies in students should never be given lightly and that, most of all, counselling of a thoroughgoing and sensitive nature should be given to any who request an abortion.

Another area that I was repeatedly asked to speak on in the early 70's was that of drug taking amongst students. In fairness, comparatively few drug-users would come to the Student Health Service to discuss their habituation. Anthony Ryle in his *Student Casualties* (1969) estimated that only 10% of regular drug-users would be known to the Health Service or University authorities.

Smoking Pot was a widespread habit and seemed to leave most of its experimenters none the worse for wear. However, I saw a number of students whose memories, concentration and ability to meet deadlines were all impaired by the frequent use of Cannabis.

More serious was the use of the hallucinogens, including LSD and Mescaline. These so-called 'mind-expanders' were given almost religious significance by Dr. Timothy Leary, the discredited professor from Harvard medical school. He eulogised about LSD in his book *The Psychedelic Experience*, writing: 'The scope and content of the experience is limitless, but its characteristic features are the transcendence of verbal concepts, or space-time dimensions, and of the ego or identity'. An eighteen-year-old student Sheila was typical of many who were beguiled into using this drug by such rhetoric. Since 'tripping' on LSD and smoking Pot, she had experienced depressed feelings, a fear of being alone, claustrophobia, a lack of concentration in her studies and a general puzzlement about herself. Despite my warnings of the way these symptoms could be perpetuated by either drug, she smoked Pot again a few months later and returned with feelings of unreality and fear. A fortnight after that she came to tell me that she wanted to leave university after only seven months to travel round the world with her new boy-friend.

The use of the 'mind-expanding' drugs was often linked with an interest in Eastern mysticism. Theodore Roszak in his excellent analysis of the Alternative Society *The Making of a Counter Culture* (1968) argued the need to rediscover the 'shaman' with his 'good magic'. He saw the desirability of the transcendent to oppose the dehumanising effects of the Machine Age. It is this reaction which seemed to draw many to the relativism of Eastern thought. David was ensnared in this way by the Divine Light Mission and became a disciple of the guru Maharaj Ji. Struggling to maintain four hours meditation a day, he became more and more unkempt and cut off from his studies and everyday functioning. A sad, pale and lost figure he eventually had to withdraw from university. His state seemed to echo the words of the Buddhagosa: 'I am nowhere a somewhatness for anyone'.

In the many hours spent in trying to help young people caught up in the more subversive aspects of the Counter Culture, there were occasions when I was able to talk directly of Christ. One such instance was with Adrian. He was a final year student of English from a well known public school. He was an insecure person who had experimented with LSD and also had sado-masochistic tendencies. He came to see me for a series of six long appointments, each lasting about fifty minutes. At the end of these he muttered, 'The trouble with me is my attitude to life'. I said, 'Would you like to discuss this?' He assented, and so we picked up our dialogue during the next term. At one of these sessions, he said, 'I've talked a lot about myself—what makes you tick?' And so, after many hours of listening, it seemed I had won the right to tell him something of Christ's transforming claim on his life. Sometime later he booked a ten minute appointment instead of the customary one of fifty minutes. He entered with, 'I haven't time to sit down but I've got a query you might be able to help me with'. 'Go ahead' I said, expecting a fresh batch of symptoms from this hypochondriacal young man. 'Is Christ as real to you as I am?' came the startling question. My affirmative answer with explanatory footnotes seemed to satisfy him—at least for that brief consultation!

It was a great privilege to be part of the team of doctors at the Health Centre. As well as Derek Sylvester, the competent and respected 'Boss', there were two other colleagues. Mary Dixon was a large and lovable character who always seemed to have a long-haired dachsund at her heels. Jan Swallow, who had been a fellow medical student at Bart's, was contrastingly diminutive and possessed a lively and penetrating wit. Between us, two men and two women, Derek and Mary in their middle years and Jan and I in our mid-thirties, we made up a usefully balanced team for counselling and psychotherapy. In the broadest terms: a father and a mother figure, along with an older brother and an older sister figure. Or so I fondly imagined until, the mid 70's, I realised that many of the student's fathers were my exact contemporaries!

The 1970's saw the beginnings of many very special friendships. Of these, a number came out of our contact with students. In some instances, the original involvement was in a doctor-patient context. As there was improvement and as the student concerned left the University the professional link gave way to one of growing friendship. One depressed and lonely medical student stayed with us one weekend and delighted our children by reading extracts of *The Lord of the Rings* to them. I wrote in her Health Service notes: 'Conifers', under the date of the weekend. She was seen subsequently by a colleague who quizzed me as to where this excellent rest home called Conifers was because the student felt much better after a weekend there!

Another circle of close relationships grew out of the Bristol Christian Arts Group which was based for some time in a ground floor flat in Clifton, initially under the chairmanship of David Shotton, a research scientist who also ran a 'L'Abri' group in Bristol. Blessed by prophetic insight from Jim Packer, then the Principal of Tyndale Theological College, and by the occasional visit by Nigel Goodwin from the Arts Centre Group in London, the small gathering of artists, sculptors, potters, musicians, dancers, actors, photographers, writers and poets—both professional and amateur—met and shared and thrived. These contacts extended our thinking a great deal as we rubbed shoulders with Christians immersed in the Arts, wrestled with the concept of aesthetics and came to terms with the Dutch Calvinist theology of Kuyper and Dooyewerd.

When David Shotton left for the States in 1972 I was asked to take over the chairmanship of the Arts Group. This proved to be a challenging experience as there was something of an identity crisis afoot—and artistic people in the throes of perplexity can be wayward company. There seemed to be at least three potential factions, each with a different vision for the group. One lobby had strong links with Youth for Christ and saw the Arts as the servant of evangelism. Another was specially inspired by the teachings of Francis Shaeffer and felt the organisation could be most productive as a Bristol based 'L'Abri' group. The third was grounded in the Kingdom Theology of Kuyper and his successors and saw this as the most appropriate basis for the future. Through God's grace, released by much prayer, these differences were accommodated, issuing in a period of great consolidation and deep fellowship.

It is invidious to single out particular friendships formed at this time but, amongst the many, the Days and Winters were of special significance. When we first met them, Lynne and Steve Day were colourful examples of latter day Hippiedom. Long-haired and outlandishly dressed, they brought a unique contribution to the Arts Group. Reacting to the straightjacketing of a Bible College background, they prodded at many of the sacred cows that evangelicals hold dear. However, their faith in and love for the Lord were strong and were richly expressed in their individual style of music-making. Forming a group called Tallow, they wrote and performed a style of rock music with roots in Hebrew and English Folk traditions. With two guitarists, a flautist, Steve on the drums and Lynne's powerful contralto voice competing with the walls of electric sound they made an arresting ensemble.

The Winters had recently arrived in Bristol and were initially based at Barrow Hospital where Richard was working in a junior post in Psychiatry. He and Jane began to attend the Arts Group and Joy and I responded to them immediately as kindred spirits. We learnt that they had met in the States, where they eventually married following Jane's conversion. They then spent a year's honeymoon travelling round the world from Jane's American home to England. This journey, coloured by the delightful romanticism of the late 60's, headed south through the islands of the West Indies to Colombia, and so north again through Central America and Mexico to California; from there the Winters crossed the Pacific to South-East Asia and India, where they began the 'Hippy Trail' in reverse and so journeyed from Nepal to Afghanistan. As they travelled they read widely the writings of the Eastern religions and were thus able to help many disillusioned Western young people who had trekked east along the Trail to the fantasy-world of Cannabis and the mysticism of Buddhism and Hinduism. As they approached Kabul, the need for medical aid amongst the drug-addicts and drop-outs cared for at Dilaram House was being prayed for. Richard and Jane, dusty and footsore, arrived out of the heat and stayed for three months to help. During this time, Jane was amongst a small group of Christians who were baptised publicly—possibly the first in Islamic Afghanistan for a thousand years.[1]

1 For more detail, see McClung, Floyd, *Just Off Chicken Street* (Fleming H. Revell Company) 1975 pp 57-59, 70-73.

In 1971, Joy and I were asked to join a group of four other couples to meet regularly for prayer, Bible study and discussion, and to arrange, from time to time, a pre-evangelistic outreach amongst other businessmen and professionals. These 'Think-Ins' comprised a good evening meal followed by a twenty minute talk and discussion. Subjects tackled included ambition, bringing up children, pleasure, family tensions, the Third World, 'art for art's sake' and living with handicap. Each of the five Christian couples invited one or two other couples and so, typically, we might have a total of twenty five to thirty on the evening, over half of whom might be uncommitted. These supper parties were seen in the context of continuing friendships and as helping to take the lid off existing communication. One couple we asked told us later that they were awake virtually the whole of that night discussing the evidences for the Ressurection!

As the years slipped by, the ten of us began to see the need for our own growth in Christian maturity within the group and so increasingly we started to share the joys and pains of our personal, married and family lives together. And so these 'Share-Ins' became a vital part of the fabric of life. They were times when we could be honest with one another and so exercise mutual love and support. An essential ingredient of this growing together was the element of conflict. One evening Joy and I were rounded on for appearing to be too self-contained and coping. It took some time for certain members of the group to accept our very real fallibilities!

During our first four years in Bristol, my health as a diabetic kept up extremely well. The regular hours of the job had a restoring effect and the quality of our friendships in medical, artistic and Christian circles had a healing influence on our lives. I was well enough to be involved as local secretary to the Christian Medical Fellowship, chairman of the Bristol Christian Arts Group, and reader at Christ Church, Clevedon, as well as coping happily with a wide range of speaking engagements and the demands of my interesting work with the students. The years 1969 to 1973 were our hey-day; we had the staying power for the pleasures and pains of what, in the West, we might call a full life.

However, there were three episodes which reminded us, amidst the busyness, of the frailty of human life. The first two were in 1971 and 1972; the third took place in 1973 and I will give that event the space of a short next chapter.

On a Monday morning early in October 1971 Joy woke at

5.00 a.m. with persistent chest pain. She was in some distress with the discomfort and so, propping her up in bed, I listened in with my stethoscope to hear a faint but definite pericardial rub, evidence that she might have developed acute pericarditis following a recent viral infection. Throughout the day there was a series of learned consultations between our General Practitioner, a visiting Cardiologist and the patient's husband. Fortunately, this illness proved to be a mild form of pericarditis although it took Joy quite a few weeks to feel really well again.

Our second reminder of the tenuous nature of life was in the summer of 1972 in the middle of a delightful holiday on the edge of the Berwyn Mountains in North Wales, where we stayed in a friend's cottage for a fortnight. Towards the end of the two weeks, we picnicked along the banks of the River Dee just above Llangollen. The afternoon was hot and so Simon, then aged seven, and I waded out into the shallows. The river was about thirty yards wide at that point and the current brisk. Finding a good sized stick, we enjoyed ourselves throwing it upstream and then retrieving it as it sped back towards us. Rachel, aged four, called from the bank and as I turned towards her, Simon lunged after the stick which was about to float past him where the water was deeper. The main force of the river occupied a rock channel, over the edge of which Simon vanished. The deep, turbulent waters mid-stream snatched at him and threatened to carry him away. I managed to turn quickly and plunge after him, pushing him back towards the safety of the shallows. As I thrust him over the lip of the rock ledge I forced myself back into the powerful surge of the spate. With considerable effort I managed to scramble out of the channel to wade ashore with Simon—two crestfallen, but profoundly thankful, Hurdings.

Joy and I lay awake for some time that night—relieved, but shaken by a near tragedy.

CHAPTER TWELVE

A SCOTTISH INTERLUDE

'Some are weather-wise, some are other-wise'.
Benjamin Franklin: *Poor Richard's Almanac,*
Feb 1735

'Because you have made the Lord your refuge, the Most High your habitation, no evil shall befall you, no scourge come near your tent.
For he will give his angels charge of you to guard you in all your ways. On their hands they will bear you up, lest you dash your foot against a stone.'
Psalm 91:9-12

TORRIDON, IN NORTH-WEST SCOTLAND, HAD A MAGNETIC appeal. I had first glimpsed its rugged mountains and pine forests from a moorland track as 'Percy' Price, my fellow medical student, and I trudged up from the coast at Applecross in 1957. My romanticism knew no bounds—'That's where I'll have a honeymoon, one day' I said. At that stage no bride was in sight but post-nuptial plans were already taking shape!

Glen Torridon was visited once again, though briefly, on a wild, wet and windy day in 1960 when I was on holiday with my parents near Ullapool. On that day the buffeted clouds were shredded and regathered by the winds, and the steep flanks of the mountains hung darkly between cloudbase and loch-side.

In April 1962 I stood once more by the shores of the sea-loch, Joy Elizabeth by my side, our marriage consummated and the whole of life before us. This time the hills were etched sharply against a cerulean sky, their crests white with snow. The ramparts of dark pines, rising from the water's edge opposite to where we stood, glistened in the tangy, sun-soaked air. A drake eider crooned softly from the shallows as if expressing surprise at his modest find: a dun-coloured mate of subtly-barred beauty.

Now, eleven years later, our marriage having emerged from a time of testing during the previous winter, we were back again—on our way even further north to join my parents, my sister's family and two Parisiennes (an undoubted bonus!) for a holiday at Coldbackie in Sutherland. In the meantime we were to spend four nights camping as a family on an isolated rocky promontory, jutting out into the waters of Loch Torridon, a mile east of Inver Alligin. Facing into the prevailing wind, the large frame-tent was further anchored by an apron of sandstone boulders. Although Joy was a reluctant camper, we could not but enjoy our glorious setting—at least for the first three of the four days of our sojourn.

One of my main restlessnesses in life is to be within reach of interesting mountains and yet not able to assail at least one of them. Circumstances and weather did not permit any such attempt over the first three days but, on the last day before our northward drive continued, I could contain myself no longer.

Let me pick up the tale essentially in the words I used within a few days of the episode as I tried to recapture its atmosphere on paper.

The sprawling moorland north of the Inver Alligin road had soaked up the heavy rains of the previous week like a vast sponge. The sponge was saturated; and water was standing in every poorly drained hollow on peat-bog and sandstone alike. The burns were alive with the rush and tumble of iron-laden water, and the steady roar of the great waterfalls in the glen of Coire Mhic Nobuil could be heard for a mile or two.

It was during that rather sleepy hour after lunch; I had said that I would be back at the tent by 7.00 p.m. and so there was no hurry. As I trudged the sodden heathland I was aware of the pain of an ingrowing toe-nail, the weight of my fifteen-year-old climbing boots and one or two superfluous items that burdened my rucksack. Apart from the presence of myriads of hungry midges, it was a place to linger in and my various discomforts encouraged this. The browns of the moorland were studded with the tiny, yellow flames of bog asphodel and the soft pinks of cross-leaved heath. On closer inspection, upright clumps of fir clubmoss were seen to contrast in form with tightly knit, ground-hugging junipers and prostrate alpine club-mosses.

It was a mild day. The surface of Loch Torridon was calm and reflected the pall of grey cloud with a cool, gun-metal sheen. From a hill-walker's point of view the level of cloud cover was borderline. The banks of strato-cumulus obscured the higher summits of Ben Damph, Liathach and Beinn Eighe, but the top of Beinn Dearg, five feet short of 3000 feet in height, was sharply defined. Ahead of me loomed my quarry, Beinn Alligin—the Jewel Ben—its summit-ridge alternately blurred and then clearly visible as the cloud gathered and dispersed. Entering its steep, south-facing corrie, I decided to climb to the lower limits of the intermittent cloud cover and then reassess.

The burn which tumbled down the southern flanks of the mountain between two precipitous buttresses did so in a series of small waterfalls. These were delightful places to pause in before assailing the heights above. As I slaked my thirst at one of the lesser falls, my eye was arrested by clumps of starry saxifrage gleaming from cool, water-splashed recesses. Even if I did not reach the high tops, my desire to feel the mountain underfoot was at least partly assuaged by the magic of this alpine corrie.

I had originally, and over-ambitiously for my unfit state, planned to walk the length of the spectacular, cliff-bound ridge of Beinn Alligin and its satellite peaks, and so complete the horseshoe by descending the north-eastern extremity of the mountain, and then trek south and west across rough moorland back to the camp-site. Now, reaching the lower fringes of the hill-top mist, I glanced back at the vanishing view of the head of Loch Torridon. The summit-ridge could not be far into the swirling cloud and it was not easy to turn back after such a laborious climb without setting foot on at least one end of the horseshoe. After all, the ingrowing toe-nail had stopped hurting!

Taking a compass reading for the nearest peak—Tom na Gruagaich (3021 feet)—I entered the cloud and strode resolutely forward on a bearing just east of north. The rock-strewn ground began to level out on to the backbone of the mountain and soon the conical mound of the peak loomed hesitantly out of the dense vapour. A few minutes later, shrouded by the grey pall of mist, I was standing on the summit peering down into the nothingness of

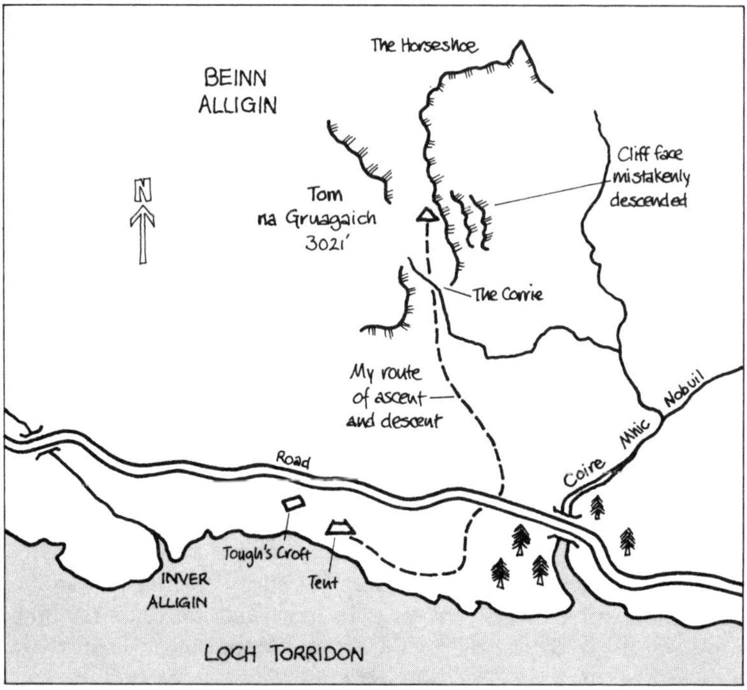

the steep eastern face. There was no time to linger; I would take a quick compass bearing (a little west of south) and soon be stepping briskly down the well-worn path in the corrie I had left minutes before.

I was too confident! Hurrying down the gentle incline south of the summit, I suddenly realised that the terrain was unfamiliar. Instead of the shelving upper lip of the corrie I had approached a massive promontory of rock, below which the mountainside plunged steeply away into obscurity. I reasoned with myself: 'Keep calm! It's still only a quarter to six—what is needed is another compass reading.' And so, following the tiny magnetic needle, I lumbered once more up to the summit cairn, this my only reference point in the veiled landscape. 'Not so fast this time—follow the compass southwards—check frequently—take it slowly!'

Concentrating on the flickering needle, I had failed to notice that the stillness had given way to a breeze, the breeze to a wind and the wind to a gale which was forcing my downward steps towards the left, towards the east and towards the line of precipitous cliffs which plunge down to the wide sweep of the Coire Mhic Nobuil.

The blizzard, for such it was, driving relentlessly across the exposed ridge, gave a new dimension to the predicament. Momentarily I detected a divine humour in the situation as my audible prayer 'Lord, get me off this mountain!' was lost in a sudden, vicious gust of wind which all but swept me over; I hastily added 'but not *that* way, please!' Such was the fury of the wind, now carrying sleet and hail, that I was forced on to hands and knees to find shelter. Ironically, the same frowning outcrop of sandstone that I had earlier spurned offered now some respite from the teeth of the gale. In the lee of the rock I pulled off my cagoule, donned a thick jersey and then replaced the waterproof outer garment. Next, I hurriedly downed a draught of hot water from the thermos and ate the remainder of a slab of Kendal mint cake.

Thus fortified, I considered once more my descent of the mountain. I reasoned that my rock-shelter must be above a steeper rim of the corrie and the sooner I drove my tired and sodden body down to below cloud-level the better. I slipped, slid and slithered down the narrow declivity of a plunging small burn. The attractions of alpine plants were ignored as I concentrated on speed and survival. After some minutes of precipitate descent I stopped. My numbed mind was making its voice heard: 'This *can't* be the way down. It's far too steep for the corrie.' The mountain-side was sheer and there was no sign of thinning in the cloud-cover. I began to realise that I must be on the eastern face of Beinn Alligin—a mile long curve of terraced cliffs dropping 1500 feet in a series of vertical bands of Torridonian sandstone. To continue would be to guarantee a most speedy downfall!

Still short of breath from my hurried descent, I looked down at the dark drop of the crags and then gazed up through the swirling mist to the shadowy buttresses that loomed above. Reason prevailed. I must climb back up the mountain-side, up an incline which, in more favourable circumstances, I would never have attempted. The ascent seemed interminable after the breathtaking descent of 500 feet or so.

The laborious climb of the cascading cliff-face eventually brought me back to the summit-ridge with its rock-shelter and its raging westerly gale. In the lee of a broken outcrop I battled with an animated map and a suspect compass while the blizzard hurled itself out over the abyss behind me. Once more I resolved to obey reason rather than intuition; logically the compass could not be faulty—its needle swung freely and as far as I knew I was not in a zone of local magnetic rock. Although it *felt* suicidal to trust the accuracy of its reading, I set out yet again on a bearing just west of south. As I did so, the full brunt of the gale tore at my wildly flapping cagoule, stinging my face with freezing rain. Battling against the broadside of wind and sleet, my obedience to the compass did *not* lead me over a precipice as I had feared. The magnetic needle exonerated, I found myself descending the shelving upper reaches of the corrie.

The wind, which had clearly veered as the front progressed, was now blowing straight down the line of the steeply sloping amphitheatre of rock and was thus funnelled by the converging lower buttresses, between which the burn cascaded in the sequence of falls where I had stopped to drink in the stillness of mid-afternoon. The resulting increased force of the gale speeded my descent still further as I leaped from rock to rock, at the same time trying to avoid an injured knee or ankle. Through the mist the dull silver of the burn glinted feebly and I was soon hurtling down the more familiar track above its banks.

It was now past 7 o'clock and thoughts of my troubled family took shape as I plunged down the corrie as fast as safety permitted. Entering the wide expanse of the moor, the rain-laden cloud was still with me and with it the unabated fury of the storm. I rushed headlong across pool, burn and sandstone, spurning the brief glimpses of unfamiliar flowers and ignoring the tell-tale flags of cotton-grass that marked the more treacherous stretches of peat-bog. Dimly through the driving rain I could make out the pine forest and sweep of road above Torridon House. It was a relief that the road was empty and that there was no sign of a white Maxi parked near the bridge with its implications of an anxiety-ridden family or, even worse, a full scale mountain search.

The firm tarmac of the road was pleasant underfoot after the instability of loose rock and soggy moss. The security of familiar territory and the return of brisker circulation made me realise how very wet I was. The squelch of my boots, the tenacity of my sodden jeans and the cold clamminess of saturated underpants gave my tired mind the same message—I was well and truly soaked!

I pushed through the bracken from the road to the footpath by the chapel and manse, and so trudged along the northern shore of the loch for the last quarter of a mile towards the tent. So far so good—I only hoped that Joy was not now patrolling the road behind me looking desperately across the moor to the vanished mountains. Two tall, male figures, clad in oilskins, strode purposefully out of the murk towards me. No-one else but rescuer and rescuee could be out in that weather. I soon discovered that these were the sons of Mr Tough, whose croft lay nearest to our tent, and they were out looking for a wet climber. I learnt that their father was in his car up at the bridge, that my family was safe in their house and that my wife was extremely worried. They said that they had been allowing me a delay of two hours before launching a full scale mountain rescue and they seemed impressed that I was only one hour late—for it was just 8 o'clock. They did not know until later that evening that I had merely climbed to one of Beinn Alligin's nearer peaks and back, and had not traversed the complete horseshoe!

While I had been following compass-bearings to and fro on the mountain top, Joy had noticed with anxiety that the cloud-cover seemed to be descending. At the time when I had first become aware of the onslaught of the blizzard, Joy and the children had been watching the sons of the local crofter fishing on the loch. Suddenly the summer tempest was upon them and they rowed feverishly for the shore as the storm-waves quickly grew in size. Joy turned to glance at the mountain and saw with dismay that it had disappeared completely, obscured by sea-level cloud.

In the nerve-racking hours that followed the storm-battered tent became an intolerable hiding-place. The cooking area had become a quagmire and one of the central poles had come adrift. To add to the anxieties about a husband lost in the mountains and a tent straining for lift-off, Sarah, then aged ten, had a middle-ear infection and a mounting temperature. At six o'clock, at which point I had been descending the cliff-face, Joy had battled through the wind and rain to the Tough's croft 100 yards away. There the three men of the family had weighed up the situation. 'Is he fit?' one of them had asked. 'No,' Joy had replied without hesitation. 'Well, then, he'll be at least another two hours. If he's not back at eight, we'll begin to set out an' look for him. We'll not be raising a full alarm till 9 o'clock.' These conservative estimates were, of course, based on my originally expressed plan to complete the horseshoe.

And so, in spite of the capricious nature of a Highland storm and the wilful nature of a Sassenach hill-walker, the Lord God once again kept our family of five intact. In 1973, we did not know that the next year would bring the stirrings that heralded the gloom of a more protracted storm.

CHAPTER THIRTEEN

THE GATHERING GLOOM

'Prognosis for vision in proliferative retinopathy is poor, especially in those who develop new vessels on the optic disc. Out of 40 eyes with disc vessels seen at Hammersmith Hospital, only four had normal vision at five years.'

Eva Kohner: *Diabetic Retinopathy* (Medicine)

'What shall we say then? Is there injustice on God's part? By no means! For he says to Moses, "I will have mercy on whom I have mercy, and I will have compassion on whom I have compassion." '

Romans 9:14,15

In 1974, I had been a diabetic for twenty-three years and, over all, had kept reasonably well. I knew that it is not unusual for certain complications of diabetes to become evident after a couple of decades or so of the disease. With this in mind, and as a check for general stability of the condition, I had seen a series of physicians on a regular basis throughout. To my knowledge, there had never been any serious queries concerning major complications and, being an optimist, my thinking was not disturbed by considering their possible emergence. However, following a routine check-up by Dr Martin Hartog that summer, I was referred to Mr Vincent Marmion, an ophthalmologist working at the Bristol Eye Hospital.

It seemed routine enough but I realised that a small percentage of diabetics can go progressively blind over a few years and so I awaited the results of Mr Marmion's painstaking scrutiny with bated breath. In time, new, fragile blood-vessels grow on the retinas of some diabetics. These recalcitrant channels can bleed readily so that there is a danger of an accumulation of blood in the jelly-like core of the eye which, in turn, can obscure vision. Initially, the eye is able to absorb each fresh bleed quite speedily but, if the haemorrhages keep recurring, then the clouding process becomes a problem.

The specialist's verdict on the 18th of July was that there were some new blood-vessels in both eyes but that he thought he could stem their progress by light coagulation. In this treatment the offending vessels are destroyed by a powerful light source which is directed on to the retina with precision and under magnification. A wide range of machines has been built and used for this purpose utilizing a number of different sources of light, including xenon arc and laser beams. The hardware has tended to become smaller and more mobile, and the employment of light increasingly accurate with improved techniques. As a result, less light is needed for each application in the newer machines, there is less discomfort for the patient and so more and more light coagulation can be carried out in an eye hospital's out-patient department. However, in 1974 such refinements were not readily available.

On two dates in September, separated by three weeks, I was admitted for a few days to have light treatment—the first admissions of many for this purpose during the next four years. I was admitted the day before photo-coagulation to ensure stability of the diabetes and to establish pre-operative routines—medical examination, assessment of dietary needs, blood tests and giving of medication. Feeling relaxed with valium and peaceful with the Lord's presence, I was wheeled along to the operating theatre to lie beside the massive xenon arc machine. I had discussed to some extent the details of the procedure with medical and nursing staff, but I was little prepared for the actual experience of having the eye anaesthetised before its bombardment with light. A generous amount of local anaesthetic was injected around the orbit of the eye via the roots of the eyelids and then massaged by the surgeon's fingers to spread its numbing effect. This prelude to the coagulation was the least bearable aspect of the treatment and I found it difficult to avoid tensing my whole body on each occasion while the infiltration was being carried out. Once the eye was numb, although held open and in position by fine forceps, the series of light flashes which destroyed the new blood-vessels was a relatively untroubling affair.

The inestimable compensation in this procedure was my knowledge that blindness could thereby be allayed, if not prevented. I am very grateful for the thoroughness of Mr Marmion's attention through those difficult years of repeated light coagulation. I am grateful, too, to the Lord for sustaining me during the ophthalmic procedures and granting His peace throughout—not least amidst the distractions of orbital pain. It is good to know, too, that more recent developments have led to virtually pain-free photocoagulation using the newer and smaller machines.

At first, although the specialists could see the mischief taking place in my retinas, I was unaware of any impairment of sight. I had always enjoyed very sharp visual acuity—the sort that could discern through an average pair of binoculars the slight uptilt in a red-throated diver's bill as the bird floated on a rough sea half a mile away—and I found it hard to believe that it could ever be otherwise. Loss of vision was something that happened to other people.

However, on a fine morning in May 1975 I woke to witness the descent of an inky dark curtain of opaqueness which gradually obscured the vision in my right eye. I had known that this might happen at some stage and the reality of it did not seem as threatening as the anticipation. The visual obstruction was already translucent by the time breakfast was finished and I concluded that the haemorrhage was dissipating quite quickly. Joy agreed to drive me to work whence Dot, one of our nursing sisters, took me to the eye hospital for assessment. The bleeding was confirmed by a junior ophthalmologist and I was advised to take life more gently for a while. I did; and the vision was fine again after ten days.

During the next ten months there were a few minor bleeds in the right eye but, on the whole, the sight maintained well on that side. However, the left vision began to deteriorate appreciably and this was our main concern by the spring of 1976.

Little daunted, we set out on Joy's birthday, the 27th of March, for a fortnight's holiday on the Isle of Mull. (This was the first of several holidays that we took over the next two years, believing that each might be my last in terms of serviceable vision!). The five of us stayed in a weatherboarded bungalow which had served as a shepherd's croft in the recent past. From the sitting-room window we looked south across the upper waters of Loch Buie to the woods beyond the ruined tower of old Moy castle—the former stronghold of the MacLaines of Lochbuie—and to a wild sweep of upland deer forest. From the head of this sea-loch, on a clear day, we could see the grey smudge of the Island of Colonsay twenty miles away to the south-west. To the south the Paps of Jura rose in arresting symmetry beyond a nearby headland. Behind our cottage we could clamber at will up the line of an exuberant burn which cascaded down from a remote lochan. This in turn was flanked, to the east, by the impressive upsweep of Ben Buie whose peak dominated the immediate landscape.

This was to be, perhaps, our most memorable holiday. The children's ages ranged from eight to thirteen and they were ripe for almost any adventure. During the days we explored the surrounding hills and shores of the loch, enjoying the exhilaration of alternating spring sunshine and squally hail-storms, and, on a day spent in the shadow of Ben More, a frenzied snow-fight between the Camerons and Campbells. On another occasion we spent seven hours on a thirty-foot coaster with two local fishermen; while they checked their lobster pots, we gazed up at the huge basaltic sea-cliffs and scoured the scene for a glimpse of a soaring eagle.

In the evenings we gathered about an open fire with our books, water colours and a series of cushions which Joy was embroidering with Red Indian totem symbols. After the children had gone to bed, we talked and prayed about the future. How far should we allow my sight to deteriorate before questioning my present job? If I could no longer work as a GP to the students, what else might I do? How would we cope if I went blind? How should we think about healing? Should we pray with teeth-clenching faith for a miracle? Should we seek out someone with a gift of healing? How should we share our hopes and uncertainties with our family and friends? With many of these questions still unresolved, we determined to share our quandary with our fellow Christians at the church we attended, asking them to consider joining us in a service of commitment—of ourselves and our situation to our sovereign God. At this stage, we did not feel it right to pursue anyone with a known gift of healing. We were convinced that God alone is the source of healing and that He would be pleased to encounter us through the body of the church to which we belonged.

And so our Hebridean holiday came to an end. We felt deeply refreshed and there was a new sense of consolidation between the five of us. While we waited for the car-ferry at Craignure, I wandered back along the road by myself. The sky was stippled with skeins of high-flying greylag geese following their migratory route northwards above the Sound of Mull. The still air carried the needle-points of their plaintive contact calls as I gazed upwards. Suddenly another flight of dark flame-shapes moved across my field of vision. Tears of self-pity welled up as I recognised that fresh bleeding was taking place in my hitherto better-sighted eye. There was a poignancy for me in the juxtaposition of the orderly flight-patterns of migrating wild geese and the sinister pyrotechnics produced by a ruptured retinal vessel. The two displays contrasted in every respect. The one spelt freedom, the other frustration. The one evoked atavistic memories that seemed to reach back to Eden, the other gave the present and the immediate future the harsh reality of the Fall. The one soared in the limitless ether, the other was confined to an orb one inch in diameter. I returned to my four, waiting loved ones aware, yet again, that beyond the tears there was a promise of boundless joy.

In the summer of the previous year we had begun to attend Christ Church, Clifton, whose spire we could sometimes see from Conifers on a clear day. Up to that year we had lived a trisected existence: living in Portishead, worshipping at Clevedon and working in Clifton, Bristol. It seemed right to lop at least one of these three branches of influence and involvement, and so I discontinued my Readership at the church in Clevedon. For a while we tried attending the local church as a family but we quickly realised that our young children were bored by the formal services and that, at that stage, there was little for them in the vicinity in the way of biblical instruction in a church setting. And so it seemed to make sense to attend the Family Service on Sunday mornings at Christ Church, Clifton, where a number of our closer friends worshipped and where my contact with students could be continued. In the evenings, Joy and I alternated in our attendance at the parish church but, in time, our increasing involvement in Clifton made this less and less practical.

On our return from the Isle of Mull, Joy and I discussed with our vicar, the Rev. Paul Berg, the possibility of a special service of prayer for our situation. We explained that, although statistically I was likely to become blind within the next few years, we believed that God was in command of our lives. We understood that in His wisdom and love He might grant healing—immediate or gradual—or, again, He might stay the process of deterioration or, finally, He might allow the condition to worsen into blindness. We knew the medical figures favoured the third outcome but we also believed that the Lord was the Lord of the Statistics!

And so, at the end of a hectic weekend delivering five ill-prepared talks to Tuesday Club (a Clifton-based Christian group for the twenty-one to thirty-fives), a Service of Commitment was held, following evening worship, at the front of Christ Church's large nave. About one hundred people gathered—friends, family and fellow Christians—to worship God and pray for one another. Joy and I sat side by side in the front pew surrounded by the love of the Lord and His people. At the climax of the service Paul Berg laid his hands on our bowed heads and prayed a prayer of commitment to the Lord God, for His safe keeping through the coming months. As he prayed, I found my own prayers ranging over various individuals in the pews behind—many of them in need in different ways from our own—some with marriages under stress, others depressed and lonely. Throughout the gathering and afterwards we were aware of the Holy Spirit's presence, breaking down barriers and reconciling one to another. We were in no doubt that the sovereign Lord was abroad to heal in areas of our lives that desperately needed His touch. We did not feel that we had a mandate to claim physical healing then and there, and our thoughts repeatedly came back to the Lord's promise to Paul as he prayed for deliverance from his 'thorn in the flesh': 'My grace is sufficient for you, for my power is made perfect in weakness.' (II Cor 12:9). We came away from the church that evening with the continuing conviction that whatever the future might hold we were in secure hands.

Throughout 1974 to 1976, while we were intermittently distracted by matters ophthalmological, life by and large continued in an orderly way. Joy, whose ambition to train and work as an Occupational Therapist had been quelled many years before when she turned her steps towards Nursing, found a job at Barrow Hospital in September 1974 to work amongst psychiatric patients as a part-time OT assistant. Working three mornings a week, her mind and fingers were soon busy with ideas to involve her clients with therapeutic activity. Joy had always been able to find plenty to do and, prior to her post at Barrow, she had a number of commitments in the community, including work for both a Shelter group and for the World Development Movement. Along with her new, part-time job, she was also able to acquire a good sized plot of deep, rich soil at some nearby allotments in which to grow vegetables.

However, at heart Joy was most fulfilled as a wife and mother, thriving on the domestic front. In time, she found the cost of travelling, to and from the job, the limitations imposed on her creativity at work and the loss of valuable, home-based time frustrating, and so she handed in her notice in the New Year.

My work with the students continued to have a high priority, especially in the areas of psychotherapy and counselling. One particularly worthwhile facet of this involvement was that we could offer anxious, depressed or obsessed students the valuable commodity of time. In this way we were able to help many through to the point of functioning adequately once more without the need to refer them for formal psychiatric consultations, with the stigma that still seemed to attach to such referrals. In the September of 1975 I organised a Bristol based conference for the British Student Health Association on 'Brief Psychotherapy'; this was attended by over sixty doctors and smaller numbers of counsellors and nurses. During this residential weekend, we explored together the methods and aims of a psychotherapy which sought to help students through a much briefer commitment of time than in traditional forms of psychoanalysis. Amidst the serious-minded professionalism of the conference we were able to sit back and laugh at our own profession on the Saturday evening while we watched a production of P. Nichols' hilarious *National Health* at the Theatre Royal. I was very grateful for some divine engineering since a block-booking at the theatre had been made long before the management knew what would be performed that night.

During these few years, Joy and I became involved with a very different type of gathering in the Wessex Conferences—seminars held in North Devon to consider Christian perspectives on marriage and family, and attended largely by farmers and their wives—mostly with Brethren backgrounds. The leading light of this admirable venture was 'K.G.' Hyland, a retired dentist with a shining face, a transforming smile and a persuasive manner. He was of that rare breed, a blend of traditional Brethrenism, with its profound grasp of the Scriptures, and neopentecostalism, with its fire of the Spirit. At a hotel in Ilfracombe in 1974 and in a low-ceilinged 17th century farmhouse near Umberleigh in 1975 we shared with fifty or so others something of our understanding of a scriptural view on relationships between husband and wife, and between parents and children—all under the loving, yet watchful aegis of 'K G'. On both occasions we were overwhelmed by the amount of personal need within the marriages of many of these farming families. Between the talks and seminars every available minute seemed to be packed with requests for counselling, including a high percentage for help with problems concerning marital sex. The general difficulty that most of us who are married have in first plucking up courage to share in this area and, then, in actually finding someone who will listen is increased by the isolated existence of people in the more rural regions.

In between these two autumnal conferences, in August 1975, we were invited as a family to 'Breakaway', a week's holiday for nearly 200 young people at Milton Abbey School in Dorset organised by the Church of the Nazarene. In return for my giving four talks on sex to the teenagers and taking two seminars on marriage for the young marrieds, we were given a rumbustious holiday with these lovely Christian people. At one point during this hectic week Joy grinned hesitantly when asked whether her husband was 'an expert on sex'.

Joy and I returned from these various conferences with a great burden for the needs of individuals and couples in the church where we worshipped at Clifton. In some ways it seemed illogical to spend so much time in other corners of Wessex when the fellowship we were part of at home seemed to be scarcely touched, at least at that stage, by systematic teaching in the area of relationships.

I shared my concern with Paul Berg on several occasions (usually over fish and chips) and he cautiously agreed that I might do something in this field of pastoral care in the New Year of 1977. And so, for five consecutive Wednesday evenings in January and February one hundred or so people gathered in the Crypt of Christ Church while I spoke on the theme of Christian caring and counselling. In these talks, illustrated by 'stick' men and women on the overhead projector, I spoke on the subjects of the principles included, adolescence, singleness, marriage, family and the three 'voids' of divorce, retirement and bereavement. A wide range of people listened avidly, the discussions in small groups buzzed busily and the Lord spoke to many of us.

During the following months an *ad hoc* committee grew up to discuss and pray about the possibility of a Christian counselling service in Bristol, complementary to the caring concern of the local churches. We were a group of about ten Christian lay leaders—men and women, Brethren, Baptists and Anglicans, charismatic and Reformed. In our discussions we found much confusion in the different ways we used the word 'counselling'. Some used the word as a synonym for evangelism, others as a more esoteric term, saddled with a great deal of mystique. In due course I was asked to repeat the series I had given at Christ Church, in order to clarify thinking in this area. This time a wide range of Bristol's churches was circulated, albeit at very short notice, and the 'neutral' territory of Prince's Hall at the city centre was booked for five evenings in June. Again the response was impressive, indicating something of the vast reservoir of need in the sphere of personal relationships. It was heart-warming to meet Christians of many different persuasions —from Roman Catholics to members of small house churches— united by their pastoral concern. We planned a further, briefer series in the autumn but my health problems prevented my participation. Excellent talks on anger, guilt and depression were given by Dr Glynn Harrison, Jerram Barr from L'Abri and Dr Richard Winter.

Our debate continued through the second half of 1977. The majority on the *ad hoc* committee favoured the development of a Christian counselling service in Bristol. Richard Winter and I were less convinced, partly because we represented churches where an increasing amount of counselling was already taking place, and partly because, at that stage, we felt that bodies like the Samaritans, the Citizens' Advice Bureau, Alcoholics Anonymous and the Marriage Guidance Council were covering many of the needs of the population in the areas of crisis intervention and longer term problems. In time, we came to a common mind that *both* aspects of Christian counselling were probably needed: that based in and through the local churches where an educational role and continual pastoral care could be carried out; and that expressed through a central service, known to be Christian, where distinctive help could be offered to the wider community.

The main snag, at that time, was that we could find no one to head up the latter venture. One of Bristol's churches kindly offered a venue and telephone but we felt that a church-based Christian counselling service intended for the city at large would only have a limited appeal. As an interim measure the Bristol Family Life Association, under the chairmanship of a local farmer, Anthony Bush, publicised in the local papers its availability for marital counselling. This offer narrowed our original vision to one important sector of society but was an important contribution which, in time, bore greater fruit. In April 1981, four years after our first deliberations, a Christian telephone counselling service called Marriage Repair was started in Bristol. This was an endeavour of faith, instigated by the BFLA, providing a dozen trained 'telephone counsellors' and thirty or so married couples who were ready to visit the homes of those in need to help prevent marital breakdown and to encourage more constructive approaches to marriage.

Throughout the earlier part of this period, my burden for wider instruction amongst Christians in the sphere of caring for one another and for the community within which they lived, led, by degrees, to the publication of my first book: *Restoring the Image*. Paul Berg, in his far-sighted way, was the first to query the possibility of at least printing my initial lecture on the principles of Christian caring and couselling. This original idea expanded and in the autumn of 1978 Christ Church generously backed the production of *A Handbook for Christian Caring and Counselling*, printed locally and incorporating my own illustrations. A thousand were printed and sold within a few months, without publicity. The speed of sale indicated a market hungry for some British writing in this area and so I was encouraged to approach some key Christian publishers. In due course The Paternoster Press took up the gauntlet and *Restoring the Image* was published in February 1980.

As a back-drop to all the excitement of progress, in both the theory and practice of counselling on the Christian scene in Bristol, was the nagging question of my eyesight. Between the two series I took on couselling, we were able, as a family, to escape to the hills once more—for an Easter holiday at a friend's cottage near Machynlleth in Mid Wales. This property comprised a sturdy farm-house flanked by disused barns and surrounded by larches and pines—all set in open, hilly country above the valley of the Dovey. We had a relaxing time whose memories include the discovery by our three children of the delights of Radio Four in our television-free environment. This was well before their collective teen-years exposed their ear-drums to the bombardments of Radio One!

Somehow my vitreous haemorrhages seemed more disruptive while we were on holiday, partly because time was more fleeting and therefore more precious in terms of a week or two's break. By now, I was coping well with the diminishing sight of the left eye but was, of course, all the more vulnerable to trouble on the right.

Nearing the end of the fortnight, I had a small but significant bleed on that side which robbed the Welsh landscape of its finer definition for the last few days. On one of those days, Simon (then aged twelve) and I ventured up the beautiful, glaciated valley of Cwm Cywarch to climb a modest horseshoe-ridge in the Aran hills. I was beginning to sense the shape (or rather the lack of shape) of things to come as we clambered amongst the boulders of Glasgym. Hearing a bird call, my instinctive reflex to raise the binoculars led to frustration. I turned and said to Simon, 'You're going to have to be my eyes—at least as far as birds are concerned.' He accepted the challenge and the binoculars readily, and we were soon chatting about the finer distinctions of this or that 'small, brown bird.'

On our return down the slopes of Y Gribin we discovered a new alpine sport—'moss-gliding'. In this activity, you glissade down the gradient on your rear-end over a cushion of heather and damp moss. The steady incline of the eastern slopes of Y Gribin is ideally suited and we built up an impressive speed of descent. The only hazard we encountered was a deep impregnation of our underpants by chlorophyll!

A further bleed in the right eye on the 30th of November meant that 1978 opened with the need for me to give up driving. I still had quite serviceable vision for most purposes but at the wheel of a car was not the safest place for me to be, both for myself and for those on the road at the same time. In 1975, as an economy measure, we had sold our second car, a Mini, and I had bought a Honda 50 motor-cycle, later graduating to a Honda 125. And so, for a couple of years I commuted in and out of Bristol and made my visits on a motor-bike. This entailed some delicate manoeuvres in terms of attending patients. I had a large box on the back of the bike which took my black Gladstone bag. I would park the Honda round the corner from the visit, remove the bag, doff gauntlets, crash-helmet and over-garments, place this gear in the box, and thus arrive at the patient's door—not very cool or calm, but certainly collected—ready for my best bedside manner. In spite of these complex rituals, riding on the open road and overtaking long streams of near stationary cars were exhilarating experiences. However, the mixed pleasures of both motor-cycle and car had to be relinquished in the New Year.

For most of 1978 I was indebted to the kindness of neighbours for the journey in and out of Bristol. For urgent visits during the day one or other of our two, lovely nursing sisters would ferry me.

The Hurding family in 1978 during a period of my unilateral blindness

At night, and this was the most trying aspect of our arrangements for transport, Joy would chauffeur me for any necessary calls. Night visits are always a challenge but it was doubly disruptive for the two of us to have to leap out of bed in the small hours. Further, we were rightly uneasy to leave our three sleeping children for an hour or so in the middle of the night. However, we developed a good system and Joy's aid was indispensible not only for the driving but for locating the precise address. My night vision was already deficient and Joy saved many a turned ankle and banged head as she guided me into dark basements or up rickety stairs.

Amidst the uncertainties of our situation, the greatest of unpredictabilities hit us in the April of 1978. One weekend, early in the month, I received an unexpected phone call from my sister Anne. We had arranged a trip together in the West Country for the following Tuesday to pursue our combined interest in Family History, and so I anticipated some practical query or other concerning our arrangements. My shock was profound when her strained voice declared that she thought her marriage with Rob was breaking up. I had organised a week off to encompass our genealogical escapade and so I was available to catch a train to London where Anne met me in order to drive us out to their home in suburban Surrey. Over the next three days I learnt at first hand something of the agonising unhappiness of a formerly strong marriage being disrupted.

Anne and Rob's union had been something of an ideal one in the eyes of both relatives and friends. Anne, vivacious and extroverted, and Rob, quieter and more reflective, had brought complementary qualities to their marriage. They had four delightful children, then aged thirteen to nineteen, known by our three as 'the Cousins'—a term always used by them with reverential endearment. Rob and Anne had brought them up in a Christian context and there was a great deal of loving contact between their family unit and ours. However, problems within their marriage had been covertly at work, had now festered and were rapidly becoming a running sore.

My emotional attachment to them both was very deep—to Rob as a specially close friend over thirty three years and to Anne as a most companionable sister. By the Lord's grace, aided by my experience in counselling, I was able to listen to them both, individually and together, as they wrestled with their changed awareness of each other. Within the next fortnight both Rob and Anne came independently to stay with us at Conifers for a few days as they tried to readjust within their exploding situation. Tragically, the wounds seemed to be too deep for mutual reconciliation and so Rob moved out. Anne's repentance was profound and through the pain of it all she had an acute sense of the Lord's forgiveness and sustaining power. Their divorce was finalised two years later.

The break-up of any apparently happy marriage has, of course, widespread repercussions amongst both friends and family. Four months after this sad severance, I had arranged two consecutive weeks' holiday in Radnorshire and then Carmarthenshire for my parents, Anne's depleted family and ourselves. The vacuum that Rob's absence left among us gave our explorations of the hills and valleys of Central Wales a bitter-sweet taste. As we lay together in the sun on our last day of holiday, the other sombre aspect of our family life loomed once more as the Welsh sky became peppered by the now familiar meteorites of another retinal bleed.

October came and Joy and I drove north to the Lake District for a week together. From the beginning of our marriage we had tried to establish a weekend or a week away by ourselves each year as a necessary part of our continuing relationship. We had understood that there was no way of preventing vitreous haemorrhages in a so-called 'proliferative diabetic retinopathy'—short of avoiding climbs above 15,000 feet! As alpine mountaineering was not a hazard of our everyday life we felt reasonably secure in the insecurity of unpredictable bleeds.

We had rented a house belonging to the Forestry Commission amidst the coniferous plantations of Whinlatter Pass in the northern Lakes. During this week we became acquainted with Herdwick sheep, the market at Cockermouth, breezy ridge walks on Hopehead Gill and Mellbreak, and the Cumberland sausage. On the Thursday evening, sitting opposite Joy by a comforting coal fire while the Cumbrian winds shook the window panes and rattled the back door, I had a massive haemorrhage in my hitherto serviceable right eye. I was reading John Fowles' intriguing novel *The French Lieutenant's Woman* and had just reached the last page. In this book the author presents two alternative endings, one fulfilling the wishes of the hero Charles Smithson, the other frustrating them. Ironically, there seemed to be a third ending provided for this particular reader as the inky, red effusion steadily blotted out the page in front of me, but not before I had glimpsed the rapidly fading sentence with which the book ends: 'And out again, upon the unplumb'd, salt, estranging sea'.

CHAPTER FOURTEEN

LIGHT AND DARKNESS

'And I will lead the blind in a way that they know not, in paths that they have not known I will guide them. I will turn the darkness before them into light, the rough places into level ground. These are the things I will do, and I will not forsake them.'

Isaiah 42:16

'God who took away my eyes that my soul might see'.

Marguerite Radclyffe-Hall: *The Blind Ploughman.*

WHILE JOY DROVE US SOUTH DOWN THE MOTORWAY TWO days after the devastating haemorrhage in my right eye, our minds were a whirl of thoughts as we wrestled with the implications of blindness. How would we break the news to the children, to the rest of our families, to our friends, to our fellow-Christians and to my colleagues at work? How long would I need to be off work? How much would I need to rest? What, if anything, would I be able to do? Whom could I get to speak for me on a panel at Badminton School in three weeks' time? How easy would it be for my fellow-doctors to find a locum to replace me? Would I ever see again?

While our thoughts whirled so did my impression of the landscape. What we had rejoiced in on our way north was, for me, a thing of former beauty, now heavily scored with a raging black snow blizzard. I had always been irked at seeing colour transparencies of exquisite scenery marred by dust. This minor irritation was now evoked on the grand scale as visual reality itself was overlaid and distorted by a retinal bloodstorm. One of the few comments I could manage out of the mental, emotional and sensory chaos was a bland axiom: 'I don't think I'll make work on Monday, Joy.'

As a family, we had never before experienced a home-coming like this one. Sarah (15), Simon (13½) and Rachel (10½) had been well looked after during the week by two very good friends, Janet and Caroline, who, independently, had spent nights at Conifers on a rota basis. The three children were enjoying an adult-free Saturday waiting for the sound of the Maxi and the return of their parents. Here they were at last—looking well and weather-beaten. But why was Mum holding Dad's arm and why was Dad so slow in looking at us?

I had anticipated with some dread the meeting up with the children on our return. Here they were now. Bursting out of the house and running up the short, concrete path to greet us. A few whispered explanations from Joy, the pain of dimly seeing their featureless faces, the thrill of hearing their laughter and feeling their tight embraces . . . .

Although I carried the visual storm with me, home was a personal haven that first weekend in the dark. Suddenly the family's weakest vessel, I spent most of the time sheltered in an arm-chair while Joy took command of a list of painful phone-calls. These distress signals assured family, friends and colleagues that, although my navigation was in serious trouble, I was by no means a complete wreck. I was safely harboured at home and would be happy, after a few days, to be inspected by visitors.

We need not have feared for our children's adjustments. Sarah was the quietest in her response, but the warmth of her hugs and the firmness with which she squeezed my hand were messages of solidarity. Within a few hours of our return, my attention was arrested by a long sequence of determined hammer-blows from the direction of the garage. On seeing his Dad out of action, Simon had removed his wardrobe doors and was now making these into a rough and ready work-bench for the coming weeks. There still needed to be a 'man about the house' and he had to have a base from which to carry out his DIY jobs. Rachel, lively and demonstrative in her affection, assured me within the first few days of my enforced exile: 'You can't read to me now, Dad, can you? Never mind. I'll start reading to you!' and, during the following evenings, proceeded to enthuse me with the adventures of Wilbur the pig in E.B. White's book *Charlotte's Web*.

Joy responded to my sudden handicap with compassionate practicality. She unravelled the complex chains of my involvements with work, church and speaking engagements and handled the stream of enquiries that flowed in with patience and sensitivity. Within the first week she tracked down a large, high-winged, second-hand armchair to provide me with a comfortable base for my new, sedentary existence.

In the advent of my dramatic loss of vision we realised something of the Lord's foreknowledge and preparatory guidance. Eight months before our holiday in the Lake District, Joy had reluctantly applied for a part-time job as a receptionist at our local Health Centre. Although her priorities had always been home-based, we both realised that if my earning capacity became curtailed through illness then it would become increasingly important for her to boost our income. She was duly interviewed and offered the post out of sixty-four applicants. This financial provision, although modest, could not be refused. In the event, Joy's link with the Health Service proved invaluable in other respects—both from the point of view of medical advice and from the equally important, although tedious, aspects of certification and other administrative matters.

On the Tuesday following our return from the Lakes, Joy and I visited the Eye Hospital to see Mr Marmion. I asked him how much I needed to rest. 'If you think of doing anything—don't!' was his simple reply. He also initiated a second opinion on the situation suggesting that we visit Cambridge in a month's time to see a Mr John Scott, an internationally known specialist of diseases of the retina and the vitreous humour.

In the meantime my adjustments to an indeterminate world continued.

During our recent holiday I had said to Joy: 'I can cope with deteriorating vision—as long as I can still read.' Now that particular life-line had been broken. I remember my extreme reluctance to even enter my book-lined study. When I did I could just make out the vertical clusters of learning upon the shelves. I touched my roll-top desk and fingered a line of paper-backs that I had been reading prior to our trip north—a book-mark in each indicating the point where the flow of study had been arrested.

Friends quickly came to the rescue. Rose, one of our 'Think-In' friends, brought me a portable tape-recorder and others spent hours putting short stories and whole books of the Bible on to tape. There was a double boon in listening to the familiar voice of a much loved friend or member of the family reading the precious words of a gospel or epistle. I quickly appreciated how frequently, in normal reading, one's eyes dart to and fro to take in the meaning of a section of the printed page. However, in my novel situation, I soon became used to winding the tape back again and again to capture the significance of a particular passage of the spoken word.

During the few years leading up to my sudden blindness, I had revived a long-standing gift of painting. This ability had been culpably neglected since my late teens and I had become belatedly convinced of the importance of my stewardship in this area. As a result, I had painted up to a dozen water-colours over about four years and, at the point of visual loss, was planning further studies. I reasoned that this creativity could be channelled elsewhere and so I began to formulate some poetry in my mind and, in time, dictated this on to tape. The poems that begin and conclude this book were worked out during this period.

Another sphere of creativity that I missed acutely in my restricted state was gardening. During our first nine years at Conifers I had built up a series of shrub borders which, by 1978, clothed both front and back gardens with harmonious compositions of foliage and flower. I could now but dimly make out their architecture but, nonetheless, I knew the positions of each plant so precisely that I could wander about the garden to check on their health by feeling—albeit cautiously in the case of roses, Spanish gorse or other prickly subjects. By the early spring of 1979 I found, to my delight, that I had learnt a technique of feeling the dormant buds on our climbing roses confidently enough to prune the bushes. Once or twice I became too confident with the secateurs, on certain shrubs that needed a general shearing over in March, and had to retreat indoors with a bleeding finger.

Although the acute withdrawal of the delights of reading, painting and gardening were compensated for to a modest extent, the greatest bonus of these months of blindness lay in the worlds of radio, and, more generally, music. Within my first week or two of curtailment our neighbours—Doug and Kay—lent me their stereo music-centre. We had a considerable number of records—mostly of Baroque, Classical and Folk music—and had enjoyed them through the years on a reliable mono record-player. It was a great joy now to listen to Bach, Mozart, Beethoven, Joni Mitchell, Ralph McTell and Fairport Convention reproduced stereophonically.

The radio had always been a close companion and so it was the extension of an already established relationship to listen to the delights of Radio 3 and Radio 4 from dawn till bedtime. My appreciation of a much wider range of music, particularly that of this century, my enjoyment of plays, discussions and debates, and my awareness of the finer details of affairs at home and abroad filled the long hours with pleasure and stimulus.

In the February of 1979 my exploration of the enriching world of music was taken a stage further by the purchase of our own music-centre. Berj Topalian, a very special friend who is mentioned more fully later, recruited two students from Bristol University for a collective blitz on the Broadmead shopping centre in the heart of the city. The four of us entered (three confidently, one tentatively) a series of chain-stores and smaller shops in search of the ultimate music-centre—within the price range that had been generously set by a gift from my parents. Berj was armed with records of Schubert's Ninth Symphony and Holst's 'The Planets' to test the quality of the machines inspected. Leaving a trail of disrupted and disappointed salesmen behind us, we eventually tracked down a superb JVC machine that had been reduced in price as it was shop-soiled. Next, the four of us sat back, our arms folded, to discuss the individual merits of the shop's extensive range of speakers while Mars, the god of war, thundered forth.

With the help of these determined allies I was able to sit in the centre of the sitting room at home while wave after wave of delectable music washed over me. Through record, radio and cassette, I was transported into the symphonic vistas of Beethoven, Brahms, Mahler and Shostakovich on the one hand and into the intimate world of chamber music on the other.

Music and radio were companionable but my relationship with them was obviously one-way. However, many of my days of listening were enhanced by the visits of friends. These occasions were of intestimable value to me as we talked and shared, sat silently or listened to a record or two. Amongst my numerous visitors were friends old and new, young and not so young, male and female, married and single, Christian and agnostic. It was a joy to share with some the peace that the Lord was giving me amidst the frustrations and to listen to others as they talked of their own pains and pleasures. The staff members from Christ Church were specially faithful well-wishers and they had clearly put me on their rota of weekly visits. Amongst these, the visits of Berj Topalian—the orchestrator of the hunt for the definitive music-centre—were a unique delight. Berj, an Armenian who was then completing his PhD thesis in theology, was Organist, Choirmaster and full-time Pastoral Assistant at Christ Church. His shock of curly black hair and swarthy beard framed a face of genial kindness and explosive humour. We drank numerous cups of tea together while we discussed complex theological and philosophical issues, listened to Mahler, or rocked, in our respective chairs, with side-splitting laughter at this or that zany perspective.

When I had anticipated the possibility of blindness I felt that my future career could at least be based on psychotherapy and counselling. However, I also wondered how I would really manage with the loss of so much invaluable non-verbal communication. It was not long before a friend needed to come to see me about his marriage and I awaited his arrival with some trepidation at the prospect of counselling 'in the dark'. As he talked, out of the murk, about his difficulties, I realised that I was still able to pick up a great deal of information about how he was thinking and feeling. Although I missed studying the maps of facial expression and observing the clues from bodily gestures, I was still able to 'read between the lines' of what he said and, with my heightened sense of hearing, I could pick up the sounds of changed posture and restlessness, and the different silences of thought, confusion and apprehension. Following this encounter, I decided that, if I needed to work as a blind psychotherapist in the future, I would briefly explain my disability on meeting new clients and would stress that if they wanted to communicate anything it would have to be done verbally because they could not rely on my discernment of more covert messages. I thought that some people in need might find an encounter with a visually handicapped counsellor less threatening as they would not have to fear being transfixed by over-persistent eye contact!

In early November, following our visit to the eye specialist in Cambridge, I was released from my sentence of inactivity, and so we were able to respond to a few invitations out. Of these, the most memorable for me were our attendance at various concerts. At the end of the month Garry and Jeannette Guinness, two more of our 'Think-In' friends, offered us tickets to accompany two other good friends, Monty and Rosemary Barker, to the Colston Hall to hear, amongst other music, Bruckner's Third Symphony. I had never listened to Bruckner with undivided concentration before and my imagination, provoked by the music, was filled with powerful images of snow-covered mountains, troops on the march, and town squares loud with ringing bells and the cries of victory—all set in a vast, Central European landscape at the begining of the last century. The epic of *War and Peace* still fertilised my mind even though stimulated by the music of a later age.

Even more venturesome was our response to the invitation of a very dear friend, Julie , to attend a performance in Wells Cathedral of Verdi's *Requiem*, in which she was singing. Disoriented within the cathedral's axis, I sat with Joy and two other friends, to listen to the walls of arresting music which rose from the nave some distance ahead of us. Somehow the lack of accurate, visual impression—I could but dimly discern the upsweep of the cathedral's floodlit architecture—exposed me more to the powerfully operatic work. The cataclysmic chords of the *Dies Irae* erupted over me, in my feeling of comparative nakedness, with great waves of sound. My spine tingled at the sheer musicality and its evocation of Judgement Day. 'It is a fearful thing to fall into the hands of the living God' and something of that fearfulness was felt and then, in time, assuaged by the peace of Christ as I continued to listen.

During the winter months, through the faithful ferrying of Joy and certain friends, I was able to attend various other functions, including a series of addresses on Christian perspectives in philosophy and some lectures in the course for candidates for the MRCPsych. (Member of the Royal College of Psychiatrists) examination. Early in the New Year I was booked to attend a day course on Psychodrama at the Jenner Centre, a complex for postgraduate study at Bristol Royal Infirmary. Although I had attended seminars, courses and workshops on a number of aspects of psychotherapy, including Gestalt and Transactional Analysis, this was to be my first taste of Psychodrama. The double impact of coping with many strangers and adjusting to the unknowns of this form of therapy was compounded, for me, by the nerve-racking novelty of coming to terms with new situations in a visually handicapped state. Left at the Centre by Joy early on the Saturday in question, I was tempted to turn round and ask my way to the nearest bus for Portishead. However,I was encouraged to persevere by my close ally, Richard Winter, who was also attending the course. We soon discovered that he, another colleague, Graham Rooth, and I were the only men amongst about thirty women

—mostly young, and working in Occupational Therapy and Social Work. We were divided into four for the day's activities and this arrangement left one group complainingly man-less.

I need not have feared for the day ahead. The group I was part of was understanding and caring, and we survived the trust-exercises, role-play, modelling and 'acted out' dramas with a great spirit of accord. In spite of my limitations, I found myself emerging as an apparently undisputed leader in a long and complex drama designed to bring out leadership qualities.

Generally, I found encounters with people difficult during this period of blindness. Old friends were most considerate but even with these there were problems. Although I could see so little—blocks of strong colour, large areas of light and darkness, and the general forms of people and large objects at close range—I was able to appear to focus my eyes on a speaker's face with some accuracy. As a result, I looked to be in less difficulty than I really was. This meant that I did not always receive the explanatory words 'Hello Roger; this is John (or Mary) . . .' at the beginning of a conversation. I would ask Joy afterwards, 'Who was that I was talking to?' to discover that I had been chatting to someone that we had known for months or even years. I also found participation in a more general discussion between, say, four or five of us difficult. I missed, of course, the eye contacts and facial expressions that are an integral part of lively interchange. Was that last question for me, or not? Who is that speaking now—is it Jim or Jack—or is it Jill with a fresh bout of laryngitis? Unanswered queries like these stultified my contribution to conversation and I gravitated towards silence.

Meeting strangers is always interesting and, even though blind, I enjoyed the novelty of conversing with a new acquaintance. The brain will not permit a voice to stay disembodied and I found mine rapidly filling out the imagined features, contours, form and bearing of a fresh contact. Sometimes I was disappointed afterwards when I asked Joy to describe the person I had just talked with. I may have been captivated by the richly sensuous tones of a newcomer's voice to learn subsequently that she had straight, greasy hair, at least two chins and a dumpling figure. Reflecting on this revelation. I might have a sequence of three lines of thought—the first unworthy, the second contrite and the third forward-looking. Initially I might have wondered how truthful Joy was being—perhaps the stranger had *looked* richly sensuous as well as sounding it and Joy, in her wifely wisdom and on my behalf, felt that disenchantment was the better part of ardour. Further thought might have been more penitential—that, even in my physical blindness, externals were far too important and that I still, reflexly, looked, unlike the Lord, on the outward appearance rather than on the heart. Finally, I might have reflected more positively that other people I felt I already knew had unexpected qualities that I had missed when my mind was preoccupied with exteriors. I would learn, as it were, to look on them with new eyes.

As an undercurrent to the intermittent flow of contacts with friends old and new was the frustration of trying to cope with the hitherto simple manoeuvres of life. This feeling of frustration must have been as acute at times for the onlookers, especially for Joy and the three children, as my restrictions meant the loss of much spontaneity in response to their visual world. Further, much forethought was needed on their part to look afresh at all the reflexes and habits that help to make up a well-knit family life. There was pain for them, as well as for me, in my inability to comment on Rachel's latest purchase from a jumble-sale, to admire Simon's most recent painting that had won acclaim at school, to see Sarah's new boy-friend or to observe the subtlety of tone and colour in Joy's freshly acquired, matching blouse. Again, there was reciprocal unease in the way Joy had to step into my shoes in the areas of an often complex correspondence, in the paying of bills, in decision-making, in the handling of the children's requests and plans, and in a host of other practical issues. We had never seen our partnership in terms of rigidly defined roles and there had been a great deal of overlap in our functions as husband, wife, father and mother. However, Joy had now to exercise all four roles to a greater extent although I was, of course, available to talk through and support her in her decisions, and help generally in verbal comunication with the children and their friends. Most appropriately, it was my job to turf out Sarah's boy-friend if he overstayed his welcome, although I had only the vaguest visual impression of his appearance—perhaps that was as well, as he had the physique of a boxer!

For my own part, the frustrations of domestic life were often at their most acute when I was alone for long hours in the house, with the children at school and Joy at work. Most mornings I would dress after the others had left. This was a laborious procedure. Initially, I battled with a pair of underpants, discovering at least eight ways of putting them on—seven of which were incorrect and uncomfortable to a varying extent! Shirts were easier as the extreme difficulty of doing up the buttons when they faced inwards prevented mistakes in the final result. I had a wonderful supply of chunky jerseys—mostly knitted by Mum and Joy—that could be worn either way round and could even be acceptable inside-out in some company. The biggest challenge came with the socks. First, I

Joy and me during my first period of blindness

preferred to wear socks that more or less matched the rest of my clothes. Secondly, I liked to wear socks that matched each other accurately. Thirdly, I would rather wear them with the more presentable aspect on the outside—*both* of them, that is. Joy thoughtfully tucked one sock inside the other to make a pair. That was fine until I undid the bundle and then dropped one of them! Some mornings I spent up to fifteen minutes on hands and knees groping about the study floor for the miscreant sock, banging my head or ribs from time to time on the edge of the desk, the side of a chair or the end of the open wardrobe door. Sometimes I wept with frustrated rage—sometimes I collapsed on the carpet, silly with uncontrollable laughter.

I gradually became used to this exhausting ritual as well as the general delineaments of the house—although I was sometimes caught out by the unexpected. The free edge of an open sitting-room door was an unpleasant obstacle to encounter when trying to move quickly to respond to the front door bell. A pair of wellington boots or a school satchel left in the main thoroughfare between the sitting-room and my intended destination could lead to a precipitate arrival at the loo's closed door. The family responded to these painful acrobatics by leaving fewer traps around for me to walk into or trip over.

Living in a chalet on a steep hillside, our bedrooms were downstairs and the toilets upstairs. At night the manoeuvre up and down was, of course, little different from the day-time from my point of view, except that I exercised more care at night to prevent unnecessary noise. Although I quickly assessed that there were thirteen steps to descend on returning to bed, I rarely remembered to count them while I made my way down. Somehow I always seemed to misjudge the final step—either expecting it too soon so that I plunged sickeningly down the last two or, believing there was still one more to go when I stood on the last, trying to push my over confident, leading foot down through the floorboards so that my sleepy frame was jolted mercilessly by the floor's upward thrust.

Throughout this period of enforced twilight, the Lord spoke most tenderly to me through Paul's second letter to the Corinthians. Although friends and family had produced tapes of most of the epistles as well as Mark's and John's gospels, this Pauline letter became the most precious with its powerful perspectives on light and darkness. Although Paul was clearly writing about spiritual realities in this respect, the contrasting imagery spoke strongly to my situation. I was in physical darkness and yet God graciously showed me more and more of His light during this difficult time. Perhaps this inner sight was best expressed for me in Paul's words in II Corinthians 4:6:

> 'For it is the God who said, "Let light shine out of darkness", who has shone in our hearts to give the light of the knowledge of the glory of God in the face of Christ'.

I will look more fully at chapters four and five of this letter, with its wonderful insights on suffering, towards the end of this book.

When Joy and I visited Cambridge in the November of 1978, Mr John Scott had examined my right eye and suggested that we spent a month considering his offer to operate on it. In the early '70's, he had pioneered an intra-ocular operation which actually removed the jelly substance at the core of the eye—the vitreous humour—in cases of blindness due to repeated retinal haemorrhages. The results of this procedure had not been very promising in the diabetic eye as other complications, including adhesions and retinal detachment, so often jeopardised sight even though the obscuring blood was removed. Some time before, I had read graphic accounts of these vitrectomies in the medical journals and prayed inwardly that I would never need such an heroic operation. Mr. Scott had now proposed a vitrectomy on my right eye but, with the special problems of the diabetic retina, had offered us four weeks' grace to say 'yes' or 'no'. With even the remotest possibility of restored vision as the outcome, we could not bring ourselves to turn down the operation—however much my flesh quailed at the prospect.

And so, on Sunday the 29th of January 1979, Joy and I drove eastwards through an ice-bound landscape to an even more frozen Cambridgeshire where we were to be based with two long-standing friends, Alan and Helen Bullock, at their home in Ely. The next day, my birthday (!), Joy took me the fifteen miles or so to Old Addenbrooke's Hospital, Cambridge, where I was to spend the next week in a small, box-like cubicle off the main Eye Ward. Our arrival at the hospital had been pre-empted by family and friends who had sent birthday greetings, get-well cards, loving letters and flowers. That evening, I learnt from Joy, our very dear 'Think-In' friends were meeting specially to pray for us and the children at our time of greatest need.

The Tuesday dawned with the Lord's deep peace pervading my being as I lay there anticipating the day ahead. Throughout the morning there seemed to be a constant flow of nurses, anaesthetists and ophthalmic surgeons in and out of the cubicle. My imagination worked overtime putting faces and figures to voices and movements. After a protracted search for a co-operative vein, a drip was put up to help balance insulin and glucose in my blood stream during the pending operation; an anaesthetist arrived to discuss details of pre-medication; nurses came to put innumerable drops in my eyes and, in the early afternoon, to cut my right eyelashes short with a pair of scissors, greased to prevent the lashes from falling into my duly prepared eye. At about 2 o'clock a beefy porter of inestimable good cheer came to wheel me on his trolley to the operating theatre while I chatted almost euphorically, buoyed up by that rare mixture of the Lord's peace and powerfully tranquillising drugs. During the next two and a half hours of the vitrectomy Joy was cloistered in King's College chapel, praying amidst a snowbound Cambridge for my restored sight.

While I slept the profound sleep of deep anaesthesia, John Scott carried out his precise and intricate operation—for him one of many similar procedures and yet, so the porter told me later, heralded by his comment, 'I'm going to make an extra effort on this one.' I strongly suspect that this gifted surgeon works equally hard to save the sight of all his patients, but the repeating of this comment filled me with gratitude later in the day. Along a curved line just above the iris three probes, each less than one millimetre in diameter, were introduced into the eye under the direct vision of a microscope. Through one of these hollow filaments the opaque vitreous humour was sucked out while, through another, the eye's inner fluid was replaced by Ringer's saline, the intra-ocular pressure being automatically maintained throughout. With the third probe adhesions were cut away and new blood vessels freed to be, in turn, removed by suction. Other potentially troublesome capillaries were destroyed by an argon laser.

Later that day, I gradually woke to find my eye heavily bandaged but remarkably free of pain. Mr. Scott arrived, removed the dressing, and bade me look at him. Through the reflex tears, I perceived a tall and smiling surgeon in his middle years. The eye-patch was replaced and the familiar darkness reasserted itself.

The thrill of this dramatic glimpse of the physical world after the murk of the previous five months was eagerly shared with Joy when she visited me later. However, the exuberance was short-lived as over the next few days the retina began to bleed once more with depressing persistence. Towards the end of the week I was released from the hospital with the assurance that, in spite of the initial disappointment, the haemorrhages would stop and my sight should then gradually clear. We stepped out into the arctic air of Cambridge, arm in arm, with a deep sense of relief that the dreaded operation was over and that there was still some real prospect of restored sight.

We drove back to the warm and loving home of the Bullock family—close to Ely Cathedral and Oliver Cromwell's house. Their painstaking attention did a great deal to ease the considerable strains that had been with us through the months. At night I had to be propped up by half a dozen pillows into a sitting position to sleep so that my eye was disturbed as little as possible. I was now beginning to experience an intense ocular pain that was aggravated viciously every time I blinked. As long as I could fix my dimmed gaze steadily ahead it was survivable. However, with the Lord's grace, patient endurance and pain-relieving tablets, the discomfort began to relinquish after another ten days or so. During this time, we returned to the West Country and to the generous love of friends, family and colleagues.

The fresh, post-operative bleeding had clouded my vision considerably once more and, as the weeks slipped by, I began to wonder whether I would see again after all. It was small comfort to be told by the eye specialist in Bristol that he had only known two patients who had bled after vitrectromy and I was one of them! However, once the pain in the eye began to lessen, I felt the need to do more and, perhaps, to begin to accept once more that I had to make the most of possibly permanent blindness.

I started on the home-front and decided that I would do as much house-work to help Joy as possible. I began by doing the washing-up on a regular basis and become adept at avoiding breakages. I graduated from ablutions at the sink to sweeping and washing the kitchen and bathroom floors regularly—each twice a week. As I became more confident, I decided I would spring-clean the house. It became an intriguing, though time-consuming, challenge to tackle each room in turn; dusting, polishing, sweeping, vacuum-cleaning and beating rugs became the order of the day as I groped my way from one corner of a room to another.

All was not plain sailing. There were hidden rocks on this course which I sometimes went aground on—at times with angry tears and at other times with a sense of the ludicrous. Knocking a recently filled dust-pan over to scatter its contents across a newly washed floor, treading on the brush end of an obliquely placed broom and finding its handle thumping against my chest or discovering I had used a brass cleaner on the hearth tiles were more tear-jerking than laughter-producing at the time. Two incidents with food were somehow more conducive to mirth.

One day, during the early spring, I was feeling extra virtuous as I cleared the kitchen table after lunch and washed up an impressive number of plates and dishes. Life really was not too bad—I had plenty of visitors, Radio 3 seemed to be broadcasting more and more intriguing music, my sight might return one day, the children would be home from school soon and the washing-up water was comfortably warm. In the middle of my reverie my hands closed on an unexpectedly bulky but yielding form floating in the bowl. I had just removed a fair-sized plate from the table and had plunged it into the sink—not realising amidst my musings that it supported a large, freshly-made fruit cake. I fished the soggy object out of the bowl on to the plate-rack to drain, joking later as the children arrived that Mum had made a sponge and not a fruit cake after all!

On another occasion, on squeezing a final item into the crowded fridge, my attention was arrested by a steady dripping sound from amongst the clustered contents. My hands probed the shelves to discover the source of the slurping; as I did so my fingers entered a variety of unidentified and chilly substances that sat upon saucers and half-filled, topless cartons. Eventually, I found the source of the disturbance. A large bowl of natural yoghurt had been tilted by my first manoeuvre and its contents had gently cascaded down through the shelves. I rationalised the situation with the thought that all foodstuffs—both sweet and savoury—can tolerate the presence of yoghurt and that I had probably done our immediate, nutritional future a service. An empty flan-case, prepared by Rachel and sitting at the bottom of the fridge, was filled to the brim with natural yoghurt when she returned from school a few hours later.

Thoughout this winter and spring of partial blindness, I established a series of short walks in the vicinity which I could manage by myself with the aid of a walking stick. I quickly learnt where the potential hazards lay and was able to avoid tripping up kerbs, walking into lamp-posts and falling over the low cliffs that fringe the local coast. Listening carefully for approaching cars and motor-bikes at the few road-crossings encountered on my way and believing that anyone on a push-bike would see me and take avoiding action, I greatly enjoyed visiting Battery Point, a spit of land which ran out into the Severn estuary nearby—like the bows of a ship pushing through the waves. I would stand or sit above this rocky promontory imagining a far grander scene than was actually offered by the muddy sweep of the bay to the south-west. When the modest waves broke on the dolomite of the point I could half see the water's spume out of the corner of my impaired left eye. Then I could believe that I looked down into some dizzy Cornish cove while Atlantic rollers broke on the rocks and shot their spray thirty feet up the cliff face. At other times, when the weather was calmer, I squinted across the bay to the vague shadow of Portishead Down and conjured up a vast coastline in Sutherland with weird, monolithic mountains rising in the background above the sand-fringed waters, which rang with the mournful cries of red-throated divers. It was during these walks that some of my attempts at poetry took shape along with the metamorphosed scene.

During the early months of 1979, one of our closer friends, Julie, who attended Christ Church and had recently finished working as a district nurse in a rural corner of the Mendips, offered to accompany me on some more venturesome walks. We had both, independently, enjoyed stepping out and exploring the remoter parts of the country and it was a great boon to me to have her company on a series of rambles through some delectable areas in mid- and south Somerset. I was able to introduce her to three much-loved walks that I knew fairly well from earlier trips with family and friends. It was good to have her eyes, to confirm the identity of the birds I heard and to describe the sky, hedgerow and woodland around us, and her humour to see the funny side of my often stumbling progress over uneven ground. She even got me running on one occasion, arm-in-arm and helter-skelter across a sandstone ridge that branched south from the Polden Hills.

Just as I was grateful to such friends for their time and company in keeping me in touch with the beauty of God's world round and about, I was also indebted to my medical colleagues as I tried to keep abreast of matters psychiatric. Graham Rooth worked as a Consultant Psychiatrist at Barrow Hospital seven miles away and he had shown a great interest in the possibility of my working with him as a Clinical Assistant, starting in the summer of that year. At his invitation I visited the hospital most Wednesdays to participate in ward rounds, group therapy and the medical meetings that were held before lunch in a room next to the library. I was specially impressed by the care and sensitivity of Graham and his team of doctors, social workers and nurses, both with regard to their patients and to my own physical handicap as I moved about the wards and the hospital grounds.

On one occasion at Barrow, just prior to a lunch meeting, I needed to visit a loo and was taken to an unfamiliar one by another consultant friend. We entered the toilets with their mixed smells of ammonia and disinfectant, and the background sound of flushing latrines. Thinking that I was orientated, I took aim at what seemed to be the correct, vertical surface, only to be grabbed by my friend and repositioned with the slightly anguished cry, 'No! Not there—it's over here!'

As April passed and we entered May, I began to wonder, from time to time, whether my vision was improving in the eye that had been operated on. One day, while washing up at home, I saw through my befogged vision the vaguest indication of lettering on a 'squeezy' bottle on the window-sill in front of me. I leaned forward to scrutinise carefully and to my joy achieved my first reading for eight months: 'Fairy Liquid'. It was a modest piece of information and would not satisfy me intellectually for long—but it was a start!

Friday, the 18th of May 1979 will always be remembered. Joy and I attended a meeting of a Bristol-based group of Christian psychiatrists that evening. As we rose after our learned discussion, Rosemary Barker crossed the room to chat with us. As she approached I realised that she had 'grown' the first eyes, nose and mouth that I had spotted since the previous September. I could scarcely contain myself as I shared this revelation with Joy on our way home.

And so, over the next few weeks, the extraordinarily novel beauty of the world around gradually emerged through the gloom as the vitreous haemorrhages at long last dissipated. The view before me imperceptibly changed from the obscure blocks of abstract art through the subtleties of an emergent impressionism to the exquisite detail of the real world—albeit a little lacking in definition, a little distorted in shape and a little washed out in tone and colour. To change the analogy, my visual experience moved from the effect of trying to see the bed of a stream obscured by the muddy and turbulent waters that flowed over it, through gaining a hazy impression of a river bottom seen through less disturbed, though mineral-laden, water to perceiving all the intricacies and wonders of fish, rock and plant-life in the bed of a tranquil lake of unclouded waters whose surface is becoming progressively still and whose sub-aqua panorama increasingly revealed as a result.

Thank God, the image was being restored.

CHAPTER FIFTEEN

RESTORING THE IMAGE

'Human kind cannot bear very much reality'.
T.S. Eliot: *Burnt Norton*

'Two are better than one, because they have a good reward for their toil. For if they fall, one will lift up his fellow; but woe to him who is alone when he falls and has not another to lift him up'.
Ecclesiastes 4 : 9, 10

During April 1979, a month before my vision began to be restored, Simon spent three weeks in Aix-les-Bains in south-eastern France as part of a school exchange. He greatly enjoyed the mountain air, cross-country ski-ing and visits to various monasteries and wine-cellars in the area. He returned laden with gifts—including some fine French cheeses. One of these, a soft cheese produced locally in the hills near Aix, was devoured with special relish by the two male Hurdings and was, some months later, thought to be the source of a mysterious illness that afflicted us both.

At the end of May, three weeks after my parents had moved from Harold Wood to a house a mile away from us in Portishead, I began to notice some intermittent flu-like symptoms. My sister Anne visited us during the Half Term and I remember feeling some puzzling aches in my neck and back along with bouts of shivering as we walked out along the local coast-line on a hot, late spring day. These sensations were forgotten until a fortnight later when both Simon and I were smitten with devastating symptoms. On the

Thursday in question I developed recurrent aches in the cervical spine and lumbar region together with extreme malaise, feverish feelings and a troublesome dry cough. This was just prior to an exceptionally busy week-end with a whole range of visitors coming and going from Friday evening through to Sunday tea-time. Joy was working on the Saturday morning and somehow I had to find a stiff upper lip to see the week-end through. On the Saturday, Simon became similarly afflicted and retired to bed with an illness that prostrated him for the next few weeks.

Having just begun to enjoy a recovery of sight over the previous four weeks, I had entered the fray of catching up with jobs, in the garden and house, that had been neglected during the previous eight months of blindness. I had also rapidly filled my diary with a number of new engagements that I could at last undertake. My sense of disappointment was profound as I emerged into a new visual freedom only to meet the extreme enervation of an extraordinarily unremitting disease. I cancelled commitment after commitment and ground my teeth with frustration. A comment from a professional friend that implied that my symptoms were simply a delayed, and perhaps neurotic, reaction to blindness did not help while I tried to fathom the cause of this new illness.

After three weeks or so of joint-aches, nocturnal feverishness, lethargy and the most anti-social of coughs, I felt that Simon and I had contracted something more persistent than influenza and we arranged for our GP to visit us. The family doctor and I discussed the possibilities of what the medical profession calls a PUO—a pyrexia of unknown origin. Amongst other considerations, I dismissed the possibility of brucellosis (or undulant fever) because we had not been in contact with any milk of doubtful origin in the previous few months. Various blood-tests were carried out and proved negative, the weeks slipped by and still we suffered. Over about two months Simon's symptoms gradually cleared with occasional relapses later; my own continued unabated. Eventually, in the late summer, repeat blood-tests revealed evidence of brucellosis after all and a local specialist in this disease incriminated our eagerly ingested cheese from Savoie!

One of the many by-products of this long-term infection was my difficulty in agreeing a date with Graham Rooth when I could start to work with him at Barrow Hospital. He and I had worked together on a number of psychiatric workshops, we got on well with each other and we both looked forward, it seemed, to being colleagues. He had the finances available for eight sessions a week for a Clinical Assistant. This seeemed most suitable as, by now, it was established that I would have to retire from my former work as a doctor in Student Health. I had hoped to return in the capacity of a psychotherapist but the University felt unable to finance such a post. My previous contract was for full-time General Practice and that appointment would need to be replaced. My inability to drive at night ruled out my continuation in that role and the lack of money to support me in a newly defined post meant that I had to leave. Many friends and colleagues agreed that Graham Rooth's job looked tailor-made. Frustratingly, he needed to make an appointment as soon as possible and I was unable to commit myself because the brucellosis dragged on. In the end we agreed that I would start on the 1st November and the relevant documents were drawn up.

With the diagnosis of undulant fever established, I was started on a three month's course of Oxytetracycline. The more acute forms of this condition can respond dramatically to antibiotics whereas the more chronic varieties are little affected. It seemed I was assigned to the latter category because I continued to feel unwell for most of the time throughout the autumn. In the days before antibiotics, brucellosis used to be called 'the 300 Day' disease because it typically lasted for ten months. Most doctors I discussed the situation with thought I should begin to improve after six months of the illness.

By the autumn Joy and I felt more than ready for a holiday and so, aided by gifts from the Bart's Nurses' Benevolent Fund and from my parents, and further encouraged by the generosity of some Christian friends who paid for our Motor-Rail fare, we set out for a week's break on the island of Colonsay—the member of the Inner Hebrides that we had glimpsed from the shores of Loch Buie, on the Island of Mull, two and a half years before. I was particularly keen that we should see something of the migration of wild geese as they headed south for Islay, the Solway Firth and beyond, and so we booked at the island's only hotel for seven nights at the beginning of October.

Although I spent a feverish night of coughing on the northward bound Motor-Rail, we boarded the car-ferry at Oban the following evening with eager relish. As the boat chugged its way out from Oban we looked back at the innumerable lights of the town reflected in the still waters of the harbour. My illness and the general strains of the previous year had tired both of us; the tranquil scene and the gathering dusk shrouded us with the promise of rest and refreshment. The ferry cleared the straits at the bay's exit and headed south-west—the dark bulk of the isle of Kerrera on our right—to enter the open waters of the Firth of Lorne. After two hours of steaming we picked out a tiny pin-prick of light just to starboard of the boat's bows. Fifteen minutes later the single light had become two, and after another ten minutes we could discern that the upper illumination came from the flood-lit hotel on its hillside perch, the lower from the small jetty of Scalasaig. We had reached our destination.

Joy drove our Maxi out of the ship's hold, past a flock of sheep —penned to one side of the pier ready for shipment, their dull eyes brilliant in the car's headlights—and so up the short stretch of road to a traveller's welcome from Kevin and Christa Byrne at the Isle of Colonsay Hotel. Initially the only guests, we had the pick of the rooms and were soon ensconced in a comfortable double-bedroom with a view down to the jetty and so across the dark waters towards Jura.

Colonsay is an elongated island with its axis running north-east to south-west; ten miles long and three miles across, it lies thirty-five miles south-west of Oban, on the Scottish mainland, with the larger islands of Islay and Jura ten miles or so to the south and south-east. With its highest point less than 500 feet about sea-level, it seemed to offer us quite modest challenges commensurate with Joy's lack of pioneering spirit and my own physical debilities. We had also brought the car on to the island just in case there was more trouble with my eye-sight. I had read a great deal about the island and its history during the preceding weeks and we looked forward to exploring the spectacular sea-cliffs, the sweep of Kiloran Bay and the wooded environs of Colonsay House in the north, as well as the sandy *machair* and beaches of the south-west. We also anticipated crossing the sands to the adjacent island of Oronsay at low-tide to watch grey seals and wander amongst the ruins of St Columba's Priory, with its stone memorials to long-dead MacDonalds and McPhees.

After the steady rain of our first full day on the island, we set out on the morning of the next day, a Friday, to explore the coast-line of Ardskenish, which marks the south-western extremity of Colonsay. It was a beautifully mild, sunny day with a soft breeze wafting in from the Atlantic. Every rock and stretch of sand was defined sharply in the pellucid air. The sensuous double uplift of the

Paps of Jura queened it over the more low-lying contours of Ardskenish and Oronsay. We meandered our way south over the *machair*, along the fringes of tidal sand and through the maze of dunes which have been driven across the northern end of the peninsula of Ardskenish by the westerlies. On our way back, we watched (and were watched by) several groups of six to eight grey seals—buoyant, rounded heads and soulful, dark eyes—peering from the waters at us while their pale pups lay in ones and twos on sea-weed covered islets a short distance off-shore. We ate well at Christa's board that night and retired early to bed, eagerly anticipating a day in the north of the island looking for golden eagles.

I woke to the sound of our alarm-clock the next morning and sleepily cancelled its exuberant ringing. I opened my eyes. I must still be dreaming because the room swam in obscurity. I closed my eyes again and prayed that I was still asleep and, if not, that all would be clearly seen on opening them once more. It was some minutes before I could open them on the awful truth that I had had another massive haemorrhage in my recently cured right eye. I lay there paralysed by a sense of unbelievable hopelessness. Was there no end to the apparent querks of divine providence? Could we not have been allowed at least seven days of Hebridean bliss rather than two, one of which had been grey and overcast throughout? Joy snuggled warm against my unyielding back. How could I tell her the appalling reality that, once more, she had a blind husband on her hands? I must move soon before Christa enters with her sparkle of Scottish hospitality and our morning tray of tea. 'Joy, I think I've had another bleed', was the best I could do as the tears began to flow. Christa must have wondered at the cause of our upset as Joy rose to take the tray from her, while I gazed sightlessly towards the window and the rising sun. Joy followed our hostess out into the passage to explain the predicament; later, breakfast was brought up for me as I could not face the limited exposure of the dining-room so quickly.

During the morning, Joy and I walked down the road to the jetty, arm in arm, and then across some rough moorland to the south. The wind lashed our faces as we stood motionless and wordless, holding each other while the tears flowed. Not only words for each other but prayer to our God seemed to have deserted us.

Later, we drove across the island to park on the *machair* so that

Joy could read aloud the opening chapters of Edith Schaeffer's recently published book *Affliction*. As we considered her thesis that God allows suffering to His people to win all sorts of victories for Him, we began to take stock once more. The authoress argued that, sometimes, God changes our circumstances in answer to our prayers—at other times He does not, but assures the sufferers that He is with them and will give them the strength they need to glorify Him. It seemed a bitter pill to swallow. We had been through eight months of my blindness together; I had emerged from that into the debilitating symptoms of brucellosis and now, to add to the trials of that chronic infection, I had lost my sight once more—quite possibly for good. We thought we had grasped the necessity of depending on God in all situations. Why the need to keep underlining the lesson? We had been convinced that our island holiday had been provided by God through the generosity of His people. Why did He allow it to be disrupted after two fleeting days? What was God up to? The questions crowded and clouded our minds.

And yet, as we sat in the car and grappled with unwanted reality, our troubled thoughts slowly latched, once more, on to the sovereignty of God—not the kingship of a perverse and sadistic dictator but of a loving Father who had sent His only Son to suffer the cruellest of deaths that we might be made whole. Jesus endured the agonising question of 'Why?' when He hung on the cross. The same question was in our own hearts and on our lips as we sat in the car together. For Jesus, His hours of darkness made sense ultimately—for us, too, we struggled to believe, our months or perhaps years of continuing affliction would also make sense, albeit retrospectively. As we thought and talked a little more freely, we were drawn closer to each other and to our loving God. We did not fully understand our plight and yet His compassion surrounded us and invaded our innermost selves. We prayed, while the Atlantic pounded the shore-line and oyster-catchers bickered from the rocks.

It took us two full days before we could bring ourselves to phone home to break the sad news. I felt too choked to trust myself to speak and so Joy bravely talked with my parents and our vicar, Paul Berg. He, in turn, would share our situation with the house-group which I led in Clifton and they, like many others, would be praying for us.

Our sense of peace mounted during the remaining days of our stay. On the Monday we visited Kiloran Bay and my imagination soared too as Joy described a spiralling golden eagle which circled high above us. Later, that same day, we wandered over the springy *machair* at Machins—where we had prayed together two days before. Suddenly I heard the fierce stuttering of an angry peregrine from the sky behind us. 'There's a peregrine back there somewhere', I cried to Joy. She was just in time to see the falcon stoop on a wheeling buzzard a hundred feet above the hill to our north. The peregrine shafted away up the coast-line while the complaining larger bird circled to gain height and so prevent another insulting attack from above.

It was extraordinary how my much-loved birds of prey closed in on us once my vision had gone, for the following day, during a visit to the peaceful island of Oronsay, we experienced another raptorial episode. We were walking back from St. Columba's Priory towards the tidal strand when I heard the shrill, whickering call-notes of a pair of merlins. Joy was able to watch with the binoculars while a male and female of this tiny falcon made repeated aerial sorties on another unfortunate buzzard—like gad-flies around a lumbering beast. The larger female was the more tenacious in these quicksilver forays before the two diminutive hawks sped away towards the north.

Although I missed the spectacle of these three avian encounters (the last two of which would have been unique sights in my bird-watching experience), the cries of the falcons and Joy's description of their aerobatics were enough to fill my mind with the wonder of it all.

Two days later, we began our long journey home by boat, car and train to another winter of gathered gloom.

In the April of 1979 we had discovered that I was eligible to use the Talking Book Service for the Blind. This facility, administered by the Royal National Institute for the Blind, provides a comprehensive tape-library of recorded books. The catalogue of general titles is further supplemented by the Student Tape Library which has more specialist works available for the widest range of disciplines—from Mexican History to Computer Science and from Classical Literature to Astrophysics. Throughout the first seven months of blindness, during the winter of 1978/79, we had assumed that I had to be registered blind to have access to these invaluable libraries. By April I was officially registered, only to discover that I could have profited from this reading material through the previous long months of darkness! This revelation made me bitterly angry—but not for long. Through the tears of anguish I reflected that the path of self-pity is always a dead-end, both for the sufferer and for those around. I asked the Lord's forgiveness and, with Joy's help, began to order an impressive list of interesting book-titles. In due course a play-back machine was delivered and its simple controls explained. Sleek, black plastic envelopes, each containing a large, six-track cassette, started to arrive in the post, and I began to luxuriate in fine literature once more. Soon after this belated but exciting discovery my sight gradually returned. The tape-machine was switched off and I reached out to my bookshelves, magnifying-glass in hand.

I read avidly that summer although my right eye tired readily while I strained to see through the powerful glass. With the renewed entry into blindness, I came back from Colonsay determined to soak up as much as possible from the Talking Book Library. Progress was slow in that listening to a book being read verbatim was a more lengthy affair than reading at my former, normally sighted rate. However, the beautifully written narrative of Richard Adams' *Watership Down*, the struggles of the oppressed human spirit in Solzhenitsyn's *The First Circle* and the poetry of D. H. Lawrence's *The Rainbow* filled the dark hours with a kaleidoscope of light and colour. Furthermore, a great sackful of tapes on sociology, psychology and psychotherapy arrived and I was thus able to study, speaking my 'notes' on to blank cassettes.

There was much to keep me busy that autumn. I believed it extremely likely that I would be permanently blind and set about adjusting to that probability with some resolution. We ordered a set of tapes that had been prepared to help blind people learn to touch-type. We bought a portable typewriter and I set to, following the instructress's recorded voice obediently. Joy assured me that increasingly what I typed made some sort of sense. I tried writing some poetry this way but soon realised that, without someone sighted at my elbow, what I had just typed was irretrievable! This loss of the 'inspired' led to further loss of inspiration. The Muse was muzzled. However, although I found creative writing simpler using a cassette-recorder because my first efforts could be played back, touch-typing did at least open up the way for writing my own letters once more.

Throughout these readjustments in the autumn of 1979, I had

the task of revising my first book *Restoring the Image*. Peter Cousins of The Paternoster Press obligingly taped his comments on the original text, Joy and a very good friend, Janet, read the five chapters of the book's prototype, *An Introduction to Christian Caring and Counselling*, on to another tape and so, with the help of three tape-recorders, I was able to make my revisions on to a third cassette.

This was a very time-consuming process—but I had the time! I would identify the paragraph that needed altering or extending, listen to it a few times and then go on one of my local walks, stick in hand, to wrestle mentally with sense, grammar and colour of language. On return, I would re-check the paragraph and so speak my final draft on to tape. I think that this situation was providential in that I was sore tempted to develop many of the concepts in the original booklet in a way that might have robbed *Restoring the Image* of its aim to be introductory and therefore accessible to as wide a readership as possible. I was trapped, mercifully, by the limitations of memory and machinery to keep quite close to the initial text.

Having my vision restored during the summer of 1979, I had inevitably begun to take on a few speaking engagements for the coming autumn and winter. These presented the novel challenge of preparing talks, lectures and sermons without the advantage of study in the conventional sense. As a long-standing diabetic I also suffered from peripheral neuritis, a condition that can lead to shooting pains in the limbs as well as, more significantly for the lover of books, to a loss of normal sensation in both hands and feet. My own fingers had become relatively numb and so the learning of Braille would have been exceptionally difficult, if not impossible. In the short term, at any rate, the only way to assimilate enough suitable material to form interesting talks was to use the Talking Book tape libraries, supplemented by the direct help of family and friends.

Apart from working out some case studies for the biennial Christian Medical Fellowship's conference in Bristol, my first challenge was in the preparation of a completely new talk on the psychological development of boys and girls, from the cradle through to their late teens, for a seminar run by the Association of Christian Teachers—again in Bristol. Modelling my thinking on Lidz's book *The Person*, I spoke directly on to a series of blank tapes as the address gradually took shape. I found that I could memorise the over-all structure as well as most of the filling, enabling me to follow a reasonably clear line of thought, together with illustrations and some application from the teacher's point of view. I was looked after for the day by our friend Janet, whom we had known for eight years or so since her student days at Bristol as an undergraduate and then as a teacher in training. I had been given twenty-five minutes to make my case and Janet had agreed to signal a distinctive cough from a predetermined part of the auditorium after twenty minutes. By the Lord's grace, keeping my memory sharp and my mind working in the right direction, I was able to finish precisely on time; Janet, mesmerised by the progression of thought, had not needed to cough!

An even bigger challenge came in the New Year. We had planned a series of sermons at Christ Church for the evening services on the theme of coping with life-situations. Appropriately, I had been asked to preach the second of the series on 'Coping with Illness'. With the help of my sister Anne and other members of the family, I was able to build up a tape library of quotations, illustrations and relevant bibical passages. I was specially conscious of the Lord's presence while I meditated on the book of Job and studied Paul's second letter to the Corinthians. Anne read me extracts from John Job's *Where is My Father? - Studies in the Book of Job*, a book I had been reading when the second retinal catastrophe struck on Colonsay. From an extensive amount of material the potential talk was honed down and the sermon took shape.

It was a strangely moving experience to have to rely so completely on the Holy Spirit's promptings of memory as I climbed up into the pulpit to face a congregation I could not see. I had been assured that the large church was packed by the volume of singing in the hymn prior to the sermon. While I preached I wondered briefly whether the silence in the pews meant that most of the congregation had quietly slipped out! However, the sense of prayerful attentiveness that pervaded the church convinced me otherwise. I felt enormously encouraged that blindness need not be a bar to my speaking engagements. Moreover, I knew most convincingly that the Lord would enable me in the preparation, memorising and delivery of talks in a way that promised a new freedom in communicating. My tendency to rely heavily on carefully made notes—a sort of insurance policy against lapse of memory or loss of inspiration—could be set aside.

The loss of sight in October, along with the persistance of the brucellosis, inevitably led to the forfeiture of the post as Clinical Assistant to Dr. Graham Rooth. I had not before experienced the situation where a uniquely suitable job—from the points of view of content, colleagueship and cash—had been snatched away at the eleventh hour. My unwellness with brucellosis softened the blow because I had seriously wondered how I would cope with the work's demands while battling with lethargy, joint-aches and feverishness. Both Graham and I were disappointed but one must believe that God is as expert at closing doors as opening them and that He had perfectly good reasons for doing so in this case. Although severely handicapped, I was still able to study, write, lecture and counsel people in need. I was beginning to appreciate, with David Scott Blackwell, the blind broadcaster and writer, that blindness could be regarded as a 'gift from God'.

In many ways, the most difficult thing for me in 1978 and 1979 was adjusting to the alternations of blindness, sight, and blindness again in the space of just over one year. I remember praying to God after the bleed on Colonsay: 'I really am prepared to accept *either* sight *or* blindness but please let's settle for one or the other'. The readjustments from books to tapes, from seeing to listening, from independence to dependence were difficult enough to want to avoid their repetition. However, I found the reversion to blindness in October 1979 was manageable in the ways already described. Further, and perhaps surprisingly, there was an almost attractive lack of complexity in the loss of vision—a stark reinforcement of the sometimes trite saying, 'What the eye doesn't see the heart doesn't grieve over'! Again, and ironically, the debilitating effects of brucellosis were almost easier to survive when the many involvements that normally beckoned could not be responded to due to a second bout of blindness. In retrospect, the combination of freshly restored sight and an inhibiting physical exhaustion during the previous summer seemed more frustrating at times since these conditions worked in opposing directions. In the autumn of 1979, loss of vision and loss of strength joined hands and threatened to wrap me around with a cocoon of undemanding simplicity.

This threat of quietism was not to persist as, to my amazement, Mr. Marmion suggested, one day in the Out-Patients, that I might be helped by a second vitrectomy! My response to this possibility was a mixture of encouragement and fear. Encouragement because the specialist told me that some diabetics had done well visually following two or even three vitrectomies on the same eye. Fear because my experience of the operation and its after effects had been quite harrowing and I remembered feeling enormous relief that, so I thought, I would never need to face such a procedure again. One of the worst aspects previously had been the nausea and vomiting post-operatively. Because I had been unable thereby to keep drinks and food down, the doctors had kept a glucose-drip going. I had become convinced, in my semi-stupor, that the intravenous infusion was pushing my blood sugar up abnormally high and that, in turn, was completing the vicious circle by producing more nausea. I feared most of all a repetition of this unpleasant situation. Good sense prevailed though. A discussion with the anaesthetist might prevent post-operative vomiting and, above all, the prospect of restored vision once more was a bait that could not be refused.

And so, one year after the first operation, and this time precisely on my birthday, I was booked at the Old Addenbrooke's Hospital, Cambridge, for a second vitrectomy on the right eye. This time it was impossible for Joy to take me without jeopardising her limited holiday quota of three weeks a year. It seemed wiser to her to have some time off for my convalescence. Julie, the friend with whom I had had some delightful walks during my previous winter of blindness, was free to drive me to Cambridge and give some moral support over the first couple of days in hospital. Her companionship was a great source of strength during the waiting hours. The Lord's loving provision always seemed a step ahead of us. As well as Julie's ready friendship, I was greeted on the ward by Debby Appleby, the daughter of some good friends of Joy's and mine, who was nursing on the Eye Ward at the time. Her supply of bonus cups of tea, her chats while the bed was being made and her prayerful attention generally were further, precious tokens of God's love through His people.

My birthday came and, garrisoned by the Lord's peace and surrounded by the prayers of friends and family, I once again awaited a potentially sight-restoring operation.

I came round from the vitrectomy in the open ward where the nursing staff could keep a better eye on this troublesome diabetic. While my consciousness came and went, I realised that I was lying flat, that my right eye was bandaged and that the operation was over. While I lay there I began to feel waves of nausea and panic. I should not, and indeed could not, move my head and yet I had an overwhelming need to sit up. Feeling increasingly claustrophobic in my prone position, I longed to rise and take deep breaths of life-

The image restored: During a sailing holiday with
Paul Berg on the Norfolk Broads, June 1981

saving air. I reached out to the bedside locker for a small, hand-carved wooden bird that Julie had given me the day before, to experience its reassuring tactility. This brief contact with the world of man-made beauty calmed me for a while. However, the sense of isolation and helpless prostration continued to torment. I wanted to cry out but could not.

I tried to pray and evoke an awareness of the Lord's presence. He was, of course, there all the time, watching me. I had a sense, in my own anguish, of His infinitely greater suffering. As I lay there I could feel something of His far profounder isolation and hour of darkness. Through it all, the agony of Golgotha seemed to supersede and engulf my own moderate sufferings. No human affliction could quite match the enormity of a God who died, naked upon a Roman cross, bearing the horror of Man's guilt from time immemorial. I saw, while I wondered, that at least the busy nurses were on my side—they comforted, reassured, gave sips of water—but this Man had been completely bereft and rejected. I suffered a little, surrounded by care—He had suffered inestimably, surrounded by a cursing crowd. In my brief span of helplessness, I drew great comfort from His all-helping helplessness. He had overcome the darkness of the abyss. His victory encompassed all.

Although there was a small bleed within a day or two of the operation, I did not experience the repeated haemorrhages of the previous year. Joy came with her practical love and comfort, I was discharged from hospital, we spent a few days with our faithful friends in Ely and so returned home.

In February 1980 *Restoring the Image* was published amidst the wonder of another restoring of the image, while the exquisite details of God's fallen but glorious world impinged once again on my battle-scarred retina.

CHAPTER SIXTEEN

THE HEALERS

'When Peter saw this, he said to them: "Men of Israel, why does this surprise you? Why do you stare at us as if by our own power or godliness we had made this man walk? The God of Abraham, Isaac and Jacob, the God of our fathers, has glorified his servant Jesus." '

Acts 3:12,13a (NIV).

(1) 'We do not allow sickness in our new home because we know faith and scriptures can drive it away, and Jesus bore our diseases for us'.
(2) 'Blessed are those who expect nothing for they shall not be disappointed'.
Two views quoted in Francis MacNutt's *Healing*

'Twenty years ago I believed that absolutely, come hell or high water, it was God's will for everybody, without exception, to be healed. But I've watched this thing very carefully. Now I see that we can't demand or command that God do anything . . .'

Francis MacNutt: *Healing*

DURING THE 1960'S AND 1970'S THE SO-CALLED 'CHARISMATIC movement' gathered momentum, initially in the States and later throughout many other countries of the world. This influence of spiritual renewal has become increasingly well documented. Some of its initial excesses—in insisting that all Christians should have a second, post-conversion experience of empowering called Spirit-Baptism and should speak in tongues, and that all illness should be healed by faith in the Holy Spirit's power—have been modified in many circles by a more circumspect theology which seeks to pay attention to the whole of the scriptural revelation. Along with its over-defined understanding of the long neglected gifts of the Spirit, charismatic renewal, following its more divisive adolescence, has been maturing healthily, infusing church life with a greater freedom in worship, a more loving commitment to fellowship, a more self-sacrificial concern about mission and community—all undergirded by a greater faith in an all-sufficient God.

Inevitably, as a Christian doctor who had also been a diabetic for over two decades, I had to sort out my thinking in relation to the pressing issues raised by the 'charismatic movement'. In the late 1960's I had studied scriptural perspectives on Spirit-Baptism and speaking in tongues to try to help the 'Young People' at Galleywood in their own spiritual growth. In the autumn of 1974 I became part of a lively correspondence in the *Church of England Newspaper* in response to a leading article by Michael Harper in which he seemed to be arguing for a two-stage experience for the Christian: regeneration and being 'baptised in the Spirit'—although acknowledging that the two are 'sometimes experienced at the same time'.[1] Soon after, at the first Senior Evangelical Anglican Conference, an important dialogue began between some key 'charismatic' and 'non-charismatic' church leaders. It was a joy to meet Michael Harper at a meeting in Bristol in December and to be strongly aware of our oneness in the Spirit.

In 1975, at the end of January, I attended a local study evening in which another Anglican minister argued very powerfully and systematically a two-stage theology with signs following. As a friend suggested afterwards, I felt like 'dog eats dog in front of cat' in retrospect because I had allowed myself to question the speaker's deductions too insistently in front of an audience of believers, mostly of a 'charismatic' persuasion, and of more traditional church attenders. I wrote and apologised to the speaker but still felt uneasy at some of the pastoral implications of his views. It seemed to me

1 Michael Harper: 'Different sides of the Charismatic Divide' CEN 11 October 1974
Roger Hurding: my first letter 25 October and following correspondence.

that all Christians are subject to the regenerating work of the Holy Spirit by definition and that Paul's statement in 1 Corinthians 12:13 is all-inclusive for believers: 'For by one Spirit we were all baptised into one body—Jews or Greeks, slaves or free—and all were made to drink of one Spirit'. Similarly, I was convinced that all Christians are charismatic, i.e. gifted by the Spirit 'who apportions to each one individually as he wills' (1 Cor 12:11). This view did not deny that many believers are muddled about their birthright of Spirit-Baptism and neglect their God-given gifts. More positively, I felt the essential challenge to Christ's disciples was one of continuous filling by His Spirit (Eph 5:18), of an openness to the receiving and right use of His supernatural gifts (1 Cor 12:31, 14:1) and the need to walk the path of fruitful obedience (John 15:4-8, Gal 5:22-26). I realised that many Christians experience a 'second crisis' in their spiritual growth; this event may, for example, be a fresh (or first) infilling by the Holy Spirit, a new awareness of sin, a greater opening up of the life to the Lordship of Christ or a new commitment to mission. Others, of course, have more than two crisis-points in their Christian pilgrimage. My difficulty was that I could not see how it helped an understanding of these crises to apply the New Testament dimension of Baptism in (by, of) the Spirit (which seemed to be so closely allied to Christ's work of regeneration in the lives of *all* believers) as a label to cover an experience which all Christians should seek as a *further* and distinctive work of the Spirit. Such systematisation seemed to rob God of the freedom to bring individual men and women into willing submission to Him in His own ways.

It saddened me that the wonder of God's sanctifying work in our lives should be the subject of so much heated interchange. I have to admit that I contributed to that heat in the ways I have already mentioned as well as in private conversation with fellow Christians. It is against this background that I tried to wrestle with the issue of miraculous healing for my patients, for those who came for pastoral advice and, later, for myself.

Sometime before I entered the more public fray of the 'charismatic debate'—back in 1971—I had an experience of trying to help one of my patients who had been attending a local church where the importance of healing was strongly stressed. The episode had powerful connotations for my own situation because my patient was not only a medical student but a diabetic! She had been persuaded by one of her church leaders, quoting scriptures such as

1 Peter 2:24b, that the Lord had died for her healing and that, therefore, her cure could be claimed by faith. She was convinced by the argument and so, during the evening service later that day, she went forward to seek prayer for healing. The next morning she stopped her insulin.

Three days later I was phoned by her spiritual adviser who told me the outline of the story and that Hilary—the student—was now ill. I drove to the hall of residence where she lived to find a drowsy patient, her lips cracked with thirst, tossing and turning in bed while a girl-friend mounted guard in a prayer vigil. 'Hilary', I said, 'you are obviously in the state of an untreated diabetic. You know that in time, medically speaking, you could sink into a coma and perhaps die. I propose therefore to give you an injection of insulin—we can then talk things over tomorrow when you should feel better'. There was some resistance to this course from both patient and friend—but Hilary acquiesced to the sense of this approach, at least for the time being.

The next day she was something of her old self although clearly perplexed at her physical deterioration following the 'prayer of faith'. I gently asked her how she had been so sure that the Lord would heal her miraculously of diabetes. Was she certain that He would be more glorified in such a healing than in the disciplined life of a well-controlled diabetic? We talked, considered other scriptural perspectives on God's power to keep us in and through affliction, and prayed together.

I learnt many years later that, three months after this experience, she was repeatedly assured by her fellow Christians at the church she attended that, in time, she would be healed. With this consideration in mind, a few weeks later again, she asked a church elder what he thought about increasing her insulin because her symptoms seemed to warrant this adjustment. He replied, 'If you can't believe the Lord for healing, I believe you will fall away from Him'. Within herself she felt this sweeping assertion to be nonsense.

Even so, it took another three years of readjustment to her continuing need for insulin for Hilary to be able to visit me once more and talk through the implications of her initial conviction of the accessibility of miraculous healing, of her subsequent pre-comatosed state on stopping insulin, of the apparent insensitivity of some of her spiritual advisers and of her present good health as a controlled diabetic. Six years later again—in the summer of

1980—now a successful general practitioner working energetically in a rural part of the West Country—she was able to reflect that she was probably a wiser and more understanding doctor as a result of her years of diabetes.

What can be said following a story like Hilary's? Does it mean that her faith was insufficient, as was implied by some of her fellow Christians? If so—what did Jesus mean when He talked of faith as small 'as a grain of mustard seed' (Matt 17:20) being sufficient to move mountains? Does it mean that God does not—or even cannot—heal diabetics? Surely not! The healing of a condition of chronic deficiency of one of the body's hormones cannot be beyond an omnipotent God who can raise the dead. Does it mean that God does not heal physical ills miraculously today? Again, there is surely too much evidence of miraculous healing throughout the world in the last decade or two to hold this view rigorously. Does it mean that God is sovereign and, although He delights in the trusting prayers of His people, He has the prerogative to say 'Yes', 'No' or 'Not yet' to our requests? It is this last possibility that I believe is the key to an understanding of a story like Hilary's.

As I have described in Chapter Thirteen, Joy and I began to face the issue of God's will in relation to my progressive blindness in the spring of 1976 following our family holiday on the Isle of Mull. After the Service of Commitment at Christ Church, Clifton in the May of that year, a good friend lovingly criticised the service for its lack of expectancy of healing. He felt that definite healing should have been prayed for perseveringly and that the tenor of the readings chosen over-emphasised God's all-sufficiency to keep His people in the midst of their sufferings and neglected His power to heal miraculously. Our friend's assessment may have been well founded but Joy and I were seeking to respond to the Spirit's direction for our precise situation, and He seemed to point us repeatedly to Paul's experience of the 'thorn in the flesh' and the way God answered the apostle's prayer for its removal by His assurance of His more than adequate grace for Paul's state of weakness.

Through the winter following my first serious loss of sight, the issue of my blindness was a pressing one not only for our family but for many of our Christian friends and for the fellowship at Christ Church in general. God's people in Clifton, at St. Peter's Harold Wood where my parents still worshipped, at Shamley Green—Joy's mother's home village, in Surbiton where my sister lived, and in many other pockets up and down the country, prayed constantly and believingly for my healing. Twice during the sixteen months of intermittent blindness, a group of church leaders from Christ Church visited Conifers to lay hands on me and pray for healing. The house-group that I led was specially faithful in prayer and, on one or two occasions, we broke bread together while we joined our worship of the crucified and risen Lord with our requests for health.

Against this background of sustained and sustaining prayer, we considered the possibility of seeking out someone with a gift of healing. We still saw God as the source of all wholeness but were prepared to see that He may choose to mediate that health through certain of His servants. A curate from another parish recommended a retired clergyman who exercised a healing ministry from his home in the Mendips. So, in the April of 1979 soon after Simon's return from France with the fateful, Savoie cheese, Joy and I visited this godly man. We talked through the issues at length and, although our theology gently parted company with his at one or two points, we saw this meeting primarily as an encounter with Our Lord and His power to heal. At this stage, my first vitrectomy and its subsequent bleeding were three months behind us. Just over three weeks later, Rosemary Barker's facial features began to appear out of the fog!

Later that year, after a month or two into the second period of blindness, I was urged by a friend to seek healing through a woman from the Midlands who was a key member of a house-church and was said to have had many experiences of dramatic healings through her ministry. Again, it seemed wrong to refuse any legitimate channel of healing and so Joy and I arranged a rendezvous with this lady at the vicarage in Clifton one Saturday morning.

There were five of us present: the healer, probably in her early thirties, two younger women (one who worked with her and our mutual friend), Joy and myself. We sat in a semi-circle about the hearth of an upstairs' room and discussed my condition—the diabetes and the resultant blindness, as well as the undulating symptoms of brucellosis. Gloria, the healer, guided the conversation and at one point early in our discussion queried whether I had been baptised in the Spirit. I replied that I had because Jesus is the Spirit-Baptiser and I had opened my life to Him. She was not happy with this apparently unexpected reply and urged that healing was commonly contingent with receiving the Spirit. I gently but firmly said that I could not set aside my understanding of the scriptural perspective on the matter so readily and, if she persisted with my need for such a 'second experience' then and there as a passport to healing, we would have to agree to differ and go our separate ways without rancour. We were not simply quibbling over words—we seemed to differ fundamentally in our understanding of the Spirit's work in the life of the believer. Although I was open to new blessings and insights from the Lord, it did not seem right to seek, as a Spirit-baptised Christian, the Baptism of the Holy Spirit as a novel entrée to healing.

Our dialogue continued with an occasional contribution from her younger co-worker. I had to declare in reply to another leading question that I could not be completely sure that God would heal me miraculously either immediately or gradually this side of Glory. She was most unhappy with this apparent lack of faith. I said that, in all honesty, I could not read the scriptures and, at the same time, dismiss the story of Job's divinely permitted suffering and delayed healing, and the account of Paul's triple prayer for deliverance with God's loving answer 'No—not that way, Paul'. The healer's replies took the wind out of my sails. 'You can only claim Job's experience if you are as good as he was; you can only identify with Paul's situation if you have had the sort of visions of God that he had'. I had not the heart to argue with these extreme particularisations of the experiences of two great men of God. I have wondered since, on the principle she enunciated, whether one can draw any comfort or teaching from the life of Christ Himself. Gloria rendered me further speechless when she capped her second point with the story of a paralysed man who was dramatically cured when he repented of the view I held with regard to Paul's 'thorn in the flesh'.

We had reached an impasse in our discussion and so, wisely, we set theorising aside and prayed together, looking to God for His healing. After some minutes of collective prayer, Gloria rose and came to stand behind me, laying her warm hands on my head. She had seemed rather tense and, perhaps, unnerved by her encounter, but now she prayed with single-minded vehemence. She cried to God for my healing, commanding diabetes, blindness and brucellosis to depart. While she agonised her fingers kneaded into my scalp. We each echoed her prayers in our hearts, reaching out to God in our trust. Joy and I thanked and embraced our sisters in Christ and made our way out into the winter streets of Clifton. Over the following days my prayers took on a more confidently expectant note for God's continuing healing. Two months later I had the second vitrectomy and the clearing of vision began once more. The symptoms of brucellosis continued to undulate through the next two years or so.

CHAPTER SEVENTEEN

COPING WITH ILLNESS

'So I went down to the potter's house, and there he was working at his wheel. And the vessel he was making of clay was spoiled in the potter's hand, and he reworked it into another vessel, as it seemed good to the potter to do'.

Jeremiah 18: 3, 4

'Weakness and pain helped me to study how to die; that set me studying how to live'.

Richard Baxter (1615-1691)

WHAT UNDERSTANDING OF THE SIGNIFICANCE OF ILLNESS AND the place of healing can we glean from experiences like those of Hilary and myself? Or, more relevantly, what principles can we learn from the scriptures in these areas and how do our personal life-situations fit in with those principles?

First of all, we see that illness, or more generally adversity and affliction, was not part of God's original design. 'God saw all that he had made, and it was very good' (Gen 1:31/NIV).

Further, stresses and strains were inevitable results of Man's disobedience. Sexual embarrassment (Gen 3:7), a sense of guilt before the Lord (3: 8,9) and blame-shifting (3:12, 13) point to new stresses in self-awareness and in relationships with others and the Creator. These inner disharmonies are reflected in pain, toil and trouble in the fabric of everyday life; the creation ordinances of family and responsible stewardship (Gen 1:26-30) were soon contaminated (Gen 3:16-19) and further sullied by jealousy, unrighteous anger and murder (Gen 4:2-8).

Man's sinful rebellion has been very productive, and the rest of history has been lived out in the face of a multitude of stresses and strains. Illness, with its physical, psychological and spiritual aspects, needs to be seen against this general background of the disruption of God's good creation.

Let us now consider the situation where you or I become ill. Let us see how far we can achieve an understanding of *why* we have become ill. Let us go further, though, and try to clarify what we can, and should, do about our affliction. In turn, let us look at the wider question of coping with illness.

I. *Why am I Ill?*

Quite often behind the question 'Why am I ill?' lurks a more disturbing query: 'What have I done to deserve this?' There is a presentiment that illness is something of a punishment and the greater the wickedness, the greater the affliction. This view of a simple and inevitable connection between sin and suffering has always been widespread. The disciples, with their Jewish backgrounds, seemed to regard illness in this way. On meeting the man born blind they asked Jesus, 'Rabbi, who sinned, this man or his parents, that he was born blind?' (John 9:1-3). They assumed that someone within the family circle *must* have sinned for the tragedy to have arisen. Jesus's reply does not argue that the link between sin and illness *never* exists but that, in this instance at least, there were quite different perspectives on the issue : 'It was not that this man sinned, or his parents, but that the works of God might be made manifest in him'. The Lord was not claiming the sinlessness of two generations of this particular family but that there was no direct causal link between their individual sinning and the particular affliction of one of its members.

Of course, there are many illnesses which we can bring upon ourselves through neglect, excess and other sinful behaviour. Common examples in our consumerist, hedonistic society include coronary artery disease and osteoarthritis related, in turn, to being overweight from undisciplined eating; cancer of the lung, emphysema and recurring bronchitis from heavy smoking; and a wide range of venereal diseases contracted as a result of sexual promiscuity. Furthermore, our anxious, resentful and self-absorbed attitudes can contribute to an even longer list of psychosomatic conditions which include, in at least some instances, intractable headaches, muscular tensions, skin rashes, wheezing attacks, duodenal ulcers, spastic colon, various forms of colitis, high blood pressure and some types of arthritis. Our wrong ways of thinking and their linkage with bodily symptoms may be reflected when we say, 'You're a pain in the neck', 'You make me choke', 'He makes me sick', 'I can't stomach her', 'So-and-so makes my flesh creep'. The psalmist indicates the way physical symptoms can relate to unconfessed sin : 'When I declared not my sin, my body wasted away' (Ps 32:3).

There is no doubt, too, that many of the world's diseases result from Man's inhumanity to Man. The materialistic self-centredness of the richer nations and the richer minorities within poorer nations continue to contribute to a vast amount of human misery in terms of malnutrition, tuberculosis, leprosy, many parasitic diseases and a wide range of infections that can be killers amongst deprived peoples—such as measles, typhoid fever, cholera and diphtheria. The only attention that Lazarus's skin ulcers had at the gate of the rich man was from the street dogs. Diseases of neglect can be laid at the gate of those who feast 'sumptuously every day'—those who expose themselves to the diseases of excess.

However, many of us do not suffer from illnesses for which we, or others, are directly culpable. In trying to understand our own situation we can, I believe, take comfort from the story of Job for his experience argues for all time that there is no *inevitable* link between suffering and sin—between becoming ill and deserving to.

As well as experiencing the loss of sons and daughters, servants and livestock, compounded by the loss of his wife's respect and the tedious diatribes of his judgemental friends, Job contracted and endured an appalling state of illness, whatever the exact diagnosis was. Covered with intensely irritating sores, he looked so emaciated and disfigured that his friends hardly recognised him. His foetid breath, pain-racked body, insomnia and profound depression must have been the sorest of trials for himself, his family and anyone strong enough to visit him. His sense of desolation was such that he cried : 'Let the day perish wherein I was born, and the night which said, "A man-child is conceived" ' (Job 3:3).

It is extremely unlikely that, whatever illness you or I may get, it will be quite as devastating as Job's wide range of afflictions (although at the time we may find it impossible to think of anything worse than our particular lot!). John Job, in his book *Where is My Father?* makes this point very tellingly: 'Job is an everyman figure and there is a sense in which all our symptoms converge in him'.[1]

And yet we read in the prologue of the book of Job that he was 'blameless and upright, one who feared God, and turned away from evil' (1:1). There was no sense in which this godly man *deserved* his illness and suffering. If Job's grim afflictions were undeserved then you and I, in our lesser adversities, can take comfort.

How do we, then, try to answer the question 'Why am I ill?' when there is no clear, causal link with our own folly or neglect by others? Although the question can be virtually unanswerable in terms of the here and now, we need to see that any answer we attempt to make is caught up in the realms of God's sovereignty and the Enemy's subversion.

One picture that many have alluded to with respect to the sovereignty of God and the mystery of suffering is that of God as a Master-Weaver who is making a beautiful tapestry with the lives of His people down through history. Individual believers and the church generally may not appreciate that there is a loving design involved while they are undergoing affliction. It is as if that, for most of the time, we can only see the obverse of the art-work where the skeins of silk seem to make little sense in terms of colour and pattern. This apparent confusion may be rendered even more puzzling in that an Enemy is at work too, seeking to undermine the Master-Weaver's artistry. Although distorting images and discordant colours may thus be introduced subversively, God has control of the over-all design and is able to turn the conflicting elements to His advantage. Individual strands of silk that refuse to be pliant in His hands may have to be discarded. From time to time most of us will catch a glimpse of the glory of the work in spite of our tangled vantage-point.

Job was aware of God's power to interweave the affairs of men and women. In reply to his wife's taunt, he said, 'Shall we receive good at the hand of God, and shall we not receive evil?' (2:9, 10). He did not have the privilege that we have of reading the prologue to his story and therefore was probably not aware of the Enemy's restricted part in suffering. We are able to read that Satan was the instigator and perpetrator of these particular adversities (1:9-12; 2:4-7) although his activity was permitted *and limited* by the Lord (1:12; 2:6).

1 Job, John, *Where is my Father?* (Epworth, 1977) p31.

It seems that God allows the Adversary to afflict us, but He also offers to be with us in the midst of our suffering to help us win all sorts of victories for Him if we will permit it.[2] King Nebuchadnezzar, reflecting on his recent, bizarre mental illness, was able to say of the sovereign God: '. . . he does according to his will in the host of heaven and among the inhabitants of the earth; and none can stay his hand or say to him, "What doest thou?" (Dan 4:35).

When, following my first, eight month period of blindness, I emerged into the daylight to be met by the exhausting symptoms of brucellosis, I cried, 'Lord, what *are* you up to? Haven't nearly thirty years of diabetes and a long winter of blindness been enough? Why give with one hand and take away with the other? Why keep me through eight months of darkness, allow me the thrill of sight again and the eagerness to come to grips with the visual world once more and then afflict me so that I have not the strength to re-engage with life?' To some extent these questions have seemed unanswerable and they may remain so this side of Glory. However, the story of Job has encouraged me and the perspective of Hebrews 12 has made some sense of the switchback of incapacity : 'God is treating you as sons; for what son is there whom his father does not discipline?' (12:7), and again, 'he disciplines us for our good, that we may share his holiness' (10). To know that sonship can be a painful experience and that the pain confirms (rather than denies) the Father's love has helped during the darker moments of the past few years.

However, when, in the autumn of 1979, I went blind again we could not help but cry, 'Why do you keep at us so, God? We really *have* got the message that we should depend on You. Lessons One and Two have been sufficient; Lesson Three really is unnecessary!' Here again the answers lie in the mystery and wonder of God's great tapestry as well as in the distortions of the Enemy's seditious activity. Our part has been to go on learning.

II *What should I do if I become Ill?*

Given the difficulty sometimes of answering the question, 'Why am I ill?', let us now be more positive about the handling of illness if and when it comes our way.

First and foremost, we should pray—and many of us do, whether

2 For a fuller treatment of this point see Edith Schaeffer, *Affliction* (Hodder 1978).

we are Christians or not—especially if we are faced with serious illness. We may need to admit that we have brought unwellness upon ourselves by the neglect or abuse of our bodies, or by persisting in wrong attitudes. This awareness should lead us to repentance, forgiveness and new resolves to live disciplined and loving lives. Our praying may help us to see that we are exhausted and that this particular illness is really a blessing to give us some respite from our busy lives and a chance to re-appraise our priorities. Unless we have a mild condition which invariably clears up speedily, it is natural and appropriate for us to seek healing. And in doing this we should see God as the source of all wholeness and the One who chooses to heal in a variety of ways.

Healing has been defined as the 'restoration to normal health of a person suffering from an organic or psychological disorder' and we all have some idea what we mean by 'normal health'. God can restore our health (or, for some of us, give it for the first time) by natural, medical and miraculous means:

(a) *Natural Healing*: God has made our bodies and minds with amazing powers of natural healing. The vast majority of us—if we are reasonably well-nourished—recover readily, with only symptomatic treatment, from such viral infections as the common cold, influenza, measles, rubella and chickenpox. Our ability to recuperate following a sprained ankle, a partially torn muscle or a skin wound depends on a whole range of complex, God-made mechanisms in body fluids and tissues. Many of our psychological and emotional disturbances, too, have a natural cycle and rate of recovery.

(b) *Medical Healing*: The Creator God has made the Earth and its resources for Man to be steward over. Many of the raw materials of the Earth's crust—animal, vegetable and mineral—are extracted, refined and used to aid healing, e.g. hormones extracted from animals for replacement treatment as in diabetes; digitalis taken from the foxglove to help control certain cardiac disorders; various pain-relievers whose source is the opium poppy; and organic mercury compounds which can be used to help remove excessive body fluid.

Furthermore, Man has a God-given ingenuity to develop even more sophisticated drugs, to carry out intricate research to help combat disease and to engineer more effective and venturesome operative techniques and other treatments. Such aids to healing should be viewed with gratitude to our Creator. 'Everything created by God is good, and nothing is to be rejected if it is received with thanksgiving'. (I Tim 4:4).

The story of the healing of King Hezekiah is instructive in this respect. Faced with a severe carbuncle and, presumably, septicaemia (today, the latter is usually preventable through the use of antibiotics), he was told by Isaiah : 'Thus says the Lord, "Set your house in order; for you shall die, you shall not recover" ' (II Kings 20:1). We then read : 'Hezekiah turned his face to the wall, and prayed to the Lord . . . '(2). His prayer, recorded in Isaiah 38, was persevering and specific: 'I cry for help until morning' (13) and 'Oh, restore me to health and make me live!' (16). Following his prayers and tears, the King was told by God through the prophet Isaiah: 'I will heal you . . . I will add fifteen years to your life. I will deliver you and this city out of the hand of the King of Assyria' (II Kings 20: 5, 6). And then—and we should not be surprised, if we see healing on the broad canvas of our Creator God—Isaiah prescribed medical treatment—a good, old-fashioned poultice to draw out the pus from the carbuncle: 'Bring a cake of figs. And let them take and lay it on the boil, that he may recover' (7).

In my own situation, I am greatly indebted to medical treatment and the skill and compassion of general practitioners, diabetic specialists, general and orthopaedic surgeons, ophthalmologists, dieticians, nurses, physiotherapists, occupational therapists, radiographers, radiologists, ward-orderlies and hospital porters who have been party to my care and healing through the years. I have no difficulty in seeing the discovery, extraction, purification and availability of insulin, the advice on correct diet, the harnessing of laser beams for accurate photocoagulation, and the surgeon's imagination, courage and skill to pioneer and carry out operations of vitrectomy as under the mandate of the God who told Man to 'fill the earth and subdue it'.

(c) *Miraculous Healing*: C. S. Lewis has defined a miracle, in popular language, as 'an interference with Nature by supernatural power'.[4] Healing by miracle is not more divine than natural and medical healing, although God is seen more clearly and dramatically where the healing is miraculous. In our short-sightedness, we tend to say, 'Isn't the body marvellous?' when the healing is natural; 'Isn't the doctor/nurse/etc. marvellous?' when the healing is medical and, 'Isn't God marvellous?' when it is miraculous. God

3 Lewis, CS *Miracles* (Collins, 1947) p.9

ultimately should be glorified in all three aspects of healing.

With regard to Our Lord's healing described in the gospels, we find that they were mostly of people with conditions that were—and often still are—incurable: blindness, deafness, dumbness, paralysis, a leprosy-like disease, and a variety of undefined, fatal illnesses. This may mean that Jesus's healing ministry was essentially one to those where natural and medical healing were not taking place. The woman with menorrhagia 'who had suffered much under many physicians' (Mark 5:26) is a clear example of a patient where medical treatment had been of no avail. Again, this perspective fits with the wider sweep of the scriptures in terms of the Lord God being the ultimate Healer.

From these considerations, I would like to argue that if you and I develop a serious and protracted illness, especially if there is no known cure and medical treatment is unlikely to help, then it is appropriate for us to pray to God for His direct intervention. He may grant a sudden and complete cure, as in the miracles of Jesus recorded in the New Testament. He may miraculously modify the expected course of a disease so that healing comes in time. He may use natural, medical and miraculous elements in combating serious illness. He may say 'No' to the prayer for a miracle, carrying out a different miracle in supporting us through months, years or even a life-time of discomfort or disability.

I believe we see these alternative answers to our prayers for release from affliction throughout the pages of scripture. For Hezekiah, the prayer for healing was granted speedily. For Job, his fortunes were eventually restored but, in the darkness of his suffering, he was not to know this. For Paul, his prayer for deliverance from his 'thorn in the flesh' (and, whatever the 'thorn' was, its persistence and unpleasantness point to a general principle with regard to prayers for release from suffering) was answered, in effect, by, 'No, Paul. I have heard your prayer but I will not change your circumstances'. God's words, 'My grace is sufficient for you, for my power is made perfect in weakness' made sense for the afflicted apostle—and they should, too, for you and me if the Lord permits the continuance of our adversities.

Have I experienced miraculous healing during the years of blindness and brucellosis? I cannot say—although God clearly knows the answer to the question! The sudden improvements in vision have ostensibly been the result of medical treatment whose ultimate source, I have argued, is God. However, in the late summer of 1981 Mr. Marmion talked of the diabetic retinopathy 'burning itself out', something that has been seen increasingly now that the results of vitrectomies can be more fully assessed. A small bleed in the right eye only three months after this encouraging statement and the discovery of a fresh batch of new blood vessels have had a sobering effect on the evaluation of healing. The brucellosis, two and a half years afters its contraction, continued to trouble—though less severely. Here a natural healing process seemed to be operating although my medical experience told me that this infection can become a life-long companion.

Many Christians claim that, because Christ died for our sicknesses as well as our sins (Isaiah 53:4; Matt 8:14-17; I Peter 2:24), all believers have a new birthright to healing, claimed by faith, for the here and now. I do not believe that this simple linking between the death of Our Lord, our faith and the inevitability of miraculous healing in this life accords with the full biblical revelation. I do believe that all Christians have the promise of complete wholeness realised in the bodily resurrection (I Cor 15; I John 3:2) but that participation in this consummate and certain triumph is only partially experienced in this life. Just as we have no prerogative for sinless perfection or complete health of mind in the here and now, I believe we cannot vouchsafe entire wholeness of body in the present. The Lord, of course, breaks through into our temporal existence with His bounty so that many of us do discover health on the road to Glory. We cannot claim this as our right.

III *What can I learn through Illness?*

If God allows chronic or serious illness in your life or mine, and says 'No' or 'Not yet' to our prayers for healing, how can we cope? What can we learn that is positive through what may be a harrowing experience?

First of all, let us realise that we are in good company when we ask 'Why?' in the face of suffering. I suspect that King Hezekiah asked this question for, in time, he was able to say of his illness: 'Surely it was for my benefit that I suffered such anguish' (Isaiah 38:17). Job asked of God, 'Why hast thou made me thy mark?' (Job 7:20) and, although he did not know of the proving of his worth that God was allowing through satanic attack, he eventually came through into a new awareness of God's power and sovereignty, and his own unworthiness—so that he could say : 'I had heard of thee by the hearing of the ear, but now my eye sees thee; therefore I despise myself, and repent in dust and ashes' (42:5, 6). It is extremely likely that the man born blind cried to Jehovah, 'Why me?'; Our Lord's answer to the parallel question from his disciples was '. . . this happened so that the work of God might be displayed in his life' (John 9: 3/NIV). We have already seen God's word to Paul the apostle in the face of his prayers and, presumably, questions: 'My grace is sufficient for you, for my power is made perfect in weakness'.

There is a sense in which Jesus himself prayed 'Why me?' when he cried from the cross, 'My God, my God, why hast thou forsaken me?' (Matt 27:46). There is no evidence that Jesus was ill, as we understand the word. Did He ever have ear-ache or a viral infection? We do not know. However, we do know that He suffered. He endured pangs of hunger, the anguish of thirst, sleepless nights, the hostility of others in their hypocrisy, pride or dumbwittedness, the betrayal of Judas, the agonising dilemma of Gethsemane, the desertion of His friends, the most unjust of trials, the taunts of Herod, the compromise of Pilate, the brutality of the soldiers and the cruellest of physical deaths. And beyond all this, He suffered supremely in the awful spiritual darkness when He bore your sin and mine—the sins of the whole of mankind from the beginning of time to the end of history—'in his body on the tree'. We can see why the writer of Hebrews wrote, 'for we have not a high priest who is unable to sympathise with our weaknesses' (4:15).

Let us, then, as we ask, 'What can you and I learn through our illnesses?', be encouraged, not only by the story of Job and his appalling afflictions, but by the sufferings of Our Lord who was 'made like his brethren in every respect' (Heb 2:17).

(a) *What can we learn within Ourselves?*

(i) *Endurance*: We still talk of the patience of Job but as we study the book of Job we discover that he was extremely impatient with both his friends and with God. In James 5:11 we read : 'You have heard of the steadfastness of Job'. Steadfastness, or patient endurance, described Job's spirit of survival better than the simple word 'patience'.

There is a story, quoted by John Job in his *Where is My Father?*, that the Emperor Nero once sent his own mother to sea in a Roman galley. His motives were far from the best as he arranged that holes should be bored in the ship's hull! In spite of these machinations, somehow the indomitable woman stayed afloat. It has been said of her that she showed 'unsinkability'. [4]

'Unsinkability' was the quality that the suffering Job demonstrated.

(ii) *Growth in Character*: In Romans 5:3, Pauls lists a sequence of positive attributes which has affliction as its starting point: 'We rejoice in our sufferings, knowing that suffering produces endurance, and endurance produces character . . . ' We know of course that there is nothing automatic about the constructive direction that adversity can take us in. Somerset Maugham in *The Moon and Sixpence* has commented that suffering can lead to other less desirable qualities: 'It is not true that suffering ennobles the character; happiness does that sometimes, but suffering, for the most part, makes men petty and vindictive'. [5]

However, as Christians, we should seek the path that leads through suffering to a strengthening of character, remembering that that is the aim which our Father seeks for us. 'For the moment all discipline seems painful rather than pleasant; later it yields the peaceful fruit of righteousness to those who have been trained by it.' (Heb 12:11).

In her first book, Joni Eareckson described her own experience of extreme suffering and how God changed her character through it. In 1967, this seventeen-year-old American girl dived into the sea and broke her neck. Her life seemed to be devastated within seconds. However, God taught her through the tears, the anger and the self-pity. In the conclusion of the book she wrote 'I'm really thankful He did something to get my attention and change me'. [6]

(b) *What can we learn in relation to Others?:*

(i) *Negatively*: Job's wife had been through it too! She had also lost property, livestock, servants, and seven sons and three daughters. Emerging from these catastrophes, she saw her husband sitting among the ashes; he was unpleasant to look at and unpleasant to smell! Job admitted later, 'I am still repulsive to my wife' (19:17). Whatever her feelings had been initially, she was now bitter and resentful. She cried to her husband, 'Do you still hold fast your integrity? Curse God, and die' (2:9).

Job's friends sat with him 'on the ground seven days and seven

4 Job, John, *op.cit.* p.65.
5 Somerset Maugham, W., *The Moon and Sixpence* (Pan Books, 1919) p.64.
6 Eareckson, Joni, *Joni* (Pickering & Inglis, 1978) p.206.

nights' (2:13). This was taking non-directive counselling to an extreme and their group silence did not seem to help the sufferer. When they spoke, however, they helped him even less! The phrase 'Job's comforter' has become a by-word for 'how not to help a friend in need'.

It is not surprising that Job later declared: 'My kinsfolk and my close friends have failed me' (19:14).

During my few years of intermittent blindness, and brucellosis, the sheer persistence of my symptoms has been a great strain on those around me. At times, it was specially difficult for Joy—having a husband who missed visual cues with monotonous predictability, who was often passive when quick decisions needed making and who was unable to deal with some of the simplest practical tasks. On one occasion a particularly forthright friend said, on hearing that I was ill yet again, 'The trouble with you, Roger, is that your illnesses are too interesting! First diabetic retinopathy and now —brucellosis!' Behind the observation, I thought I detected something of the exasperation of knowing someone who kept becoming ill.

These anecdotal points remind us that there are at least two sides to our illness. You and I may suffer, but so do those around us often in ways that are rendered less bearable by a sense of helplessness or even hopelessness. Such problems can be made much worse where our illness is a chronic one. The sympathy of family and friends may last well for a few weeks but their resources may be severely taxed if the condition goes on for months or even years.

As we study the book of Job we see that this difficulty can cut both ways. Although Job's friends wearied him with their theological niceties and harsh judgements, he, for his part, treated them far from well. He rounded on them irritably: 'How then will you comfort me with empty nothings? There is nothing left of your answers but falsehood' (21:34).

When ill we need to remember that friendship is one of the best medicines. We need to resist the temptation to talk endlessly about our symptoms or to luxuriate in self-pity when our friends visit us. Even though we may be seriously ill, they are still our friends—and friendship demands a mutuality of interest and caring. If we indulge ourselves in our illnesses, we should not be surprised if the rate of visiting gradually drops!

(ii) *Postively*: Perhaps one of the most positive statements in the Scriptures that makes sense of suffering is this:

> 'Blessed be the God and Father of our Lord Jesus Christ, the Father of mercies and God of all comfort, who comforts us in all our affliction, so that we may be able to comfort those who are in any affliction, with the comfort with which we ourselves are comforted by God' (II Cor 1:3,4).

The Greek word *parakaleo*, which is here translated 'to comfort', occurs 109 times in the New Testament. Its meaning elsewhere includes 'to invite' and 'to exhort'. A cognate of this verb is the noun *parakletos* which is used exclusively by John and is a name that refers to the Holy Spirit—variously translated as Advocate, Helper and Comforter. In II Corinthians 1:3, 4, the idea of comforting includes the stronger concepts of 'consoling' and 'encouraging'. In the common stock of these Greek words we can sense the link between the Holy Spirit's work of encouragement and that of the Christian believer.

Bringing these strands together, we see that an important perspective of suffering for the Christian is that the afflicted believer is consoled and encouraged by the Father through the Spirit. This strengthening is not a dead-end. It is meant to be productive. The encouraged one should reach out to others in their adversities to help and console. Those who exercise this loving ministry have been called 'missionaries of comfort'.

Caroline Cansdale, to whom I have dedicated the poem with which this book concludes, was a 'missionary of comfort'. In the summer of 1979, a month or so after I had begun to see again following the first vitrectomy and in the early weeks of the mysterious 'pyrexia of unknown origin', Joy and I chatted with her during a Church picnic at Blaise Castle near Bristol one Sunday afternoon. Caroline (then in her early thirties) and her husband Michael were the parents of three fine boys and had been good Christian friends of ours for many years. She had recently noticed some ominously enlarged glands in her neck but had just heard that the hospital tests were negative. We rejoiced with her on that sunny afternoon amidst the gathering of forty to fifty people from Christ Church, Clifton. We were doubly relieved for her as there was a strong history of cancer on the female side of her family and malignancy was a real dread to her.

However, the relief was short-lived, because later that summer a most virulent form of cancer of the body's lymph glands was diagnosed. Radiotherapy and chemotherapy became the order of her day and through the autumn Caroline became too weak to be out of bed for more than a few minutes at a time. Fair-haired, beautiful and always immaculately groomed and dressed—the stress of her declining appearance was acutely painful to her. In time, X-ray treatment led to the loss of her hair and to the advent of a troublesome skin condition. The wasting disease she suffered from emaciated her body rapidly so that by the end of October her appearance was almost skeletal. Added to this precipitate decline of her physical beauty were the wretched symptoms of nausea, protracted pain, loss of voice and a recurring cough.

During the last four weeks of her life I visited her a few times, chauffered by one or two friends since I had recently lost my sight again during our holiday on Colonsay. I ascended the stairway of the Cansdales' tastefully furnished, Victorian house to be ushered into Caroline's bedroom. Our encounters had to be fairly brief because the weakness of her voice and the irritation of her cough made conversation especially tiring for her. I sat by the bed straining to glimpse something of her wasting frame while she whispered her thoughts. At times, amidst the agonies of her physical condition, she experienced a disturbing spiritual darkness when the Lord felt distant and even condemning. Nearer the time of her death in November 1979 she seemed more assured of His peace and strength, confident that she would soon be in His gloriously liberating presence. Ostensibly, I visited Caroline to comfort and console her but I always came away encouraged by her fortitude, honesty and at times tenuous awareness of the Lord's reality. In her integrity and her openness to Christ's loving help she was, for me, and many others, a 'missionary of comfort'.

(c) *What can we learn in relation to God?*

There is so much that I could write about under this heading, but supremely, I want to underline that our illness can lead us to a greater awareness of both our dependence on God and our hope for the future.

(i) *Dependence on God*: Job, overwhelmed by his bitter afflictions, wrestled with this puzzling Deity who had allowed such things to happen to him. His dependency on a loving God was put to a very sore test. Job was very critical of this God who seemed to discard the upright on to life's rubbish-tip while the wicked could snap their fingers at the Creator and still survive. In Job 38:1 we read that 'the Lord answered Job out of the whirlwind', demonstrating

His power, wisdom and detailed caring as Creator and Sustainer of the Universe, and His righteousness and wrath as Judge of the wicked and proud (Job 38-41). At the spectacle of all this magnificent wonder, Job was brought to see the sin of his impudent independence. 'I have uttered what I did not understand, things too wonderful for me, which I did not know' (42:3) and again, 'therefore I despise myself, and repent in dust and ashes' (42:6).

Paul was afflicted in Asia, along with some fellow missionaries, and described their experience in these terms: ' . . . we were so utterly, unbearably crushed that we despaired of life itself' (II Cor 1:8). It is not known for certain what particular adversity he was referring to—it may have been, for example, the threat of mob violence or of serious illness. The situation was so grim that it felt like a death sentence. However, Paul was able to see some reason for this suffering. In verse nine he declared that it 'was to make us rely not on ourselves but on God who raises the dead'.

During the last thirty years or so of my life as a diabetic and most especially within the period of recurring blindness and the development of brucellosis, I have felt repeatedly challenged on this question of my dependency on God. The human spirit is proud and, even when the life is opened to Christ, continually reasserts itself in its bid for independence. In the most difficult times I have usually come back to see my need to rely on God more, returning with my tail between my legs. When life has been easier I have often taken charge once again, taking the reins surreptitiously at first—but with increasing confidence as the weeks slipped by. However, at the times of greatest realism, whether on the crest of the wave in my God-chosen profession or in the trough of blindness, the Holy Spirit has reminded me that all I have that is worthwhile is from God's hands—both my natural abilities, given and sustained by a generous Creator, and my growth towards wholeness, made possible through Christ's death and resurrection, and nurtured by His Spirit. At such times I am reminded of the profound security there is in submission to the Father. I was made for this dependency and in living a life of trust and obedience I am most fulfilled as a redeemed human being. I thank God for the illnesses He has allowed that have underscored this insight.

(ii) *Hope*: Paul's complete statement in Romans 5:3-5 is as follows:

> 'More than that, we rejoice in our sufferings, knowing that suffering produces endurance, and endurance produces

character, and character produces hope, and hope does not disappoint us, because God's love has been poured into our hearts through the Holy Spirit which has been given to us'.

Paul was able to see the glorious link between suffering, rightly responded to, and the sequence of endurance, character-change and a hope made confident by the Holy Spirit's mediation of God's love.

This dimension of a certain hope is powerfully expressed in Paul's second letter to the Corinthians, particularly in chapters one, four and five. When God had rescued Paul and his friends from danger in Asia, the apostle was able to look both back in gratitude and forward in confidence: 'And He will deliver us; on Him we have set our hope' (1:10). More generally, at the end of chapter four, Paul proclaimed a principle which has sustained me through many long hours of darkness; 'So we do not lose heart. Though our outer nature is wasting away, our inner nature is being renewed every day. For this slight momentary affliction is preparing for us an eternal weight of glory beyond all comparison' (4:16, 17). It is as if Paul sees a pair of scales. Your affliction and mine rest upon one side. At the time, their burden may weigh us down intolerably but, in terms of the statistics of Eternity, they are as a few feathers compared with the weight of prepared glory that crashes down on the other scale. In fact the disparity between 'here and now' and 'then and there' is so vast that the comparison cannot be accurately made. Joni Eareckson in the Epilogue of her book *Joni* has sounded the right note: 'From the standpoint of eternity, my body is only a flicker in the time-span of forever.' [7]

Jesus Himself, facing the appalling suffering of Calvary, found encouragement in the prospect of glory ahead. We read of him: 'Who for the joy that was set before him endured the cross . . .' (Heb 12:2). If His affliction was more bearable because of His certain hope, we should never be ashamed to own a similar consolation as we battle with adversity.

7 Eareckson, Joni, *op.cit.*, p.205.

CHAPTER EIGHTEEN

WHAT PRICE GLORY?

'In bringing many sons to glory, it was fitting that God, for whom and through whom everything exists, should make the Pioneer of their salvation perfect through suffering'.

Hebrews 2:10 (NIV).

'If we invoke Him (the Holy Spirit), we must be ready for the glorious pain of being caught by His power out of our petty orbit into the eternal purposes of the Almighty, in whose onward sweep our lives are a speck of dust. The soul that is filled with the Spirit must have become purged of all love of ease, all self-complacence and self-reliance; but that soul has found the only real dignity, the only lasting joy. Come then, Great Spirit, come. Convict the world; and convict my timid soul.'

William Temple: *Readings in St John's Gospel*

'Weeping may tarry for the night, but joy comes with the morning'. *Psalm 30:5b.*

WHAT HAS THE LORD BEEN TEACHING ME THROUGH THE YEARS since that gusty November week-end on the Essex marshes in 1951 when, as a seventeen-year-old bird-watcher, I battled with the debilitating symptoms of an undiagnosed illness? Was this affliction a mark of God's displeasure? Have its more recent complications denoted a process of progressive punishment in the life of one particular believer? Was the addition of the ingredient of brucellosis to the recipe of tribulation a further trick to make life even more unpalatable? Or, more widely, have the adversities been a vindictive attack on the integrity of friends and family through the decades? Although at times such questions have pressed in upon me, my experience has exposed the lie that these queries sometimes hide—the lie that our God is a punitive sadist, delighting in the hurts of His children.

God is love, and His love has come crowding into the fabric of my life in a thousand and one ways. His love has been seen in the beauty of the world around me, in the nurturing of my parents, in the closeness of my sister, in the specialness of friends, in the wonder of my life with Joy and our children, and in all the glories of new life in Christ. It has been discerned too, though on occasions with great difficulty, in the darker side of life—in the struggles within our modest environments, in the pain of family misunderstandings, in the heart-ache of broken relationships, in the strain of disappointed ideals and, as this book bears witness, in the curtailments of protracted illness and the frustrations of the twilight world of recurring blindness. God's love can be perceived in both the storm and the sunshine, in both the Cross and the Resurrection.

When God, in his love, allows adversity to dog our footsteps, we may react in a number of ways. We may try to ignore the existence of stress and so become unrealistic in our relationships with God and those around us. In effect we say, 'I'm fine, thank you—there really *is* no problem', while our friends, seeing the strains we are under, exchange knowing glances. Or we may, acknowledging our troubles, grit our teeth stoically and declare, '*I'm* strong enough to cope with all this. *I'll* show 'em!', emerging as self-styled martyrs who look down on the lesser mortals who crumple under life's load. Others of us may be trapped by self-pity, bitterness or anger where blame for the affliction is laid at the door of an apparently unscrupulous God; or we may point the finger at our circumstances, our upbringing, our family and friends but the real culprit, we my feel in our heart of hearts, is the Almighty. And here is the dilemma for many of us. We may reason: 'If God *is* Almighty, what is He up to? If He has the power to do anything He chooses within the limits of His nature, then He must be *choosing* to afflict us. We object to being afflicted! God is clearly at fault.'

Thank God that there is a truer perspective on suffering. I am not denying that God's ways with us are often puzzling and even mysterious from our limited view-point. I am not forgetting, too, that God is the Judge of all the earth and the Bible shows us many examples of affliction sent as punishment on the rebellious ways of individuals, families, communities and whole nations. However, what I have argued in the previous chapter from the scriptures has been abundantly confirmed in my own experience through the years —that God the Father cares for his children profoundly and that He allows adversity in our lives not primarily for punishment but for discipline, not for retribution but for restoration and renewal. Putting this point another way—He may at times need to rebuke us for sin but His aim is always that we may become more Christ-like, bearing the fruit of His Spirit and living to His glory.

I have been deeply comforted during the dark days by realising that the passage in Hebrews 12 on the Father's loving discipline of His own (3-11) is introduced by the invitation, 'Consider him . . . '. We are bidden to reflect on Jesus, the One who 'endured the cross, scorning its shame' (2/NIV). I believe that a Father who cares has permitted the adversities, of which I have written, to reshape me as a person, to strip me of self-reliance and pride, and to instil within a further dependence on His all-sufficiency. I can join with others in declaring that 'God disciplines us for our good, that we may share in his holiness.' (10). This moulding has become bearable, and, moreover, desirable, as I have 'considered Him'. It has been the Spirit-inspired vision of the Suffering Servant that has strengthend and revived me during the most difficult hours. This God who diciplines in love is a God who suffers in love. His anguish infinitely surpasses ours for He has gathered up the pain of the whole of mankind in His Son's cry, 'My God, my God, why have you forsaken me?' His cry of dereliction on the cross puts my suffering and yours into perspective.

I have looked at the past in detail; what of the future? In terms of the diabetes and its complications there may well be more trouble ahead. My sight has held in the right eye for over two years and I am profoundly greatful to God for the continuing thrill of beholding His handiwork. The recent advent of more new retinal blood vessels may herald a return of further visual loss in the coming months or years. The brucellosis has, from time to time, seemed to be relinquishing its grip on my life although a fresh medical opinion has described the condition as 'chronic', and so its symptoms may smoulder on for a long period yet.

Inevitably, there have been perils in embarking on a 'dangerously

"What of the future?" Joy and me during some respite from brucellosis, April, 1982

personal' piece of writing and one of these has been the temptation to over-emphasise my own individual situation. My answers in the last paragraph to the self-imposed question, 'What of the future?' may suggest a pitifully narrow and egocentric framework of thinking—a framework that I have tried to reject throughout the book. Just as my past, as I have shown, is but one strand in the complex web of the lives of family, friends and fellow-believers so my future is caught up with the futures of so many others. None of us stands alone. Just as those closest, especially my parents, sister and more intimate friends throughout and, increasingly through the latter years, my dear wife and children, have been an integral part of the light and darkness of my life so, God willing, such fellow-travellers will sustain and be sustained in the years ahead.

What does the future hold for any of us? God only knows in the details of your life and mine. More generally, God only knows in the terms of the Second Coming of His Son, with respect to the de-humanising poverty and oppression of large sections of the Global Village, in relation to the threatened economics of the richer countries and with regard to every facet of international, national, community, family and individual life.

Two things are certain. One is that suffering will continue in every part of this fallen world until Christ's final triumph over evil. The people of God are not exempt from this affliction—indeed their faithfulness to the Suffering Servant often puts them in the vanguard of adversity. Apart from the stresses that may come the way of all mankind through war, famine, poverty, unemployment, earthquake, flood, fire, oppression, torture, neglect, homelessness, the breaking up of families, bereavement and loneliness, you and I may also have to face serious or persistent illness.

You may already have some idea of what facing adversity might mean for you, your family and friends. I have tried to demonstrate, by teasing out scriptural principles while I have been describing the journey through life of one individual, something of a renewed and renewing attitude to suffering which I hope will help you in the midst of your own unique experiences. Suffering is part of the warp and weft of your existence and mine. If you feel a stranger to God's love and claims on your life, seek to learn through your suffering that God, though He may seem hidden to you, is knowable through His Son, Jesus Christ; He is willing to offer you a new purpose in life as you turn trustingly to Him in penitence and obedience. If you belong to God's family through Christ and are beset with trials, allow Him to temper you in the melting-pot of His disciplining love; further, lift up your gaze in hope because, for God's people, joy follows sadness as surely as morning the night, and spring the winter.

The other, more glorious, certainty, is that we have a God who will make all things new. His kingdom *is* amongst us and is continually advancing into the doomed princedom of the Enemy. You and I, through faith in the crucified and risen Christ, can be part of this resplendent and victorious company. At the same time, we see that affliction, including for many of us protracted illness, is part of our present lot. We should pray for deliverance and for healing. At times our God will wonderfully rescue us and at other times He will wonderfully strengthen us for the continuing fray, making us more Christ-like and comforting us in our hour of need. In face of adversity let us rejoice in our dependence on an all-sufficient God, eagerly anticipating our certain hope of Glory when:

> 'he will wipe away every tear from their eyes, and death shall be no more, neither shall there be mourning nor crying nor pain any more, for the former things have passed away' (Rev 21:4).

PITCHED BATTLE

(Dedicated to Caroline and based on II Corinthians 5:1-5)

Let's go camping!

Our tents are already pitched,
Canvassed taut,
Guy-ropes straining,
Between the earth and the sky.

Some tents are pioneers,
Hanging from Eiger faces
Or iglooed in deep snows;
Martyr material,
Daring all to achieve.

More are Force Tenners,
Explorers of homelier hills,
Ready for most eventualities;
Careful, circumspect campers,
Insurance policy holders.

Away from the front-line,
With its low-profile tents in greens and browns,
Are tents gawdy and gargantuan
Crowded into convenient corners;
A comfortable world
Of knitted cardigans and folding chairs.

Others are tattered, torn,
Poles creaking and ropes fraying,
Storm-tossed, wind-shriven
And pain-racked;
They laugh
Into the teeth of the gale.

Tents are destructible;
Once jaunty upon the earth's crust,
They fade and fall apart;
Yet canvas shrouds will pitch again,
In Resurrection's glory.

Home at last!

SELECTED BIBLIOGRAPHY

CHAPTER ONE

Bloom, Arnold *Diabetes Explained* MTP (1978)
Howard Taylor, Dr & Mrs *Hudson Taylor in Early Years*
Howard Taylor *Hudson Taylor and the China Inland Mission* Morgan & Scott (1918)
Seaver, George *Edward Wilson of the Antarctic* John Murray (1933)

CHAPTER TWO

Jeffries, Richard *Landscape and Labour* Moonraker (1979)
Atthill, Robin *Old Mendip* David & Charles (1964)
Thompson, Edward *The Making of the English Working Class* Harmondsworth (1968)
Archives of Dorset Record Office, Dorchester; *Somerset Record Office*, Taunton; and *Wiltshire Record Office*, Trowbridge.

CHAPTER THREE

Bermant, Chaim *Point of Arrival: a study of London's East End* Eyre Methuen (1975)
Besant, Walter *East London* Chatto & Windus (1903)
Ezard, Edward *Battersea Boy* William Kimber (1979)
Kent, William *An Encyclopaedia of London* J M Dent & Sons Ltd. (1937)

CHAPTER FOUR

Cooksley, Peter G *Flying Bomb* Robert Hale (1979)
Deighton, Len *Fighter: the true story of the Battle of Britain* J Cape (1977)
Harrisson, Tom *Living through the Blitz* Collins (1976)

CHAPTER FIVE

Ryle, J C *Holiness* James Clarke & Co Ltd. (edn 1952)

CHAPTER SIX

Abse, Dannie *My Medical School* Robson Books Ltd. (1978)
Berenson, Bernard *The Italian Painters of the Renaissance* Oxford Univ. (1948)
Round the Fountain St Bartholomew's Hospital Journal (1949)
Bart's 850 Years St Bartholomew's Hospital Journal (1973)

CHAPTER EIGHT

Yaxley, David *Portrait of Norfolk* Hale (1977)

CHAPTER NINE

Pack, S W C *Cunningham the Commander* Batsford (1974)
Thompson, Laurence *1940: Year of Legend Year of History* Collins (1966)

CHAPTER TEN

Balint, Michael *The Doctor, the Patient and the Illness* Pitman (1957)
Berger, John & Mohr, Jean *A Fortunate Man: the story of a country doctor* Penguin (1967)
Haworth-Booth, Michael *Effective Flowering Shrubs* Collins (1951)

CHAPTER ELEVEN

Guinness, Os *The Dust of Death* IVP (1973)
Laing, R D *The Divided Self* Penguin (1965)
Laing, R D *Politics of Experience and The Bird of Paradise* Penguin (1967)
Leech, Kenneth *Youthquake* Sheldon (1973)
McClung, Floyd *Just off Chicken Street* Fleming H Revell/New Jersey (1975)
Reich, Charles *The Greening of America* Penguin (1971)
Roszak, Theodore *The Making of a Counter Culture* Faber (1970)
Ryle, Anthony *Student Casualties* Allen Lane (1969)

CHAPTER THIRTEEN

Fowles, John *The French Lieutenant's Woman* Triad/Panther (1977)
Macnab, P A *The Isle of Mull* David & Charles (1970)
Murray, W H *The Islands of Western Scotland* Eyre Methuen (1973)

CHAPTER FIFTEEN

Adams, Richard *Watership Down* Penguin (1974)
Lawrence, D H *The Rainbow* Heinemann (1971)
Loder, J de Vere *Colonsay and Oronsay* (1935)
Schaeffer, Edith *Affliction* Hodder (1978)
Solzhenitsyn, Alexander *The First Circle* Collins & Harvill (1968)

CHAPTER SIXTEEN

Dunn, James D G *Baptism in the Holy Spirit* SCM (1970)
Bridge, Donald & Phypers, David *Spiritual Gifts and the Church* IVP (1973)
Frost, Henry *Miraculous Healing* Marshall, Morgan & Scott (1961)
MacNutt, Francis *Healing* Ave Maria Press (1974)
Smail, Thomas A *Reflected Glory* Hodder (1975)

CHAPTER SEVENTEEN

Casson, James *Dying: the greatest adventure of my life* CMF (1980)
Eareckson, Joni *Joni* Pickering & Inglis (1978)
Job, John *Where Is My Father? studies in the book of Job* Epworth (1977)

CHAPTER EIGHTEEN

Lovelace, Richard F *Dynamics of Spiritual Life* Paternoster (1979)